Wishes

Gerry Duffy

GERRY DUFFY
TICK, TOCK, TEN

Ballpoint Press

Best Wishes

To Jacinta. You are always there at every step.
Thank you.

Published in 2013 by Ballpoint Press
4 Wyndham Park, Bray, Co Wicklow, Republic of Ireland.
Telephone: 00353 86 821 7631
Email: ballpointpress1@gmail.com

ISBN 978-0-9572072-3-3

Book design and production by Elly Design

Cover by Tanya O'Neill

Printed and bound by GraphyCems

CONTENTS

ACKNOWLEDGEMENTS

For me, this page is the most important.

To PJ Cunningham for his superb editing skills and ideas. This is our second ultra project together. Fortunately, I remembered a lot of what he taught me in 2010.

To Joe Coyle for his outstanding design work and to Kathleen Ivory a secondary school art teacher and very talented artist who has prepared the course maps that appear in the early pages. To Tanya O'Neill for her work on the book cover, thank you. To the proof readers of Tom Duffy Senior, Ken Whitelaw, Brian Ivory and Peter Wallace, all of you are part of my crew on this project.

To Steve, Eddie and Leigh whose names will shortly be understood by all who read this story. Thank you for putting on the big event and for watching over us all.

To Patrick Bolger (www.patrickbolger.com) for the portrait photograph you see on the book cover, as well as Nigel Farrow (www.nigelfarrow.com) for allowing me to access and publish many of the professional photographs he took during the deca.

To the thousands who followed this event online and who sent such kind messages of support. Almost two years on, I still read them regularly.

To my family for their support in the journey that was this ambition.

A special word for my exceptional crew of seven who travelled to England – Jacinta, Brendan, Ken, Doug, Jarlath, Dor and Enda. You know why you are mentioned here and soon you the reader will too.

To everyone named on this page, thank you all.

This book narrates the tale of a sporting ambition. If you consider it slightly extreme, well join the club because I do as well.

One of my passions over the past several years is long distance running and ultra triathlon events. The longest one day event in triathlon is an Ironman event or iron distance triathlon. With a cut off limit of 17 hours, competitors are required to:

- Swim 2.4 miles (3.8km)
- Cycle 112 miles (180 km)
- Run a full marathon of 26.2 miles (42.2 km).

It is not for the faint-hearted.

This story is about an event with the term DECA at its foundation. A 'deca' iron distance triathlon is one where the competitor must complete an iron distance triathlon each day for ten consecutive days. Extreme in every sense perhaps.

It involves a total of:

- 24 miles (38km) of swimming
- 1,120 miles (1802 km) of cycling
- 262 miles (422km) of running.

For our Irish readers the swim, cycle and run is the equivalent of swimming from Dublin's city centre to Drogheda in County Louth, of cycling from Dublin airport to Malaga airport in the south of Spain as the crow flies and the run is the equivalent of covering the distance between Belfast and Cork.

In a European context, it equates approximately to starting in Dover on the south east coast of England and swimming across the English channel to France, cycling from Le Havre all the way down though France before crossing into Italy and travelling to Naples in the lower west coast of that country. From there you start running and don't stop until you reach the Ionian sea at the southernmost part of the Italian coastline.

In the following pages, I will share with you a tale of ten days in June 2011, when along with a small number of likeminded individuals, I competed in the first ever staging of a deca iron distance event in the UK.

To give you a visual insight into what was involved, map drawings of the course that we competed on each day have been included.

In researching this book, I came across a statistic which stated that more humans have been in space than have completed a deca triathlon. At the time we undertook this challenge in mid-2011, approximately 65-70 people had finished one.

This is the story of how I, along with 19 others, attempted to join that illustrious list.

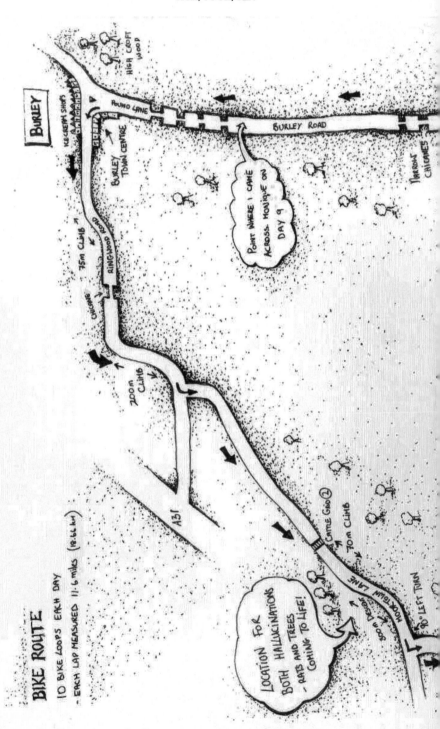

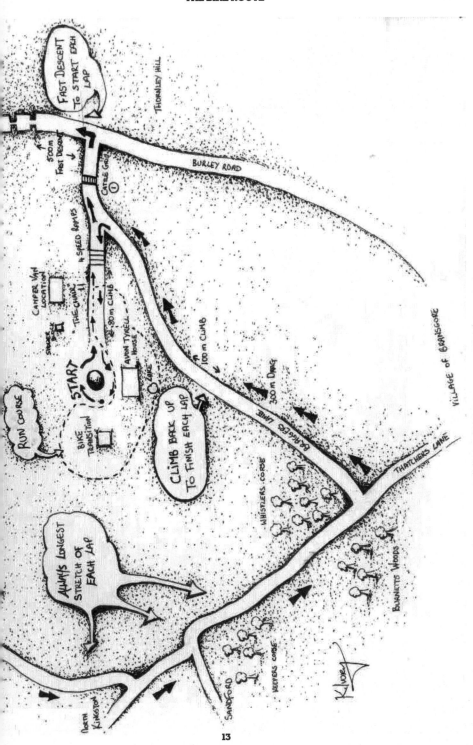

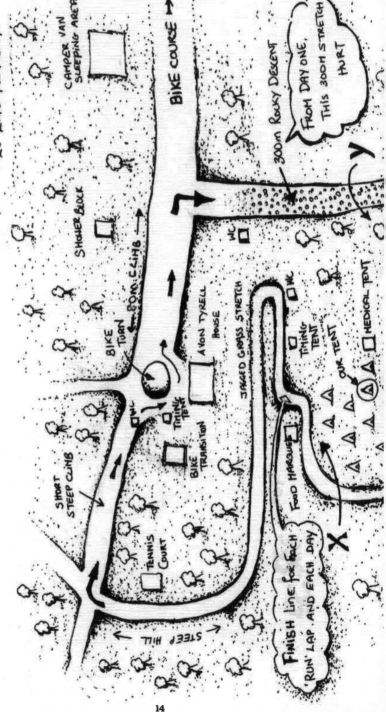

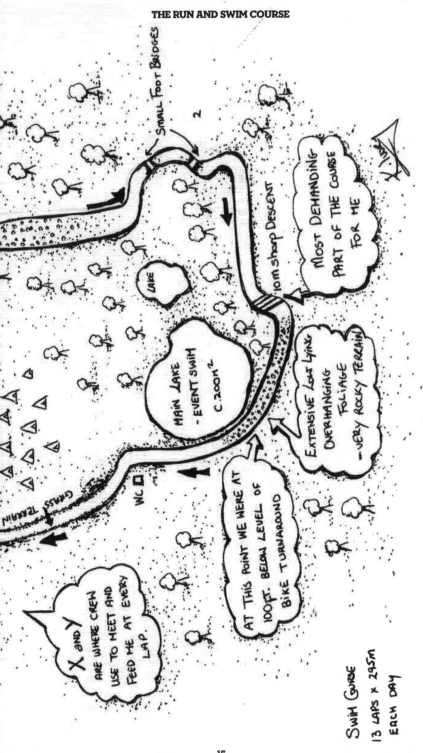

DAY ONE

CHAPTER ONE

We're Almost There

AVON TYRELL, HAMPSHIRE, ENGLAND
FRIDAY 3RD JUNE, 2011
05:45AM

Walking down towards the lake on Day One was a strange, almost surreal experience. This moment had heavily occupied my thoughts for over eight months. Now it was a reality. Given that there were only 20 competitors, the crowd of well-wishers and event crew was small in number, perhaps 40 in all.

It was hard to describe what I was feeling. By now any pre-event nerves had scattered like the ripples on the water that were being created by waking ducks as we approached. I was very excited in the lead-up to the event. Now the waiting was over and we were finally ready to go, after more than five months of specific training and 186 different workout sessions since a cold January beginning.

Some might have an opinion that we were walking towards a crazy ambition, but I felt incredibly alive. After all, extreme sports is one of the things I love and long to do. An early morning summer sun was gifting heat rays to add to my buoyant disposition.

I felt really strong.

Having a crew member of the calibre of Brendan Doyle at my side for the opening three days of effort, added both confidence and resilience to my mindset. I did feel that I had trained my body as well as I could, but knowing I had a great back up crew of seven, gave me added assurance.

Brendan was coolness personified. It was like having Clint Eastwood as your co-pilot; a rock of strength and support in every respect. Running and extreme sports is in every muscle fibre of Brendan's six foot frame. I think I even saw a hint of jealousy on his face as he helped me into the wetsuit that first morning.

If Brendan reminded me of one Hollywood icon, then Steve Haywood, the event co-organiser, reminded me of another – Tommy Lee Jones. As he began the first of 10 roll calls, Haywood commanded respect and authority in the same breath. At 5:50am he cleared his throat and demanded attention. 20 names were called out and twenty voices replied 'here'. He made eye contact with each and every one.

From then on, I would use this image as a motivation every day. If I was having a low moment at any time, I would visualise Steve at the lake the following day, calling out our names. My one goal everyday was to be one of the lucky ones that would reappear day after day dressed in a wetsuit for the next day's test. That would mean I was still in this event. There could be no firmer evidence.

At 5:55am we stepped into the water for the first time. It didn't feel cold. We hardly needed wet suits, the water an almost balmy 19 degrees celsius. I submerged and opened my eyes keen to see what lay beneath but nothing but darkness greeted me. If there were any creatures lurking below, they would have to make physical contact to make their presence known.

After three minutes of warming up and ensuring my goggles were watertight, I was ready.

Just then Steve shouted 'two minutes'.

I looked around me. Everyone was ready but Steve was the ringmaster. We dropped to our knees keen to gather our thoughts in concentration. Such was the shallowness of this part of the lake, we still rose high above the water line.

'One minute.'

All of us were experiencing different emotions. I could hear short nervous breaths from some, whilst others held their breath before exhaling heavily. As I stood half-submerged, I thought of what lay ahead. That lasted for less than two seconds. After all, I hadn't a clue.

'Thirty seconds'.

The last half minute felt like an hour. Only a bird alerting its family to our gathering below, broke the deafening silence. An awkwardness developed among the athletes as we nervously avoided eye contact.

'Three.'

Engines on.

'Two.'

Almost there.

'One.'

'Good luck,' Steve roared.

With that the droned starting horn evaporated into the morning air. As his voice faded, the clock was already ticking. It wouldn't stop for 10 more days.

We were off.

END OF DAY NINE

CHAPTER TWO

On The Edge Of Meltdown

SATURDAY 11TH JUNE, 2011
11:19PM

Finishing Day Nine was a nightmare. I was falling apart. Once I crossed the finish line and despite somehow managing to complete that Saturday's test, as soon as I stopped running, I realised I could barely walk. Uninterrupted momentum during the later stages of the ninth marathon had masked my true distress.

There at the finish line to assist me were my final rota of crew. My long suffering partner Jacinta, my youngest sister Dorothy, a veteran of three Ironman events herself, and her partner Enda. Also there was my older brother Tom who had flown in that morning and Andrew Fay, a close pal. Andrew was a lawyer. Perhaps a good time to discuss a will. In this event, from a physical perspective, I was sinking.

Once I had finished, I had no desire to go down to the lake to offer recovery to my leg muscles as I had done on eight previous occasions. All that consumed me was the pain in my right leg. Climbing the steps in front of Avon Tyrell house was agony. The house which acted as race headquarters, was a red facade and imposing 19th century stately dwelling where sometime close to midnight I dragged myself up the 10 steps that fronted it. As I did so, my face muscles contorted on every step. Every other night I had taken a different route back home through the forest. This new route might perhaps be 50 metres shorter. Every inch salvaged might aid recovery and make a difference the next day.

Once I reached the top I turned right and slowly directed my body towards the shower block. As I did so, my crew looked on with concern. Moments before and just as I had finished Day Nine, self-doubt had engulfed me like a tsunami. The pain in my right leg was excruciating. My crew had long sensed that all was not well, so silence prevailed.

After competing with a worsening stress fracture for the previous three days, my right shin was dreadfully tender and unbearably raw even to the faintest contact. Cellulitis, a nasty infection, had also set in a few days earlier. A tiny dart of pain that had first appeared on Day Six, had now ballooned into an unmasked monster. Mentally and physically exhausted after 142 hours of endurance over nine days, I was a pathetic sight as I dragged myself back towards the priceless reward of a hot shower and the sanctuary of my sleeping bag.

Normally this short pilgrimage took a slow five minutes or thereabouts. That night it took twice as long. By now it was close to midnight, with a night sky as dark as an eclipse. It would be another hour at least before I would close my eyes and less than four more before I would open them again, with a requirement to do one more day.

Once inside the shower block I stripped off and slowly manoeuvred my battered frame into the cubicle. As I summoned up the energy to turn on the shower, I thought of easing myself into a foetal position on the tiled shower floor. As appealing as it was, the reality would have been far too painful to execute.

Every other night, I had carried out a ritual in the shower, that of raising my legs one at a time until I could lift each knee to waist height. This was a strategy conceived during the early days to loosen and relieve any developing aches in the leg muscles ahead of the next day's labour. Not tonight though. Partly because I would have been unable, mostly because I didn't give a f***.

In the shower I examined my body. It was a wreck. I felt like a ragdoll with no skeleton supporting my body tissue. Every limb had been battered by exhaustion, every muscle was keen to submit. As I stood there drained of energy, I could barely muster the vigour to wash away the gathered dirt of the previous 17 hours and 19 minutes activity.

I had just completed Day Nine of the most challenging sporting days of my life. Twenty competitors had started nine days earlier but now there were only three of us left. Some had withdrawn as a result of the enormity of the challenge, others because of injury. One participant had the decision made for him when the event doctor deemed it unsafe for him to continue.

Just four had started the ninth day, Mark Padley, Tony Raynor, Monique Hollinshead and myself. Every day for the previous nine days we had swum 2.4 miles (3.8km), we had cycled 116 miles (186 km) and we had run a full marathon of 26.2 miles (42.2km). We had begun on Friday June 3rd and now it was June 11th.

Sadly Monique didn't finish Day Nine. Just like us all, merciless exhaustion had paid her a visit days before and had never left. Earlier on Day Nine, it had swallowed her up.

As I dried my body, Jacinta came in and tried to lift my spirits. I was half-dressed in shorts as she entered and attempting unsuccessfully to pull a t-shirt over my head. On seeing her, I couldn't contain the emotion of what this event was doing to me. The enormity of it was now eating into me as well. I collapsed my head totally and unashamedly into her right shoulder and began to cry.

With one day remaining I was leading by over 18 hours, but not finishing was now a distinct possibility in my mind. At that precise moment I was unsure if my body was going to allow me another 17 or 18 hours of this absurd ambition.

I wept for about a minute. It was only Jacinta and I, embraced in a moment where I was at my absolute weakest. The thought of putting one foot in front of the other, just like I had suggested to so many others to achieve any goal, felt beyond my ability. How on earth could I do this again in a little over five hours from now?

That was the reason why the tears came.

I had nine days completed. But this was a deca.

This was all about the number 10.

TICK, TOCK, TEN

CHAPTER THREE
Back For The Future

So there you have a brief insight into two very different experiences during my attempt to complete this ambition.

I have no doubt if you are unfamiliar with my story, you might think these opening pages a little delusional. When I first read the distances for the various disciplines, I myself thought they were a misprint. It's 24 miles (38km) of swimming, 1,120 miles (1802km) on a bike and the requirement to run 262 miles (422km) – extreme in each discipline and in every sense. The swim distance is the equivalent of 1,520 lengths of a 25 metre pool, the cycle distance nautically comparable to the distance between the UK and Morocco in north Africa. And then there's the requirement to run 10 full marathons.

You could be forgiven for asking if it is really possible to travel such distances in a lake, on a bike and on foot? At one time in my mid-20s, I would have asked the same question. That is the insight however that I love to share.

I don't profess to be born with an Olympic talent in my legs nor do I believe I'm blessed with an elite endowment like those whom we see competing on our tv screens in high profile sporting events. I am 44 now and a professional speaker, business trainer and writer by profession. I am also someone who is very focussed on wringing every ounce out of life that it is kind enough to offer me. Once upon a time however, I was almost the complete opposite. I was someone who had no ambition and rather ironically had a pathological fear of speaking in any kind of formal public environment.

Before going further on the journey in Avon Tyrell, it is appropriate that I fill in a little of my background to let you know where I came from to undertake such a challenge.

Back in the 1970s and early 80s I had a very contented

upbringing in Ireland. Along with my brother and three sisters, a few horses, dogs and cats we lived very happy childhoods in a town called Mullingar. Living close to a lake, many happy hours were spent around the lakeshore, swimming, eating, laughing and having fun. When I grew up I wanted to breathe and swim under water like Patrick Duffy in 'The Man from Atlantis', the equivalent of an Xbox was a BMX bike and believe it or not, back then Liverpool football club couldn't stop winning.

My parents provided us with great childhoods and we were fortunate in that we never wanted for anything. At school I played all sports. Gaelic football, hurling and pitch and putt were particular favourites. Back then I was very active.

It was in my late teens and early twenties when I had to stand up and really take charge of myself, that my early maturity began to wane. In some ways from a growing up point of view, I peaked at 17. It wasn't until 10 years later at 27 years of age that I realised it.

Once I had to take responsibility for myself I began to go downhill. I didn't realise it at the time but if I was to go back now, I would give myself a massive kick in the behind as an 18-year-old. I was already living passively. That was a period when every week was the same. Right through my mid-twenties, if I am truthful, I asked very little of myself and was happily if totally unmotivated.

A typical week day in my twenties saw me work 35-40 hours whilst carrying out a job which didn't overly tax me. I was in sales but the reality was the company was very successful with or without me. They had quality products at competitive prices and provided an excellent back up service. A proven mix for business success.

My typical work day involved four or five hours of driving around Ireland, interspersed with as many sales calls. Pretty much five days a week I had a three course lunch. I was entertaining clients you see, or at least that is how I explained it to myself. I had left school in 1985 weighing approximately 168lbs. Ten years later

I hovered around the 238 lbs mark. During that time I smoked up to 30 cigarettes a day.

I loved one sport with a passion. Golf. Almost every weekend, I strolled around my home course. On most Saturdays and Sundays I smoked my way around the 18 holes with my golf bag containing more chocolate bars than golf balls. Aside from this one exception of exercising, I was the original couch potato.

I wasn't bad company to be around but I wasn't great company either. My life was just breathe, sleep, eat, work, smoke, golf, drink a few beers on Saturday nights in the pub and on Sunday evenings when watching sport on television at home.

My diet was basic. In fact I rarely cooked. On top of work lunches, I would eat take-outs three times a week or more. Chinese take-aways and pizza restaurants got more calls from me than my family members did. Four nights a week I watched football or golf on my tv at home. I was a sports fanatic but in the armchair sense.

Looking back I was very lazy but also unhappy. I never pushed myself to ask more of myself. Week after week, I always did the same things and as a result my life was boring.

What I didn't realise was that life was giving me everything I asked of it. I didn't realise that if I wanted to get happier, I had to do it for myself. Wasn't it Einstein who once said that the definition of insanity is doing the same thing over and over again and expecting a different result?

I never did, so I never got a different result. This was my life for 10 years or thereabouts. At the time I was telling myself I was happy, but the reality is I wasn't.

If during that period my life was a house, I lived principally in just one room called 'daily existence'. Health was another room I used, but never consciously. I only used it on occasion, whenever I remembered I had in fact got another area of my life to keep. Most of my time was spent in daily existence where I just sat either at home or in work, never wanting to push out boundaries.

I did very little to improve my education or career in this time. Indeed, education was something totally off limits from 1987 to 1997. Career was an unchallenging job and I did nothing to improve that area of my life until the late nineties.

I had no keys for the doors that lead to growth and ability. Ambition and challenge were words I knew but didn't experience or perhaps understand. Fitness, personal development and self-belief were on a set of plans that I had yet to draw into my life scheme.

From what you've just read, you will see I was very much in a place called the 'Comfort Zone', a time which I chronicled in *Who Dares, Runs*, my first book.

CHAPTER FOUR

Bursting Out Of
My Comfort Zone

'It is in your moments of decision, that your destiny is shaped'.
Anthony Robbins

Don't we all have a wake-up moment some time in our lives? It makes me laugh now how 'simple' my road to redemption was. It came in the form of a photograph.

In that picture – reprinted here in the photo section – I saw myself or more precisely who I had allowed myself to become with new eyes as if for the first time.

Was I aware of the impact that photograph would have in a positive sense back then? Not a chance. Did I dream back in July 1995 when it was taken, that one day I would attempt a 10 day sporting ambition that most deem impossible? I would have thought myself mad.

I am so grateful though for that picture which was one of me with my boyhood idol, Seve Ballesteros, the late, great Spanish golfer. The reason is that it became the catalyst for me to invest in a pair of running shoes. Every journey starts somewhere and that was mine. That picture taken 18 years before this book was published shocked me into taking up physical exercise and into running in particular. In the beginning I did it purely to lose weight.

At first when I started, I simply ran three or four miles, three or four times a week. The more I did though, the more I realised what I could do. Thankfully I was in the early stages of slowly changing that old mindset. This was the time I began to reach out, to stretch myself and to make things happen.

Almost immediately, I began to add new compartments to my life. At first it was only noticeable to me.

When I gave up cigarettes for all of 1996, that was a serious jolt that took me out of my comfort zone and into a new department of health. Within a few years the more physically fit I became, the more my life began to take on a completely different appearance. By then I was up to seven or eight miles. The more I did, the more I wanted to do. By the turn of the millennium I was hovering closer to 10 miles (16km) on a normal run. Thankfully I was slowly growing all the time, albeit largely sub-consciously. Even then I had no great master plan to pursue bigger sporting ambitions. That only arrived years later, but I realised that by challenging myself to do things, I was becoming more contented and therefore getting so much more out of my life.

I have learned that we derive happiness from growth and from the way we contribute our talents to others. Now I was growing. As a result I was becoming happier.

Running got me mentally fit enough to encourage me to open my own business in 2003. It wasn't in the sporting industry but running did unlock the mental part of me which made me challenge myself to do it. By then I had spent 14 years working for the same company. Fortunately with my new mindset, I had risen to the position of Sales Manager by the time I handed in my notice. I derived great satisfaction from setting up this new business but also had a few sleepless nights in the early days.

A year later, in 2004, I took part in my debut sprint triathlon as part of a relay team. Thats a 750m swim, a 20 km bike and a 5km run, where I completed the swim section. That swim took 15 minutes or thereabouts. Back then, I was unsure of my ability to do all three disciplines consecutively.

To do that swim, I also had to exit a comfort zone as I was still a resident there in some ways. It took three phone calls from my older brother Tom to persuade me to sign up. Emerging from the water though, I was bursting with enthusiasm. I didn't realise it at the time but that swim would prove hugely significant and was a small key that would later open a big door.

Another day of enormous significance to me was the day I began to overcome that pathological fear of public speaking. It happened in 2005, having arrived at my door in the capacity of the business I was now running. In some ways I felt I had no option but to confront it, but the thought was terrifying. For me standing up in front of a crowd and having to speak, was 10 times a greater challenge than this event you are about to read. Having the courage to attempt it and achieve it, injected huge confidence into my formerly disbelieving mind.

By 2007 I had graduated to doing all three legs of an Olympic distance triathlon (1500m swim/40km bike/10 km run). Its knock-on benefits now oozed out of every pore and I lived for the thrill of competing. In '07 I also competed in my first marathon and soon after that, I got into the really long distance stuff in triathlon. That involved signing up for my first Ironman distance event.

An Ironman distance triathlon is exceptionally hard (swim 2.4 mls/3.8km, cycle 112 mls/180km, run 26.2 mls/42.2km) but then of course it's all relative and we must always keep things in perspective. Its final test is to run a full marathon before the medal is given.

Even preparing for it changed me. The discipline and preparation it places on wannabes extracted hitherto unseen ability in that arena and I surprised myself at every turn. Never once did I miss a training session and I cannot recall my motivation waning an ounce in the six month lead-in period.

Without realising it, I was stripping away any remaining doubts about my ability not just in triathlon and running but also in almost everything else as well. The words 'can't' and 'quit' disappeared from my vocabulary. It taught me so much about myself and what I was capable of achieving.

Now I was a doer. There was no secret to it. Everything I was achieving just required desire, discipline and lots and lots of practice.

> **Gretchen Rubin, author of 'The Happiness Project'**
> 'To achieve mastery, enthusiasm is far more important than
> innate ability because the single most important element in
> developing an expertise is the willingness to practise.'

I would highly recommend you revisit this quote. It is 26
words of the finest education I have ever received and is a quote
that is now a permanent fixture in my home.

After completing a few Ironman triathlons, in the late summer
of 2008, I got an idea that became a passion. It was to run 32
marathons in 32 days and in each of the 32 counties on the island
of Ireland. A close friend, Ken Whitelaw, would later come on board
and share that amazing journey with me.

In preparation for the 32 x 32 (chronicled in the book *Who Dares,
Runs*), in 2009 I completed a double iron distance triathlon 4.8 mile
(7.6km) swim, 224 mile (360km) cycle and 52.4 mile (84.4km) run.
That event took over 28 hours non-stop. It also took an even greater
comfort zone departure and involved significant empowerment
and further confidence being instilled into this then 41-year-old.

A clue to how I was successful in the 32 marathons lies there.
Until I completed that interim double iron event, the 32 marathons
in 32 days was not a realistic goal. After that double, I still had one
more full years training to do to be able to attempt running 32
marathons in 32 days.

Sometime before and in a lot of ways subconsciously, I had
started to challenge the term 'conventional wisdom' in all aspects
of my life. Why should running 27 miles be impossible just because
it is beyond the more popular marathon distance of 26.2 miles? I
had also thought speaking in front of a crowd was beyond my ability,
but it wasn't. What else did I have a limiting belief in?

I began to demand a higher standard of myself, in sport, in work
and in many other aspects. It was a welcome contagion.

CHAPTER FIVE

Setting Your Goals Higher And Then Higher Again

Part of my reasoning for sharing this story with you is to encourage others to realise that big goals are within us all to achieve. Whatever dream or ambition you have and no matter how daunting it might appear, I hope once you've finished this book you'll realise (if you don't already) that it can be done. For sure, just like me you might need a little luck, but luck is often found in the lengths that we are prepared to practise or go to, to succeed.

Recently I went to a talk given by four time World Ironman Champion Chrissie Wellington. During her one hour presentation, Chrissie explained how she only discovered her triathlon ability somewhat by accident and in her very late twenties. At first she said she took up marathon running to lose weight. She made reference on the night to how many people are at home sitting on their couches not realising what wonderful abilities might be lying dormant within them.

I share a similar belief and also the fact that this gift lies within us all, relative to whatever ambitions each of us might have, desire or have yet to identify. Once I started into exercise I just kept raising the bar. In terms of distance and duration, all I did was keep going. It was that simple.

All I needed was that wake up call in the shape of that photograph.

As you travel these pages it is important I share one fact with you. I'm no more or less talented than anyone who reads this book. If you read this and say "well it's ok for him, he's talented," then you are doing yourself a great disservice and giving me an accolade that I am no more deserving of than you are.

This book is not to encourage or discourage you from doing an event such as this. The story in this book can be just a metaphor.

I believe that a deca iron distance triathlon, incredibly challenging as it may be, is simply a symbol for what almost anyone is capable of achieving, relative to their own goals, dreams or ambitions. We must always respect that challenges are different things to different people and are all relative. For someone reading this a 10km or a half marathon of 13.1 miles (21km) might be just as hard as a deca triathlon. At school the subject of maths was immensely challenging to me and the D grade I received in my final school exams in 1985 was an achievement of which I am immensely proud to this day. (D was the minimum grade required to pass) I hadn't passed a single maths exam in the previous two years.

We all have goals. Perhaps in your life you have a sizeable one in front of you right now. Maybe it is to run a marathon? Maybe it is to build a house or in the field of education. You might be considering starting a new business venture and are unsure you have what it takes. When I opened my own business, I remember it was quite daunting. Perhaps you have been made redundant and are looking for employment. Maybe you want to start running, or to take up cycling or swimming. Maybe you just want to get fit but can't see a way. Maybe your goal is to find a goal?

Perhaps any of these ambitions may seem as intimidating or as impossible as the challenge I began training for in the winter of 2010. Believe me, I understand. I am not saying that you might doubt your ability but what I know for sure is that I once did. I'm pretty sure that even after you read this book you'll have no ambition to replicate what I attempted to do. But almost all of us have personal dreams and ambitions. I hope this book encourages you to realise (if you need it) that these dreams or ambitions may be well within your grasp. No matter how hard or distant they might seem, you should realise that there is almost always a way to get there.

Physical exercise regardless of activity, time or distance gives us so much more than just physical fitness. The late US President John F Kennedy was once asked his views on exercise. "Physical fitness is not only one of the most important keys to a healthy body. It is the basis of a creative and dynamic intellectual activity," he said.

That sums it up for me. It fills my brain with positivity. It gives me mental fitness and it has helped open new doors into new rooms in my mind. The fitter I've become physically, the fitter I have also become mentally as well.

This is a book that proves what is possible because this event did have some finishers. And even those who did not finish achieved other goals in their lives like doing three, four or five back to back days. Goals within goals.

My aim in these pages is to encourage you to align your own dream or ambition with this story.

As I mentioned earlier, Ken Whitelaw and I completed the 32 marathons in 32 days challenge in 2010. Running a marathon every day for over a month sounds crazy. There was however, a perfect logic to it all. I spent two years preparing my body to make it a realistic ambition. It was immensely challenging, but also infinitely rewarding on many levels. It was everything that we had hoped for and more and I felt very grateful to have enjoyed such a wonderful experience. That included the entire journey from conception two years before, right through to the final mile.

For months after the '32 Marathon Challenge' finished, people asked every day what was next? I felt no immediate urge to do anything. That challenge had captured people's imagination (mine included) and I loved sharing the experience with anyone who was interested enough to ask. Approximately 2,500 people became part of that unique event. It proved to be a major charity initiative that brought over 1,000 runners onto the roads of Ireland to join us at some part of our journey. Ken and I felt privileged to have devised, planned and achieved it.

That winter though, I longed for another challenge, this time something even harder. Not in terms of duration but a tougher physical challenge. The 32 marathons adventure was an average of a little over four hours of running every day for 32 consecutive days. I didn't have the luxury of another five weeks to devote to a sporting ambition but I could manage two weeks.

I began to do some research. Why not extend the daily effort and physical challenge but lessen the overall duration? It didn't take long to find something that really stirred my adrenalin juices.

Time for another adventure.

November 2010 was when I began seriously to consider this new endurance challenge. The event my internet research had earlier stumbled upon was a deca iron distance triathlon, the equivalent of 10 iron distance triathlons in 10 days.

In 2008 I had been shattered after a single iron distance event. Less than two months later however I did another. That taught me a lot. It was manageable. In fact crossing the finish line I was fine. My body was becoming used to such a demand.

The new challenge was being staged the following summer (2011) in the United Kingdom.

It would involve a gathering of ultra triathletes from all over Europe.

CHAPTER SIX

Facing Up To The Deca Challenge

When I sat down first and thought about the magnitude of what the deca involved, I struggled for a day or two to get my head around it. The distances were enormous. It's not that I doubted my ability but I was far from certain I had what it took to do it. I knew that in the months leading up to it however, I would give the training every ounce of effort I possessed.

The detail of a goal is in the preparation and in the execution. Carl Lewis, a four time gold medallist from the 1984 Los Angeles Olympics, once said about setting goals that the first thing you establish is the price you are prepared to pay. How hard are you prepared to work to get it and what is your strategy?

I couldn't take it as a given that I would achieve it, as that would have taken away from the respect I had for such a huge physical challenge. In work I am the same. While I may know how much money I might expect to earn from whatever, I will never allow myself to consider the fee as mine until I have done the job. I find this a great strategy.

That respect has helped me to guarantee a successful outcome for all concerned. It is simple mind discipline for me. To do anything else would be to take it for granted and is, I feel, disrespectful.

Like it or not, there was no way anyone could disrespect this deca ambition. It was way beyond anything I had ever attempted before and would call on all my self-belief that I had acquired to even contemplate undertaking it.

There were several other factors too and outside considerations that had to be pondered. For starters there was my family. This would have an impact on them. I needed to be sure I wasn't going to detract selfishly from the people in my life who should always come before these ambitions. They had to be consulted, especially Jacinta.

People often ask me how preparing and doing such events negatively impact on work and on family life. Perhaps Jacinta is better qualified to answer that one but I do my utmost not to allow it. I've learned to become well disciplined in time management. The key to this I believe, is to get up very early. With the exception of peak training periods for whatever event, most days I am finished my training by 7.15am. Rarely do I train in the evenings.

Other considerations that weighed heavily apart from the level of commitment needed and the extra hours I needed to conjure up, was the physical and mental effort it would take over the months of preparation. I knew too I would have huge demands in these same areas in the event itself. I anticipated and budgeted from previous experience that the shortest day of the challenge would be in excess of 13 hours. To do that day after day sounded exhausting even in my head. Attempting it and the efforts it would take to ensure success, needed respectful consideration. I also had early thoughts about what kind of a strategy would be needed. All of these things needed to be worked out rationally and with no distractions.

I needed time to think.

Completing my maiden Ironman event in France in 2008 had taught me so much. I don't just mean in terms of triathlon. I mean about sport, about work, about life, about me. It had made me realise just what I could achieve. When I had crossed the finish line of my first single iron distance event just three years before, I felt I had grown immeasurably as a person.

By the summer of 2010 and the 32 marathons I had raised my fitness to a much higher level. Running a marathon every day for a month had been a thoroughly rewarding experience and I was fortunate to remain injury free. As a result my fitness levels and my aerobic ability went to a whole new level.

Signing up for this ambition was the easy part. The devil was in the detail with the huge number of training sessions required for proper preparation.

In late August of 2010, I resumed training for that year's Dublin City marathon at the end of October. It was a strategy to some degree. I hadn't fully committed to the deca yet, but it was in the back of my mind. Over the following few months, I worked out many things in my head and by the time November had arrived, I'd decided I was going to do it. Fortunately I had kept up a high level of fitness in the interim.

The main phase of deca preparation began in earnest in January 2011.

TICK, TOCK, TEN

CHAPTER SEVEN

On The Road Again

'What you focus on, is who you become'
Author unknown

The winter of 2010 and early 2011 in Ireland was cold, exceedingly cold. Minus 10 and below was a regular occurrence. That winter virtually every lake in Ireland was frozen. I live near one of them, a lake in fact that spans over 2.5 miles (4km). On Christmas Day 2010, I witnessed a local man walk across it.

Over cosy fires that December, I plotted the main phase of my training programme. I'd kept fit since my previous marathon excursion in October in Dublin. January would be my starting block for the following five months of training.

In November and December, I'd averaged 50 miles (80km) of running and two or three indoor bike workouts every week. I trained hard but this was just concrete being poured in to give me the proper foundations for what lay ahead.

Over Christmas, I began to focus on what lay in front of me in my preparation. It was a case of paying dues in training and serving some more apprenticeships to achieve a goal.

Early January was very cold. As the heating mechanism kicked in at 5am on the morning of Monday January 10th, I knew it would have to work extra hard just to heat the four walls of the house. Sitting up in the bed, my breath was visible in the air as if I was smoking a cigarette. We were in the depth of one of Ireland's coldest winters.

At 5.30am, I evicted myself from the warmth of my bed and put four layers around my semi naked body; two pairs of leggings, gloves, a woolly hat and a brain filled with first-day enthusiasm. From Mr Bean to a crazy ambitious runner in just two minutes. As I laced my running shoes, the house was slowly warming up but I knew a definite ambush awaited outside.

I opened the door and moved forward cautiously so as to get to grips with the conditions beneath my shoes. As I did so, the ice in the winter air bit into my clothes. It was slippery underfoot with snow and ice covering the entire yard.

Given the unsuitable conditions, I decided to jog to a point one mile away and return and then to repeat this twice more. It would be a six mile (9.6km) appetiser at a slow rate of knots to begin the voyage.

The first ¾ mile required balancing skills learned as an infant just to stay upright because it was as slippery as an ice rink. The final quarter though for some unknown reason, was ice free.

Taking the underfoot conditions into account, I decided to change my planned routing and confine the majority of this workout to the furthest 400 metre stretch, continually running back and forth, like a hamster in a wheel. After 45 minutes I had to plot a route home. If you feel I'm exaggerating, let me tell you that on the return I lost my footing and upended myself three times, the last of which had me yelling like a new-born. I felt a little foolish being out there but it certainly brushed off a few cobwebs.

My diary for the next six days shows that I did four indoor bike workouts and two swim sessions in the warmth of a modern day leisure centre. Gosh, I could get used to that. The first week's total exertion was a little over six hours.

In week two, I went beyond 10 hours of combined training over the three disciplines and I didn't find it that taxing. Several years of extreme training had risen my energy levels to an unprecedented base. Normally I would recommend only a marginal five or 10 per cent increase but the truth is in that first week, I felt I was only brushing off the holiday shackles. Week two saw seven hours of cycling on my plate, all of which was done indoors due to the wintry influence outside.

Over the previous months I'd researched thoroughly how I would train. Figuring out how to prepare for a deca was put together thus.

To begin with, I reflected on the hundreds of different training sessions I had carried out over the years and a multitude of learning and successes that I had experienced. This knowledge, combined with the many books I'd read, provided me with a wealth of wisdom.

I was determined to bring a relatively simplistic method to my training and reverted to a strategy that always yielded dividends. It comprised of 'a little bit more every week'. It had never failed me in the past. Why change it? It's just that in this case, well 'a little bit more' would actually be quite a lot more than I had done before.

During the research I stumbled upon an account of a man who had completed the same challenge I was about to attempt. Bob Brown had not only completed a deca way back in 1997, he had also put pen to paper and written his story.

Over Christmas I devoured this Englishman's tale, making notes as I consumed the pages. The fact that he was 14 years younger when he did it than I would be, and that it took him a full 12 months to recover, only heightened my resolve to be thoroughly prepared. I committed to preparing with a mindset as military as Napoleon Bonaparte.

Reading the epilogue at the end of Brown's book, 'The Road to Deca' certainly didn't fill me with cheer. His efforts in completing the event in Mexico 14 years before had come at a heavy cost.

> **Bob Brown**
> 'It is now six months since I crossed the finish line. As the memories of the race fade, I am left to deal with the physical and emotional consequences of what I put my body and my mind through. My health since the race has been very poor. The supreme torment I put my body through has taken its toll.'

In the months after his November '97 exertions, Brown developed 'severe respiratory problems' and started to 'suffer from dizzy spells'. He developed asthma, possibly in his own words as a result of pushing his body 'too far' in the polluted air of the city in which he did his event.

I enjoyed Brown's autobiography and found it a source of useful knowledge and parallels. One area where I felt strongly that I was doing things differently was after an event or a race. I had no problem resting up and recuperating after a marathon, an Ironman triathlon or the '32 Marathon Challenge'. Conversely, Brown seemed to enjoy jumping right back in almost the very next day.

My biggest dilemma after a big event was usually whether to have the post-event massage on the way to the pizza restaurant or on my return. My only challenge in the days after was to muster the effort to raise the bottle of beer high enough to reach my lips.

CHAPTER EIGHT

How To Train...
And When To Rest

When Ken and I prepared for the 32 marathons a year before, our training peaked at just over 110 miles or 177km in a seven day period. This was the equivalent of a little over four marathons in a week's training block. Each week we raised the weekly total by about 10 per cent, but every three weeks we dropped it heavily for seven days to allow our bodies to recover.

For this new challenge I decided to change the way I would train and to do it instead in *hours* of effort rather than being distance specific.

Rather than run a number miles or swim so many lengths or kilometres, it would be an hour in the pool or three hours on the bike. Thus, week one was calculated at 6 hours and 20 minutes. Week two was 10 hours and 45 minutes. That second week had one hour of swimming spread over two 30 minute sessions and two runs of just under an hour each.

In reality it is still very much the same net result and with similar distances being covered. It just seemed like an interesting way to stimulate and maintain enthusiasm for this new challenge. I resolved to reach a peak of 24 hours of training in a single week.

Again my reasoning and logic was simple. When I examined old diaries of how I had trained in previous years, I estimated that weekly totals equated to approximately 12 to 14 hours for my single ironman races and about 25 per cent more for the double iron distance event in 2009.

Now in early 2011 and relative to where I was even a few short years before, I figured that my body was in very good shape. I was sure it would remember the significant fitness base that the 32 marathons in 32 days had provided.

A friend, Brian Boyle, had once offered advice for an endurance event that I had never forgotten. "Always make sure you do your long session every week. That is the key session. Everything else is secondary." Wise words indeed from someone formerly at the helm of my local triathlon club.

No matter what distractions I might encounter during the course of a normal week, it was vital that I made that long swim, cycle or run a reality. And barring injury or tiredness, it had to be executed. Everything else was secondary. I believe the rise in distance or duration when followed with sufficient rest, combines to elevate one's fitness.

I knew that over the next several months unexpected things would crop up resulting in a missed session here or there. Family and work would always take precedence over this ambition. I would just have to rely on good discipline to ensure I hit as many sessions as possible. I read somewhere once that *'you will find time for anything you are committed to'*.

Another insight Brian had shared was that in the middle of intense training if your body was saying it was tired, then it was tired. 'Take a day off, even two,' he suggested. 'Your body will thank you for it'.

It can be so hard though to convince ourselves to take a rest. As I write these words, a friend Andrew Revington, who was four weeks away from his debut marathon, took note. Andrew is a 40-year-old self-employed dairy farmer who rises at 4.30am to begin each day. Marathon running is very new to him.

Andrew had got in touch seeking advice because he was feeling very tired. Following a return text with some of Brian's advice embedded into it, he reluctantly agreed to take a few days off. An update several days later following a long run read: *"Two hours 53 minutes. Nearly made the three hours. Easier than last week I have to say. The three days not running worked a treat."*

That was his body saying: 'Thanks Andrew, I needed the rest. Now I will reward you by having lots of energy to make this next long run an enjoyable experience. You have looked after me and now I'll return the favour.'

Once we are within a training schedule it can be so hard to convince ourselves to rest but sometimes it is the smarter thing to do. People ask me all the time about injury prevention. I'm firmly of the belief that listening to Brian's wisdom here and implementing it when this warning sign appears, has served me well.

In week one of my training in January, a long run was an hour. In March it would reach two hours. Likewise a long cycle in early February was scheduled to be four hours whereas in April I planned to rise to nine hours. Early on in my preparation, I felt that getting outrageously fit on the bike was one of the keys to success.

Preparing to swim for 2.4 miles (3.8 km) every day for 10 days in a row was not to be underestimated, but previous experience had led me to believe that the swim was merely a starter before the main course. I knew that many revolutions of the bike pedals would have to be turned in the spring of 2011.

My rationale on bike preparation was to get up to nine hours in a single ride but also to have lots of rides close to that length. In early 2009 I had prepared for an attempt at that double iron distance which had a 52.4 mile run (84.4km) as the third discipline. Over those first five months of preparation back in '09, a persistent knee injury meant I had to rely heavily on what miles I could cycle. It was non weight-bearing so it became a key strategy. In August I completed that event. Before I started into the run, I'd already swum and cycled for over 19 hours. Despite having very little running in my legs leading into the event, I ran every almost every metre of the 52.4 miles. I figure therefore that the cycling must have helped.

In 2010 it was the opposite as I had done little or no road-biking. My busy life that year meant something had to give. So the bike was confined to storage for most of that year.

On January 26th 2011, I met up with an old training partner Douglas Bates for my first outdoor cycle in over 10 months. It is hard to credit that in 2009 I had peaked at 150 miles (240 km) in a single ride, yet now I had to build myself up mentally for less than a quarter of that.

On that first outdoor excursion – done in a cold northerly January wind – I was mentally fragile and still only slowly emerging from hibernation in some aspects.

CHAPTER NINE

The Happiness Of The Long Distance Competitor

Sometimes the hardest part of training for a goal is getting started. A book I once read had a section entitled the 'ultimate success formula' which proposed a number of strategies to achieve success.

Number one was – decide what you want. Number two was equally straightforward – take action.

Thankfully by the end of January 2011, my training ship had truly set sail. This was the part I loved. Going to bed sometime close to 10pm with the thought of rising at 5.30am when I would get to run, swim or cycle. How lucky was I? I love early morning workouts and the earlier the better.

What appeals to me is the solitude, the magnified silence, the free pleasure of watching the early morning dew evaporate on the grass. At that early hour, I own it all. Usually I hear the birds in the trees above my house being startled from their nests as I leave. My mother suggested a number of years ago that I should learn to enjoy nature. For years I was unconsciously among it. Now I search for it almost every day.

Being happy is what life is all about. We all want to be happy, don't we? Well, morning training ticks a box for me. I'm not saying it's always easy to get out of bed. The truth is, it almost never is. But within minutes of inhaling the gift of clean oxygen from the surrounding countryside, I'm consciously alive in the moment and experiencing the new day.

By early February I was approaching 13 hours a week in training, still a long way short of where I wanted to get to but measured progress nonetheless. An excerpt from my training diary from Wednesday February 9th showed that I was really starting to get my teeth into it.

DIARY

'Today, I know I'm back and very focused on a challenging goal. I have been officially training for the past four weeks but today I really knew I was in the zone. I attended an early morning cycling class with a group of very determined individuals. The class started at 6:40am. It lasted one hour. It was very intense and we all felt it.

I had got out of bed at 5:30am and ran the five miles to the fitness studio. I then had to run five miles back home as well. Ten miles (16km) and a hard 60 minute bike session all done before breakfast on a Wednesday morning.'

In case you think I don't have some hard days, just two days later I went for what turned out to be a four hour bike ride. I must confess that I sometimes find long bike sessions hard. My first love in triathlon is running. Running is so simple. You just put on your running shoes and off you go. You need very little because your body temperature helps keep you warm. It's not as simple on a bike. For starters, the clothing that is required is a little more complex. In February I needed four layers around my upper body to keep me warm as well as sufficient nutrition and hydration for the duration of the cycle.

Four hours alone on a bike can play on the mind. That was the part I initially found hard to re-adjust to. I hadn't done any long cycles in over a year. Getting back into that mindset wasn't easy. That in itself was also a workout which would shortly prove very useful. The deca would require every ounce of mental strength just to keep going. That Friday in February as I walked back in the door, exhausted physically and mentally by the 100km distance covered, Jacinta said that I looked like I wanted to cry.

How right she was.

The following week's diary suggested that I was feeling low.

'Tough week this week, motivation wasn't there.'

No doubt some of you might empathise. I'm not sure why this happened. Perhaps it was just normal day-to-day living pulling a little and meaning my mind was elsewhere for a period.

I can't have been too bad though because the next day I cycled for over five hours. Fast forward to the following Wednesday and I hit six hours duration in a single bike ride. That night the records indicate a clear change in mindset.

'Feeling strong and very motivated once more.'

Usually I did very early morning mid-week cycles. This was a strategy on my part to try to work as close to a regular working day as possible. Despite being very dark at that hour, my strategy was to begin the workout indoors and to venture out only when daylight appeared.

I'm a business owner. I do sport for fun. Because of that I knew that every hour out cycling, swimming or running was not generating income. It meant that I had to be very disciplined in time management. This sometimes required earlier rising than my traditional 5.30am starts. Usually though it was only necessary for the weekly long cycle. As it transpired, it wasn't as hard as it sounds because by late February I was totally immersed in the mindset of doing whatever it took. I just went to bed earlier.

By early March there were some weeks I had a few miles pedalled before 4.30am. This meant that by the time daylight appeared, I had already covered perhaps 45 miles (72km) or more.

In preparation for one of those long cycles, I recall that one morning the weather was particularly awful outside. Rather than face the elements, I decided instead to set up an indoor turbo, propping the bike into it and turning on a film. Four hours later, the gangster movie starring Robert De Niro and James Woods, 'Once Upon A Time In America' rolled its credits. I managed to keep going for a further 15 minutes before boredom took over and I climbed down.

DIARY TUESDAY, MARCH 2, 2011

'I believe the 'bike training' is key. As a consequence I have decided to work off approximately a 60/20/20 principle for the first 10 weeks of training. This means 60 per cent cycling and 20 per cent for each of the two other disciplines. This will be revised in mid-to-late March.

Within six weeks I'm already comfortably doing a weekly bike ride of six hours. In previous years I would not be there until April. Even saying 'six hours on a bike' sounds challenging and the physical execution can sometimes be even more so.

I've several two and three hour workouts in the legs already as well as a four, a five and a six hour session. All going well, tomorrow (March 3rd) will see another six hours completed. It's surprising how the mind can adapt to such training. Early in the New Year a contemplation of such a duration seemed hard to comprehend. Now I am focussed and it is not quite as hard as I envisaged. Sometimes a consideration of something can be far harder than the reality.

On average I'm doing eight training sessions per week. Two swims, two runs and four bike sessions ranging from hard one hour turbo sessions to those 'quarter of a day' cycles.

Time is so precious, I have to use every opportunity to train the best I can for each session. I've been lucky to avoid injuries for most of my life. When I see others sidelined it reminds me to have an 'attitude of gratitude' every day for such good health.

I plan to increase my weekly training sessions by 10 per cent. This has worked well over the first seven weeks and with the exception of next week, I will continue to ramp it up. Next week will see a drop of 20 per cent to allow some well-earned recovery.'

Over the month of March my weekly volume of hours grew steadily. By then 15 hours and beyond was now routine and soon it would hit 20. During the week of March 20th, I completed two hours of swimming, five hours of running and just under 14 hours of cycling. All this while trying to work normal hours.

A few weeks later, on April 11th, I made my first mistake.

CHAPTER TEN
Not All 'Train' Sailing

For the week of April 11th, I had a sizeable schedule ahead of me. This was due to be the first of two really hard weeks. Monday morning I was in the pool at 6.30am for a 75 minute swim session. Later that evening, I did a hard one hour cycle. The next day I was two hours on the bike and covered 17 miles (27km) on a run.

On Wednesday I have humorously written the phrase 'yikes' on my computer spreadsheet beside the duration of 9 hours and 15 minutes. I didn't find that cycle overly hard. I just went and did it. I got excited months before contemplating such a duration. Now that it had arrived, that morning I could see the bigger picture of what it meant.

Mentally I was fine. This would be my longest day, covering over 150 miles (240 km) in that single ride and travelling through many different counties along the way. I felt really strong both physically and mentally as well. The week before I had completed an eight hour cycle and then went off to do a speaking presentation to a group of 100 secondary school students where I was on my feet for two hours. January's mental challenge of two hours on a bike was a distant memory.

Following the 150 mile cycle, I completed another four and a half hours training between Friday and Saturday. I had planned to take part in a charity 10k run on Sunday to finish the week off. My plan was always to run cautiously but once I started I couldn't resist picking it up. It felt easy. My plan was to finish in something close to 40 minutes, a comfortable time that would exert no major toll.

I felt so strong on that beautiful sunny Sunday morning that I decided after 500 metres to pick up the pace. Soon after I finished, I realised I'd run considerably faster than planned and finished in 36 minutes and 40 seconds. No major damage was done but it was a silly thing to do. I had lost sight of the bigger picture.

Waking up that Sunday morning, I had felt super fit. On Monday I woke up like someone had attached sandbags to my legs. That four minute difference or thereabouts had exacted a heavy toll which would only become apparent in the days and weeks after. I hadn't realised it at the time.

It was silly in the extreme. That Sunday was the seventh day of my biggest training week and was not a day I should have attempted to run a fast 10k. No matter how strong I felt, the reality was I was actually tired. It was foolish and I should have known better.

The next week I managed just under 22 hours but because of this foolish exertion, every minute of it was a struggle. Fortunately I had a recovery week just around the corner. It would be two full weeks before I would feel good again.

CHAPTER ELEVEN

Increasing My Hour Power

Three weeks later, Wednesday morning, May 4th and a little before 6:30am I was in a place called Mullaghmeen, a 1,000 acre beech forest on the border of Westmeath (my home county) and Meath to the north. By that early hour, I had already cycled 35 miles (56km). Hiding the bike underneath some undergrowth, I began a 90 minute run.

Mullaghmeen, the largest forest of its kind in Western Europe offered a wonderland of elevated trail running. Arriving here was part of my strategy. As I hadn't been there for several months, it offered a new training route of sorts. For the third day in a row, I had been up even earlier than usual – 3.30 am – determined not to let the training eat into my working day. Don't worry, I hadn't developed insomnia. The early hour will shortly be explained.

Ahead in the forest lay a hard hill run before then cycling back home. That evening I swam 2km as well. I'd already done a similar workout on Monday and Tuesday. Today was Day Three of four.

Something had happened the previous Wednesday, April 27th, which meant that I felt such a punishing schedule was necessary.

A week before, I'd just reclined luxuriously against three fluffy pillows in the bedroom splendour of a four star hotel. A few days before that, I'd reached what I thought was my peak of training. The stay in the hotel was in some ways a reward for my efforts and timed to coincide with an easy week to allow my body to recover. Many hard months of training had to be respected and so only eight hours of training was scheduled for the entire seven days. I needed a rest. That fast 10k was still in my mind and my energy levels were low.

Jacinta, who is a teacher, was on midterm break so we took advantage of the fact and booked a short break. On the last night, she was preparing to go down to the restaurant for a romantic meal which we had booked. While she was getting ready, I turned on my laptop and read the blog of a fellow competitor, 'Big Ted'.

I didn't know Edward Page but soon I would. We were both members of a triathlon website where fellow competitors were posting details about their individual preparation. Edward was another deca wannabe just like me. His website pseudonym was the name 'Big Ted'.

I read on-line in the hotel bedroom that Big Ted was also hitting his peak and had just completed 35 hours of training. I had peaked at just under 25 hours, more than 10 hours less in a single week. 'You prize idiot', I thought to myself. "You haven't done nearly enough".

I stared at the screen. I had this sinking feeling that I had botched up all my planning. I immediately became preoccupied with hatching a plan to escape this riddle. My mind went into overdrive about one thing – how to catch up.

We were due to return home the following day and so I ran for three and a half hours. Only half of it was planned. The remainder was to think. During every minute of that running solace, I plotted a quick remedy for the question I was now asking myself. In my training schedule drawn up five months before I had allowed for things not quite going to plan. I had time on my side and I knew I had a week at my disposal if I needed it.

I needed it.

Doing over 24 hours of training in a week had been hard. It's a lot of exercise. Regardless though, I decided I would do 30 hours the following week. I didn't feel the need to do 35. The gap would be too great and I felt I would risk injury if I attempted it. I was certain my body would remember the endurance built up just a year before but almost 11 hours of a gap was too much. If Ted could do 35, then I should do at least 30.

With my schedule hastily rearranged, I then had to map how to make it happen. I figured I could do it by simulating four half-iron distances over four days – 1.2 mile swim (1.9km), 56 mile bike

(90 km) and 13.1 miles run (21k) but with a personalised twist. I'd lessen the run by two or three miles but go further on the bike in its place. Instead of 56 miles (90km) on the bike, I would cycle 65 miles (105km) on Day One and 70 miles (113km) on each of the remainder. This went back to my thinking that in the event itself so much rested on my ability to be able to comfortably finish each day's bike ride. Given the extra time spent in the saddle, I figured 10 miles (16km) or so of running was plenty to be doing.

I didn't fancy doing the same course four days running so I decided to create four different courses over four consecutive days.

Conscious of not letting training eat into a normal working day, I would run and cycle in the morning, then go to work before swimming each evening on my way home. That was the reason I was in Mullaghmeen that morning and also the reason for the 3:30am start. It was a sacrifice I only had to make for four days. The terrain in Mullaghmeen was very undulating and hard on the upper leg muscles and ideal preparation for the course I would soon encounter in England.

By the end of that week I had completed four and a half hours of swimming, 18 hours of cycling and just under nine hours of running. thirty-one hours in total. An impressive tally.

During that week, I felt very strong, the fittest I have ever felt in my life. As a result, my confidence soared.

For that I owed a big thank you to Edward Page.

CHAPTER TWELVE

Bags Packed And
Ready To Go

As part of my research I studied various race reports of athletes who had completed a deca iron event in the past. I have already mentioned Bob Brown's book. I firmly believe that by studying other people's stories we can learn so much about how to achieve something in a matter of hours or days. Autobiographies can serve us well here. They can provide a crash course in learning. Of course, you still have to prepare physically but it can offer a blueprint from which to start.

Brown's book provided lots of useful information. As the event came closer, I did some more research as I was keen to read up on every bit of information available to ensure success. What I found scared the life out of me. Competitors in the event who had completed a deca all seemed to share several consistencies. If they weren't cutting off the front of their running shoes to allow ballooned feet to expand, they were hallucinating about trees coming alive and trying to capture them. Taking out shares in a blister plaster manufacturer and having a good psychiatrist on speed dial, seemed a good tactic to consider.

One area that I was able to pick up some tips on, was what I should pack into my suitcases. Notice the plural here. I realised from one report I read that I would need to carry more suitcases than were on sale in the luggage department of Harrods. Such was the checklist, I opened up a spreadsheet on my laptop and began to type alphabetically the list of items I would need to bring. It took quite a while to finish.

With a week to go, I spoke to each of the crew. All of them had helped me in previous events. A rota had been drawn up well in advance and flights for the short hop to the south of England had been booked.

To share the labour of transporting all of the necessary equipment, I decided to divide out the baggage amongst them. Some clothes and other material wouldn't be needed until the latter half of the event (assuming I was still in it) so that was given to Jarlath, Dorothy and Enda. Ken was due to arrive on Day Three so I gambled that I would be ok with one bike until he arrived. For the first three days I had a dependable mechanic in Brendan Doyle.

Nutrition would be carried in its own stand-alone bag and ended up weighing more than a few of the competitors. A shopping spree at an English supermarket on arrival would top up our requirements for the opening days. Each crew member would also bring luxuries from home as well as new demands which would arise as the event evolved.

THE CREW

To achieve any major goal I believe we need to surround ourselves with great people. My crew for this attempt were not just the people at my side. I also felt those whose books I had read or advice I had sought were in my corner. Just because they weren't there in person, didn't mean they hadn't helped me. If something they did or wrote influenced me, then surely they were a part of my crew. People such as Bob Brown who had travelled this deca road before me was one of those.

In my mind I also believe 'Big Ted' was a part of my crew even though he and I had yet to meet. His leadership in carrying out such a heavy training volume had jolted me into raising my own training bar. Another person I used as a role model was Terry Fox whose influence had inspired me to challenge myself in sport. Fox – who had passed away as long ago as 1981 – is firmly planted in my memory bank as part of the crew. In 1980, he attempted to run across Canada with a prosthetic leg to raise funds for cancer research.

Half-way across his homeland, this 18-year-old was struck

with cancer for the second time in his short life and died soon after. People ask me why I do what I do? It's because people such as Terry have inspired me. His legacy and influence lives on. On many long training bike rides and trail runs I think of him. I pledged the first time I ever read of him that I would never forget him.

One example of holding my end of this bargain occurred just over three years ago when I got injured. For three months I was unable to run after a knee operation. I promised myself that when my injury healed, I'd be forever grateful and treasure the gift of simply having the health to run. I've kept this promise. Since embracing this philosophy my whole life has become more enriched. As long as I live and in every event I do, Terry Fox will always be on my crew.

My travelling crew consisted of the following: Jacinta O'Neill, Ken Whitelaw, Doug Bates, my sister Dorothy, and Brendan Doyle (all of whom had completed ironman events themselves) as well as Jarlath Mahon and Enda Munnelly. Each volunteered a few days of their time or more and brought the following qualities; attitude, work ethic, technical expertise, mentoring, respect, fear (Doug) and intimacy (guess who). Best of all, they were also close friends.

JACINTA O'NEILL

First up was Jacinta, my girlfriend, my partner, my counsellor, my mentor and my closest ally. Naturally she was my most vital crew member and my closest confidante. Now a marathon runner herself, Jacinta had run a half and a full marathon back in the summer of 2010. Fast forward 12 months and by now we had been dating for over two years and still she hadn't left.

From previous events I realised my ambitions are most demanding of her. She takes the discomforts, the pain and the demands to heart. Every groan, every moan and every grimace exacts a toll on her. During our tour of Ireland in 2010, Jacinta was one of only three people who had crewed all 32 days. Each day for her was a minimum of 14 hours labour. A primary school teacher by profession, she is an expert organiser and she would need to be. Apparently I can be more demanding than all of the 31 five-year-olds that she has in her classroom each day. Given my lack of talent in some areas of organisation, we complemented each other well. I would swim, cycle and run and leave the rest to her and the other members of the crew.

Jacinta had the presence of mind to ask before the event how to approach a situation where I might not be fit to complete the event. Who would or could make the decision to withdraw me? Would I decide? Could she make the decision for me?

The first two occasions she brought the subject up, I fobbed her off. I didn't want to countenance such a possibility. I proudly boasted that I would never pull out.

Her pragmatism on this issue won out and a series of 'what ifs' were discussed. What if I got injured? What if I finished so late into the night that I had no chance to recover? What if I was unfit to make a rational decision for myself? The 'what ifs' generated much conversation. Although I had never previously suffered a withdrawal, who knew what might lie around the corner?

We devised a plan. It was quite simple.

It involved two colours. Green and red. If I looked to be in discomfort she or the crew would ask me which colour I was. Green was the only colour I wanted to think of. If they felt I was really suffering and was on the point of pulling out then she would ask me repeatedly what colour I was.

If I said red then it meant I was agreeable for them to make a decision on my behalf. I threw in an extra caveat. I would have to give three straight red replies to three consecutive questions. Only after three 'reds' could they go and tell the organisers that they were withdrawing me. Ironically with the hundreds of things in my head in the few days before, I actually forgot to brief the rest of the crew on this.

Jacinta's work commitments meant she was unable to travel out with me. I had to travel on a Wednesday for a Friday start.

Jacinta would arrive over late on Friday night for her first of two crewing rotas. A bank holiday meant she would be able to stay that first weekend for three days.

KEN WHITELAW AND DOUGLAS BATES

Ken and Doug would take over from the Monday (Day Four). Ken was due to stay until Wednesday and Doug until Thursday. Ken and I had travelled every inch of the 32 marathons in 32 days adventure together. In fact, back then his challenge was far greater. I was fortunate to remain injury free throughout. Injury plagued him from Day Six onwards. During the course of that month, Ken had endured more pains and jabs than a voodoo doll. His determination to continue though was profound. Once he commits to a goal, he gives it everything.

Doug Bates had the appearance of a night club bouncer but had the heart of a Rolo chocolate. He was also a two time Ironman finisher. Doug had also been a crew member at the double iron distance event back in 2009, having discharged himself from hospital to be there. For two days he had stood at the turnaround point (looped course) on crutches, monitoring my pace, watching my nutrition and shouting abuse or was it encouragement in my direction. Doug, a father of four, is a very motivated individual who like me, had initially taken up sport to shed weight.

JARLATH MAHON

Jarlath was the longest serving triathlete on the entire crew having made his debut in a work-related charity triathlon event 10 years before. While his performance on the day of that triathlon was life-changing, it had nothing to do with his prowess as a sportsman. It was on that day that he met a lady called Gabriella Szabo, a Hungarian nutritionist, who had lived in Ireland for a period. Mahon's hunger to ask her out led him to travel soon after to Hungary to encourage her to move back to Ireland and indeed to marriage several years later. Perhaps their six-year-old daughter

Nessa will represent Ireland or indeed Hungary in triathlon in a future Olympic Games.

Jarlath is a national account manager with a leading global cereal manufacturer, but I have consistently refused to give into his shameless requests and bribes to give his employer a plug on these pages. Suffice to say they are the company with the green and red cockerel on the morning cereal box. Soon, I would eat one of his company's products every night during the deca before nodding off, so I have will have no option but to mention *Kellogg's* later.

Jarlath's sporting talent in triathlon was not the reason for being asked to crew. The qualities he brought on the airplane that week were a positive attitude, a ceaseless work ethic, unrelenting enthusiasm and a face full of focus.

They say if you want something done, then ask a busy person. Jarlath was always on the move. In everyday life he is a fun guy and a great friend but for this event he left that behind and brought a seriousness and conviction to help. This was demonstrated at 2am on the night after I finished Day Seven, when he spent two hours searching the forest for a pair of sandals. A difficult enough dilemma during daylight hours, let alone with only a torch as your guide.

DOROTHY DUFFY AND ENDA MUNNELLY

Dorothy is my youngest sister and Enda is her husband. Together with Jacinta, Dor as she is known, and Enda would bring up the rear in terms of crewing. They would arrive in late on the second Friday night; assuming I was still competing, and cover the final two days.

Dor – a three time Ironman finisher – and I are very close and we have much in common. She is my junior by seven years and we have travelled many triathlon and indeed career journeys together. She worked with me in business from 2004 to 2009 and both of us spent all of 2007 travelling the length and breadth of Ireland doing lots of triathlons in our first full-year competing. Dor opened her own business on the strength of all the experience she had gained in the preceding years and is now the proud owner of a 5,000 sq foot triathlon and multi-sports store in our hometown of Mullingar.

Enda Munnelly is the guy who knows it all. No, not a know it all. He genuinely knows it all – well almost. He is a natural sports man, can run a 5k in under 20 minutes even though he may not have run in a year. A degree in computer applications is but a modicum of his talents. Hand him a guitar in a bar and you suddenly realise he has a talent that could see him jam with Noel Gallagher, late of Oasis. Oh and he is an expert bike mechanic as well.

Asking someone to crew for 10 straight days seemed unfair and a poor strategy in my eyes. I knew this event would be incredibly demanding on us all. A key to success included surrounding myself with a good capable crew at my side and one that was at all times full of energy.

I knew every day would be really long. In reality though I had no idea just how long. Before the event, I felt that 13 hours a day for competition would be realistic with the crew adding an extra hour either side. For the crew in fact, the shortest day would be 19 hours.

BARRY WHITELAW AND ALAN MAYE

Both Barry and Alan never made it to the New Forest but both played a vital role. Barry (Ken's older brother) was the computer IT man who each night shared images, video content and a few quotes to the many thousands who tuned in online for updates. As the event progressed, interest escalated. Barry simply took it all in his stride.

Alan, who works with Dor in her multi-sports store, had prepared my brand new bike and had moulded my body frame into it, courtesy of a 30 minute bike fitting a few weeks earlier. I was nervous about getting a new bike just a week before the big day but Alan assured me all would be well.

BRENDAN DOYLE

Covering the lead-in and the opening three days was Brendan Doyle. He and I had been friends for just three years. A mutual friend had connected us when Brendan was training for his own maiden Ironman event in 2009. We had similar mindsets and shared ambitions for doing extreme sporting challenges.

Brendan is a married father of three, 41 years of age and has quite a distinctive appearance with long strands of curly black hair draped half way down his back. During his maiden voyage at Ironman France 2009, on-lookers could have been forgiven for thinking they were watching Ozzy Osbourne – the English heavy metal vocalist and songwriter – in lycra, pounding the streets of Nice on that day. It is fair to say that Brendan would look more at home backstage on the sound and lighting desk of a U2 or Led Zeppelin concert, than on a marathon or triathlon course.

At 8:30 am on Wednesday June 1st, 2011, he and I boarded a flight at Dublin airport bound for Southampton in the South of England followed by a short commute of 22 miles (35 km) to the 'New Forest' – our home for the deca fortnight. Both of us were very quiet on the flight, our thoughts occupied by what lay ahead.

In reality and with hindsight, neither of us had a clue.

CHAPTER THIRTEEN

What Have I Gotten Us Into?

WEDNESDAY 1ST JUNE, 2011

Wednesday and Thursday was always going to be about getting very nervous, finding our way, adapting to new surroundings, going through checklists and generally s******* myself. What the hell had I gotten us into?

I was now in the final days of a three week tapering period where I had reduced my training volume massively. This was to allow my body to conserve as much energy as possible. Taper is hard. I was very fit but relative to what I'd been doing, I had now to get lazy to store up every ounce.

My last hard session had been 18 days earlier during a half-iron distance event back on Sat May 14th – (1.9km swim/90km bike/21km run). During that workout, the cold water of a lake in May invited something close to frostbite into my fingers. Following the swim and over the following four hours or more, a hilly and windy bike course of 56 miles (90km) with some heavy showers as well, was exactly what I needed. Throw in a closing half-marathon run of one hour and 28 minutes (1:28) gave me a finishing time of 5:11 which was as perfect a preparation as I could have hoped for. I wanted a hard workout and I got it. I did hold back but only a fraction and I felt very strong throughout. Fast forward several weeks, now I was feeling very lethargic and sluggish. I wasn't at all concerned though. I knew this was normal.

Picking up the camper van at Southampton airport, Brendan and I made our way to The New Forest. Such a location sounds fanciful and conjures up an image of medieval banquet music emanating from the treetops. Well we never saw that or Robin Hood for that matter but it turned out to be a part of England that offered a stunning countryside and included the largest remaining tracts of unenclosed pasture land, heath land, and forest in the south west of England. The area covers south west Hampshire, and extends into east Wiltshire and towards East Dorset. Dorset was a place I'd last visited in 2008 when competing in the UK Ironman event.

The New Forest was created by William the First in about 1079 for the Royal Hunt. Almost 800 years later, significant new protection was granted in 1877. Why the history lesson? Well, believe it or not, for our 10 day stay a consequence of that 1877 statute would influence our concentration for every day on the bike course.

For hundreds of years inhabitants of the area had pre-existing rights of commonage to turn horses and cattle out into the forest to graze. The cattle had long since been fenced off but someone had forgotten to corral the horses. As Brendan and I arrived and merged onto what we later realised was the bike course, we saw almost as many horses on the road as teenagers at a Take That concert. Horses we soon found out, had as much right to walk down the main street of Burley – the one village we would navigate through 10 times each day – as I had to cycle through it on my Felt AR4 road bike.

By early afternoon we arrived into Avon Tyrell, a 65-acre outdoor activity centre and home for the next fortnight or so. Pulling up at the front door, we were immediately shadowed by a 130-year-old imposing 'calendar house' that dominated the entire estate. Built in 1891 by William Letharby, this sprawling three storey dwelling had 365 windows, one for every day of the year and 52 rooms – one for each week. It also had 12 chimneys to reflect each of the 12 months and seven ground floor entrances, one for each day of the week. I had never heard of a calendar house before but this was one in every sense of the word.

Having checking into the campsite, we returned to the camper to park up, unpack and to hook up to the electricity mains. A few hours later we went for a stroll to locate the race registration.

As you might have guessed, this event did not have mass appeal. There had been no need to sit by a computer to register in a panic that it might be oversubscribed. In fact just 20 people had entered.

Five more were due to arrive five days later for a quintuple event (five iron distances in five days) as well as others for a triple distance, a double, a 100 mile run (160km) and a single day iron distance event 12 days hence. That seemed light years away.

There was an almost detached feeling as we descended the hill to the small marquee erected in the middle of a field. Any atmosphere had yet to stirred but soon that would change. In the field we met two other competitors – Mark Padley and Edward 'Big Ted' Page.

I didn't recognise Big Ted at first but as soon as he introduced himself as Edward, I knew he was one and the same. I had much to be grateful to Big Ted for and informed him of this during our brief chat. He seemed grateful. Both of us had a lot on our minds. We would meet many times in the days ahead but at that juncture, it was just a brief connection. Having left Ted and Mark, Brendan and I decided to familiarise ourselves with the swim and run route.

A few hundred metres from the race headquarters, we spotted a small lake, barely 200m² in circumference. It meant the swim would involve multiple laps of the lake. Whilst aesthetically the surrounds of the lake were attractive with manicured rhododendrons and other flowers coming into bloom, the lake looked very uninviting. It was as dark as chocolate.

To our left we spotted a trail through which I knew would lead to a part of the run course. Brendan and I ventured forward keen to see that part of the exam paper. The run loop was a little over one mile (1.6km) in total which we would have to navigate 262 times. Perhaps that sounds crazy but my double iron experience had made me realise that such a short loop does in fact make sense in an event such as this. The reasons will become apparent later.

We walked the entire course keen to study the terrain, the elevation, its navigation and its routing. As we did, we examined it thoroughly, stopping every few metres. It looked as inviting as an applied math test.

The terrain was predominately trail, rock and stone but with a short grass section as well. It had lots and lots of small hills and was a maze of twists and turns. It had a few small bridges to cross, tree roots to climb over and some overhanging foliage to duck beneath. Orange paint had already been sprayed by the race organisers on all visible tree roots. At night and with tired legs, those roots could and would in later days, become as big an obstruction to scale as a crossbar of a goals on a soccer pitch. For the entire loop the course barely had a flat piece of ground. I knew this event would be hard, that is one of the reasons I had signed up for it. But this run course was a beast.

The organisers had rightly heralded that:

'Avon Tyrell hosts a true triathlon course. No closed roads, no two km flat loops, no tarmac run, no hiding place.'

We might have been forgiven for expecting and hoping that the organisers would have given us a dead flat single loop. After all the distance is the distance. Why did it need added difficulty? What I realised immediately though was that they had given us something truly special and the truth is, I loved it the moment I saw it. It reminded me of Belvedere House outside my hometown, one of my favourite training grounds.

Having to run the loop 262 times could be likened to a hamster on a circling wheel but this very special course repeatedly changed landscape, meaning we would rarely be bored. I relished the thoughts of running on it and the prospect of developing an intimate relationship with it very shortly.

Earlier when we had arrived into Burley, we had dropped my bike into a repair shop. It had been taken apart and packed into a box for the flight so I was keen to have it pieced back together by a professional. They kindly returned it to us several hours later by which time we had parked up our camper.

I retired early on Wednesday night at 10:30pm and woke at 5:30am the next morning. Even then I was in no hurry to get up. I lay in my sleeping bag, eyes open but keen to stay off my feet for another hour. I felt I was being smart because in some ways the event had already begun. Pretty soon I knew every ounce of energy I could stow away in the lead in might be called upon.

THURSDAY 2ND JUNE, 2011

When I got up we were greeted by Heather and Tony Fisher who had set up beside our camper overnight. They had travelled over 400km from Chester in the county of Cheshire. By day, Tony was head of the Department of Medical Physics and Clinical Engineering at the Royal Liverpool University Hospital. For fun, he competed in ultra triathlons.

Tony had only taken up ultra-triathlon at the age of 40. What's more, he was one of only two people in the field who had entered a deca event before. During that day, the four of us shared a fledgling friendship. They were very welcoming people and they were happy to chat in detail about what lay ahead and as to what we had let ourselves in for.

The only previous European staging of a deca was held in France in 2006. Tony was there and what's more finished it. On the one hand I was enthused by the fact that here was a man sharing our breakfast table who had done this before. Firm evidence that it was possible. The downside was his view that our course was the hardest he had ever seen in ultra-triathlon. He seemed surprised by the level of difficulty. His insight into the bike course – which he was just back from cycling – was not encouraging either. He explained that it was quite technical and had lots of climbing in it.

That morning though, I felt very enthusiastic, very positive and all of the tiredness had thankfully left my body. Adrenalin had arrived and brought with it an edge. I rarely get over-excited as events draw near but this was different. As the day progressed, I began to feel very energised. During Thursday, I really picked up my mental focus and began to think long and hard about what the next day would bring. Brendan went for a long run on the bike course; I went for a short stroll to think and plan for what lay ahead.

I had a concern after seeing the contours of the run course over what footwear I needed. The course was littered with cones from the ubiquitous spruce and pine trees. During the previous day they had regularly got snagged up in the soles of my shoes. The organisers had suggested trail shoes. I brought regular road running shoes, not ideal. I panicked a bit in my mind but realised that worrying would serve no purpose. Over a phone call, Dor offered to try to source a few pairs in the coming days. Even then breaking in a new pair of shoes for a full marathon was not very wise.

Earlier I asked Tony his opinion on the list of entrants, how they might fare and who he fancied to emerge victorious. He mentioned a few. One of the names was Neil Kapoor, a banker from London. Neil had also completed a deca in Mexico in 2008 as well as the infamous Badwater Ultra Marathon in Death Valley, California. That event was a 135 mile (217km) footrace ran in temperatures hovering towards 120 degrees fahrenheit (49°C) and involving over 2,500 feet of climbing. Tony also mentioned a German lecturer based in Oxford University, Hanno Nickau. Hanno had previous successfully completed both a double and a triple iron distance triathlon event (7.2ml swim/336ml cycle/78.6ml run).

The previous day Brendan and I had gone shopping. We returned to base with a multitude of bags containing cereals, breads, milk, sausages, eggs, bananas, butter, tea bags and much more. We had a large crew to consider after all. For this splurge we had visited the town of Christchurch, a short 10 minute drive from Avon Tyrell. It was a modest-sized town but with awkward parking options. We had to walk almost a mile to and from the shops. I know this mightn't sound like much but it wasn't ideal preparation as I had planned to stay off my feet as much as possible.

As we were driving back in the camper with our rations for the next several days, my mobile phone rang. It was a researcher from the Ray D'Arcy Show, Ireland's most popular mid-morning radio programme. I had been a guest on the Today FM programme just a month before for an interview following the launch of the book *Who Dares, Runs*. In reply to one of Ray's questions about future sporting ambitions, I revealed my deca goal to the show's listeners. As a result, many people in Ireland knew what was on my Summer sporting agenda.

Siobhan Hogan, the researcher, explained that they had kept note of when the event was due to begin and were keen to do an eve-of-race interview. We had agreed to do it the following morning (Thursday) just after the 11am news bulletin. As part of the deca event I had planned to raise money for the same charity Ken and I had run the 32 marathons for – Irish Autism Action (IAA).

For the deca I had a fundraising target of over €5,000 and close to €3,000 had already been donated before I left. I knew the extra publicity would help greatly in achieving this target. On Thursday they rang as planned. After the interview was finished, I passed on Ken's mobile number to Siobhan in case they wanted to follow my progress. As far as I was concerned that was the final interview that I would do. My phone bleeped continuously afterwards for about 20 minutes with good luck messages and texts.

Later that afternoon Brendan went to work figuring out how to piece together a new Garmin GPS watch. My job was less taxing, choosing which Blue Seventy wetsuit to wear, which runners to use on Day One and also to go for a short spin on the bike to ensure all was in order. By now the start was less than 14 hours away.

One practice that the 32-day marathon experience had taught me was to record my experiences each day on an audio device. I had brought the same recording device with me on this new adventure...

AUDIO DIARY

'Put this into perspective. How lucky am I to be out here. So many other people today, Thursday June 2, have real challenges to face. I'm doing this for fun. Remind yourself all the time, I'm the lucky one. I choose to be here.'

RACE BRIEFING

Attendance at the 6:00pm race briefing was mandatory. As I sat in a chair, I scanned the room, eager to visually study the other 19 who had entered. Regular iron distance events attract thousands. This was an event that out of a European population in the hundreds of millions, had tempted only 20 people from across a continent.

Along with the event organisers and chief marshalls, 19 men and one lady now sat gathered into the marquee. The average age was probably in the late thirties to early forties. Were you to list the entire experiences of all those in the room, it would make an interesting curriculum vitae. One condition of event entry was that each participant forwarded their previous relevant experience.

Those in charge were of the opinion that:

'Before you attempt a deca your base needs to be extensive or the body will break and fail. The athletes' mindsets and the will to continue is what will pull them through the bad periods. A weak mind fails.'

The race briefing was professional and detailed. The race organisers were the same who had organised the double iron distance event I had participated in back in 2009. Eddie Ette and

Steve Haywood owned 'Enduroman Events' and were two people whose attention to detail was of the highest order. They excelled in offering extreme events to those who wanted to go that bit further. They were not in it solely for commercial reasons. Their first reason was a passion for triathlon. If they made money it was a bonus.

For this event they had also enlisted the services of a man called Dan Earthquake. I later found out he had changed his name by deed poll. The surname certainly fitted the individual. He was a larger than life character and was a super guy to be around. He was in charge of the swim each morning as well as having responsibility for ensuring that everyone finished safely before the lights were turned off at day's end.

As Steve Haywood introduced himself, all 20 competitors sat nervously around the many trestle tables. An extreme sports specialist, Haywood was a sub four-minute mile runner and had once run from John O'Groats to Land's End in the UK, a distance of some 1,000 miles.

The briefing lasted 90 minutes where the safety of those competing was the primary concern. After that, they expressed their desire and commitment to host a great event. As part of registration we had been asked to sign a waiver passing over medical responsibility to a medical doctor who would at all times have the right to withdraw a competitor if she deemed someone unfit to continue. Little did we know that this would have to be enforced on someone.

I fully understood the logic. I was about to push my body to an extreme that I'd certainly never experienced before. In a way it was a comfort to know that there was another pair of eyes watching over us.

All aspects of the event were discussed including cut off times, meal schedules and general rules and regulations. There was a barrage of questions but we knew most of the answers already. Perhaps it was just nervousness coming to the fore.

Later that night, I triple-checked everything. Scrutiny of your kit in advance wasn't as intense as a regular one day event though. For this event I had a dedicated crew to watch over me and to manage my kit. That was a comfort. If I was to be successful, I wouldn't do it alone.

At 10pm I closed my eyes and immediately fell fast asleep.

CHAPTER FOURTEEN

Course Lays Down
A Marker To Us

FRIDAY 3RD JUNE, 2011
04:51AM

AUDIO DIARY

'Morning. Eh, I think it's Friday. Have to say I feel very good. Very pensive, very nervous, very respectful of the challenge that lies ahead. Have no idea how it's going to go but like everything in life – you just have to give it your best, and please God the best will be good enough.'

The ruffled and crumpled blue sleeping bag is strewn across the top bunk of the camper and forms a fitting backdrop on the poor quality phone video. The time on the screen indicates it was filmed at 4:51am that morning, a little over an hour before the start of Day One.

At this remove from the event I can study my body language and how I looked. A little gaunt perhaps. Five months of hard training had chiselled away any fat from my face and frame.

In the video I had a tight grip on a cup of tea in my hand. Overall, I looked fine; maybe a little sleepy which was a good sign. I had slept well. I also knew that I'd arrived in the best shape that I possibly could. Training had gone to plan and I had no injury concerns.

My plan for the first day was to complete the course in about 13.5 hours. My reasoning was that this was a 10-day event and I had to pace myself. That sort of finish would be comfortable and allow me enough time to recover before Day Two. On day one of the 32 Marathon Challenge back in 2010, Ken and I had run in a time of 4 hrs 39 minutes for the opening marathon. Back then we had to be conscious of the bigger picture. Although we knew we could run faster, it was not a single marathon event, it was 32 of them we had to do. Likewise this event was all about the number ten. Ten iron distance triathlons in ten days. Not seven, eight or nine. TEN.

Although I had yet to experience the course, a first day immersion would soon shock us all. What I hadn't factored in was the terrain. Perhaps you might think that naive and that I had not prepared as best I could. Well, I didn't live in England so I didn't have the opportunity to do a reconnaissance trip in advance. The event website had been as informative as it could be. I did have some idea of the type of marathon course that would greet us but perhaps not the complexity and topography of it. If I was guilty of anything, it was my lack of research of the bike route. I thought it would be modest in terms of elevation. It was nothing of the sort, in fact it had hills and plenty of them.

I was guilty of not knowing the exact terrain, but my legs did not fear the course. The day before in fact, I passed up on an opportunity to cycle the bike course as a deliberate tactic. To do so would have taken a few ounces of energy that I was not keen to give away. Nor did I wish to drive it. I had learned that lesson three years before. On the eve of Ironman France in 2008, a friend and I drove that bike route. I had cycled it a month before but he was seeing it for the first time. As our hire car struggled up the many cols (climbs) that hot summer's day, I had watched the blood drain from his face. It was already sapping energy from him and the event had yet to start. A lesson learned and stored in my memory bank.

I knew that within a few hours of starting, I would enter an intimate relationship with this new bike route. By the end of Day One I would already know every twist, turn, descent, ascent, corner, chicane and have knowledge and sight of every breed of horse bred in the South of England since 1877.

In the next chapter I will narrate that opening first day. In summary though, many hours after I had spoken into the video, I returned to the camper very taken aback. As soon as I climbed into bed I spoke into the audio device to log my first day's thoughts. Listening back my voice and comments portray more than a little shock.

'Brutally tough,' was how I summed it up.

Day One took 71 minutes longer than my pre-race strategy. I had earlier crossed the finish line at 20:41pm or 14 hours and 41 minutes after I started. Already I had lost over an hour of the most valuable of resources, recovery time. What really concerned me was the fact that in reality I couldn't have gone much faster.

Every day the cut-off was 22 hours or 04:00 on the 24 hour clock. If you didn't finish within that time, you would be disqualified. Before the event, I struggled to comprehend that any day could take that long, but I hadn't bargained for the course being as hard as it was.

This course was a beast, its test keen to place every hour of our preparation under the microscope. By the end of that first day, four would already drop out.

DAY ONE

CHAPTER FIFTEEN

FRIDAY 3RD JUNE, 2011
06:00AM

SWIM

Fifty minutes after shooting that piece of video footage, Brendan and I made our way calmly down to the start line. That last five minutes before Steve Haywood started the event felt as long as a prison term.

As soon as the starting horn evaporated into the air, I submerged for the first time in competition. Unlike regular Ironman triathlons there was no mad panic or rush to the first buoy. This was not about speed. This was Friday. All going well, we would still be doing this on Sunday week.

This was about two things, stamina and endurance. It would literally be a survival of the fittest to keep going until the final day. Well that and avoiding injury. That is where luck or strategy might play some part.

To swim a 2.4 mile distance (3.8km) in the lake, we were required to do 13 laps each day, each one measuring 295 metres. The short course had one inconvenience however. It meant we had to stop momentarily at the end of each lap as competitors were funnelled into a counting area, with a requirement to shout out our race number. The organisers had to be certain of keeping an accurate count. I had been given the number four. Its significance? None really, apart from the fact that on Day One I would finish fourth.

It was an anti-clockwise course with yellow buoys lining the route. A strong morning sun was emerging which added to an already excited atmosphere. As I completed lap one, I watched carefully to ensure I navigated my way around the buoys and correctly back to base. This was our debut lap so it was new. As I completed lap one successfully, I stopped momentarily and stood up from beneath the water.

'Four,' I shouted.

'Four,' they replied in confirmation.

It was the competitors responsibility to ensure that the marshall replied with the correct number. I was sure they had said four. Great. That much mastered on that occasion. One down, only 129 more swim laps to go.

Over the next hour or more, I settled into a rhythm of about 65-70 per cent effort. This wasn't difficult. Ever since my marathon debut in 2007 where I hit the wall because of an early pace faux pas, I have always been good at pacing in races. I knew I had to be clever. Quite a few swimmers had already opened up a 10 metre gap even after a few laps. I didn't care one iota. I would do my thing. I would pace my race. I was determined to ease and feel my way into this event. It would be nothing if not very long.

Shortly after 7am, six wetsuits emerged from the lake before me. When I had 12 laps completed I was informed by the counters that this was my final lap. It was welcome news. As I was completing my last lap, I noticed one or two figures heading up the field towards the transition area but they were just shapes in the distance. They might have been competitors, marshalls, crew, ghosts, groupies, bible salesmen.

The records indicate I finished the swim on Day One in 1:15:03. This was modest based on previous swims over that distance but I am pretty certain the timing also included a walk of 250 metres back to transition that took several minutes. If I had three boxes to tick each day and 10 days to complete, I credited myself mentally with already ticking the first box of 30.

My final thought the night before in breaking down the magnitude of what lay ahead, was a metaphor of eating an elephant. Impossible at first thought but not if you eat it piece by piece.

On exiting the lake we had to walk to the area where most people had pitched their changing tents. Quite a few of them had chosen to sleep there as well. That was their choice. I felt like we were residing in a luxury hotel compared to some. Some athletes had secured lodges on the grounds but by the time I called about them they were booked out, so the camper seemed a logical alternative.

The ground logistics were only becoming apparent as we became accustomed to the surroundings. I hadn't brought a tent in which to change. Now going back to the camper was not an option, as it would be an additional 500 metres of unnecessary travelling in each direction. No need to scare the natives with a sight of my naked body though. Tony Fisher had kindly offered me the use of his changing tent the day before. A lesson already learned. A phone call was put through to Ken to bring one over with him on Sunday.

BIKE

The bike transition was on a disused tennis court. In regular triathlons, identifying your bike in transition can be a challenge. Usually competitors have to memorise where they have racked, which can be difficult because so many are competing. Not for this event though. The heavy wrought iron bars holding up our transport were barely burdened by our small numbers.

Co-organiser Eddie Ette greeted Brendan and I as we exited the bike racking area. A former Royal Marine, Ette looked as fit as a man half his 55 years. Six foot or more in height and with a tanned and chiselled exterior, he exemplified someone who embraced a healthy lifestyle. He and Haywood had set up Enduroman Events, in Eddie's words to 'help adventurers just like us to test themselves'. Ette had some extreme challenges ticked off himself. He was the first Royal Marine to swim the English Channel without a wetsuit and had once swum from Lanzarote to Fuerteventura in the Canary Islands, a distance of 16km. For Eddie, that was just a warm up. A short time later he swam the entire circumference of Lanzarote in 12 stages covering 140km along the way.

As I clipped into the pedals, Eddie updated me on how I was faring.

'You are first on the bike Gerry,' he informed me, his voice full of first day enthusiasm. Encouragement from Eddie never waned for the duration. He is without doubt one of the most pleasant and sincere sports organisers I have ever had the privilege to meet.

I was a little shocked by this news as a number of other competitors had swum much quicker than me. The first out of the water had been Englishman Mike Trew who sported a distinctive army major moustache. He completed the swim in a time of 1:06:56. I found out that he and the other five competitors who had been faster were still in the marquee tucking into a large breakfast for the long day ahead.

The start of our 1,160 mile cycle (1,866km) had a sharp 80 metre hill so we immediately had to vacate the saddle to climb it. Perhaps you have noticed that this is 40 miles further than I explained on page one as to how much a deca cycle was. For our event we would cycle an 11.6 mile looped circuit 10 times every day. The simple math added up to a further 40 miles over a 10-day period.

From the top of this hill, we had to cover a further 500 metres to reach the exit of the estate. Some of the other competitors had already christened a part of this stretch the 'rat run'. It had more pot-holes than a county council museum display. To add to the navigational challenge it had speed bumps. Not like speed bumps in Ireland which were barely elevated. These were real high bumps and four in number. That meant 80 crossings every day.

Before reaching the main road we had to cross the first of two cattle grids that were on the course. In a car a cattle grid barely warrants attention but on a bike it is different. Within a few days they would have my body contorting with discomfort at every crossing. In fact after the first 10 or 12 that day, it was already starting to make a lasting impression on my groin area.

I learned two things by 9am on Day One. The first was that the turning point at the end of every bike lap was an inconvenient distance from the marquee where the food was served. It would be perfectly located on the run route where we would pass it 26 times every evening. On the bike however, it was a nuisance as it would mean a return walk of 400 metres to get food. That few minutes when added to a five minute eating period, meant you were using up close to 10 minutes. I figured I could better utilise this time and began to hatch a plan for Day Two. More on this later.

The day before I had also hatched a plan to complete one lap on the bike before eating the official event breakfast. Brendan had earlier prepared my first breakfast back in the camper at 5am but eating more than normal would become a major strategy for my forward momentum. The organisers had warned us quite rightly that this was a fifth discipline along with swimming, cycling, running and rest. I also realised that if you waited until after the first bike lap to source an official breakfast, you would starve.

When I came in on that first morning as hungry as a wolf, the cupboard was bare. The chef quite understandably had thought everyone had finished and was cleaning up as I entered. I took full responsibility for this. To his credit he salvaged some scrambled egg from the corner of the serving dish and I devoured it. There was barely enough on the plate to feed a bird though. As I jogged back to the bike, I decided there and then to change my strategy after the next day's swim. I would stop at the marquee as I passed it on the way to the bike. This meant I would consume a second breakfast before beginning the cycle.

Each bike loop took us in an anti-clockwise direction of 11.6 miles (18.6 km) where normal rules of the road applied. On the first few laps I paced myself cautiously, taking in my surroundings for the first time. What struck me immediately was the vast contrasts in the landscape and in the traffic volumes as the morning matured. The first section offered panoramic views of heath, shrub and valley bogs for as far as the eye could see. The first three miles were also hectic with a mixture of locals, car tourists, biking enthusiasts and members of the equine community all jostling for their right of way. The last eight miles or so (13km) were a picture postcard vision of English countryside, full of woodland and grasslands and where a sight of another human was a rarity.

It would have been easy to go out fast but I knew that it would serve no purpose. I was determined to stick to a pace where I would finish Day One by about 7:30pm. On one lap I asked Brendan to record my time. I wanted to find out how long it took to complete a normal lap. This information would prove useful the further I got into the event as it would give me something to compare against. Just 44 minutes later I came in for my first lunch. It was 9:50am. Already we had swum 2.4 miles (3.8km) and I'd cycled 35 miles (56km), or three laps. I was starving. Thankfully Brendan was already developing a culinary talent to rival Gordon Ramsey's and I devoured a tasty omelette of gargantuan proportions.

By mid-morning on that first day I had already begun to form an intimate relationship with the bike course. Fortunately the chemistry was good as we had no choice but to get on. On the fourth loop, I noticed the terrain in a little more detail and by the beginning of the fifth (46 miles/ 74km), I had formulated a strategy to maximise the opportunities or take advantage of the weaknesses in the route that I had already identified.

As we exited the gates of Avon Tyrell after completing a little under half a mile, we hit the public road. From here we had about 400 metres before arriving at a major T-junction where the traffic volume increased significantly. Here we had to slow, often to a standstill, while casting a quick glance over our right shoulders to watch for oncoming traffic. Then there was the luxury of a fast descent of approximately 500 metres.

At this the highest point which was just before our descent, we had a view of every car and bicycle for a mile or more. (*See bike map at the beginning of the book for reference*). The downhill gradient had its benefits. I quickly worked out that taking full advantage required exquisite timing and a little good fortune.

The entire area in which we cycled was known locally as The

New Forest and it was a tourist attraction for the young and the young-at-heart. Because of the large volume of visitors and the traffic, narrow chicanes had been built into the surrounding road network. I had never seen their like before. The chicane was a simple narrowing of the road where a high concrete curb cut into the already narrow road, with the intention of slowing down traffic. It was in fact impossible for any more than one vehicle at a time whether car, bike or beast to pass through.

With a full sight of the enemy, we could calculate who might have priority at each chicane. Over the space of 40 seconds or several hundred metres it required constant reassessment so as to time your arrival at the chicanes to the optimum. To have to slow down would not only hinder our progress, it would also drain a few ounces of mental energy.

In the overall scheme of things this short stretch and the opportunity it presented might seem insignificant. Were we to make it to the end however, by then we would have travelled it 100 times in all. It was one of only two significant downhill opportunities where you could take considerable advantage of not having to pedal for quite a distance. Multiply that by 10 times a day for 10 days and it added up to over six miles (9.6km) of potential untaxed progress. Any time you had to slow down took away this freewheeling opportunity. I can recall reaching speeds of up to 40 miles per hour (65 km) on this stretch only to have to give way on occasion to an oncoming Vauxhall, a motorbike or a New Forest pony.

The only village on the loop through which we had to cycle was the village of Burley. It was famous for two things, witches and ice-cream. It was a mecca for tourists and its single main street had more ice-cream parlours than a Los Angeles beach boulevard. It was a typical picture postcard village consisting of a post office, newsagents and a butcher's shop. It had a village store, several tearooms, antique shops, art galleries and a couple of gift shops. Those giftshops sold pointed witches' hats, long handled broomsticks and magic potions. Witches and ice-cream cones soon became ingrained into my eyelids as I became more and more familiar with this petite but beautiful Hampshire village.

Day One on the bike had very few highlights. It was more about becoming acquainted with our surroundings and finding good cycling legs. The only incident that stood out was when I momentarily lost concentration about 30 metres from a chicane. I was briefly distracted and had my head facing downward, unaware of the indent ahead. I only realised it approximately seven-hundredths of a second before I was about to come a cropper. I jammed the back brake while turning the handlebars to the right. As I did so the bike skidded beyond the pilot's control.

Hitting the high curb at 20 miles an hour, I would have come off second best. As serious as the impact might have been on the bike, it was the only bike I had. Ken was still back in Ireland packing his socks, his underwear and my spare bike. I shouted out loud as a reprimand to myself. 'What an idiot.' I needed to focus more. I wasn't concentrating. And this was Day One when I had all my faculties intact.

Ironically the climbs of which there were quite a few, actually helped me. It was a welcome opportunity to give the calves and hamstring muscles in my legs a good stretch by getting out of the saddle. It was several weeks since I had had a really good workout.

The first 10 miles or so (16km) had plenty of hillocks, some short sharp rises and a 200 metre hill to climb just after passing through Burley. It was a rise in elevation but nothing overly-taxing. Between miles 10 miles and 11, it was payback time though for the lovely descent we had profited from earlier. Isaac Newtown's theory of 'what goes up, must come down' was perhaps solidified in Hampshire. On the back entry to the estate, we had to climb back up an equivalent distance and more. It wasn't as sharp as the descent but it was longer. Almost ¾ of a mile all told. Once or twice would be fine. By the end of Day One, we still had 90 more climbs ahead of us on that hill alone.

In the mid-afternoon I returned to Brendan and base camp, 116 miles (186.6km) completed and a second box ticked. The first cycle had taken me eight hours and four minutes. It was slow but for several reasons. It was a tough course and was seldom flat. It had that long ascent on the back side that would over time take on the appearance of a test of Himalayan proportions. The route was also four miles longer (6.4km) than it needed to be. To be fair, it was impossible to shorten. It was what it was.

At 3:20pm, I dismounted and changed for the first of 10 marathons.

RUN

I am a reasonably paced runner. Not exceptionally fast but with proper dedication to a single marathon yielding a personal best of two hours, 53 minutes and eight seconds. On Friday, June 3, I ran a marathon at what I felt was a strong pace to finish off what had been a tough first day. Yes, I paced myself cautiously but I still ran strong. The time it took me to finish utterly shocked me though. The severity of the terrain shocked me too.

When Brendan and I had walked it a few days before it had looked difficult. To do its challenge justice, here are the facts. It was a loop of a little over a mile that we had to run 26 times every evening. That didn't bother me at all. In fact for events such as this a short loop makes complete sense both logistically as well as providing the athletes with regular positive bursts of energy as you meet crew, supporters, officials, food and emergency medical cover if needed and have easy access to toilets.

Before starting the run I had already swum and cycled for just under nine and a half hours. Even after three laps of the run, I was expressing surprise at the time each lap was taking. Just like in the descent at the beginning of the bike circuit, on the run route we also had a descent, this time of c.300 metres. On two wheels a descent is blissful. On two legs in this event, it was of no advantage and on two tired legs, it was actually painful. Even on the first lap my quadricep muscles were annoyed (large muscles at the front of the upper leg between the hip joint and the knee joint). I tried to ignore them. I told myself that this unexpected pain would dissipate. I told myself that it was something I would become accustomed to or that it would simply level off.

I was wrong.

How could I be as slow as I was? Sure, I had stopped for dinner in the marquee after 21 miles (33km), the only time in 10 days I would stop during the run. That stop took me 15 minutes. Even taking that into consideration, I was disappointed when Brendan handed me my split times for each discipline as we walked back towards the camper. That first run had taken me five hours and 21 minutes. This was Day One. It was unlikely I was ever going to get much faster, was I?

Later some competitors suggested the entire marathon distance was long by over a mile. When I heard grumblings of this, I simply said to myself that it was what it was and that even if it was longer, it wasn't going to change. We already knew the bike route was 116 miles each day and four miles beyond what was required. This event was meant to be hard. That is what we had signed up for. The toughest triathlon of them all. In fact, I adapted well to the fact that it might be longer. The possible extra distance didn't get to me. It was just the length of time that the marathon had taken was very unexpected.

The organisers prided themselves on setting very stiff exams. For sure, these 10 days would be.

'No hiding place,' they had proudly boasted.

You will notice I haven't gone into much detail about the marathon itself. We have plenty of time.

STANDINGS AFTER DAY ONE

Competitor	Race Position	Time
Toby Smithson	1	12:53:33
Lee Wigzell	2	13:48:14
Hanno Nickau	3	14:16:25
Gerry Duffy	4	14:41:07
Russell Clarke	5	15:17:11
Andy Kemp	6	15:39:39
Jean Yves Even	7	16:14:53
Roderick Elder	8	16:25:49
Neil Kapoor	9	16:26:21
Tony Fisher	10	16:34:58
Richard Ginn	11	16:38:51
Tony Raynor	12	16:41:06
Mark Padley	13	16:51:49
Michael Trew	14	16:57:45
Mick Barnes	15	17:46:47
Edward Page	16	18:11:34
Andrew Moore	17	18:17:38
Monique Hollinshead	18	19:28:49
Keith Laing	19	19:37:26
Simon Pearson	20	dnf

DAY TWO

CHAPTER SIXTEEN

SATURDAY 4TH JUNE, 2011

At the lakeshore the next morning, Brendan brought me up to date on how everybody had performed on the opening day. A spreadsheet had been posted in the marquee. Fastest competitor of the day had been Toby Smithson, a 39-year-old Englishman, in a time of 12:53:53.

Smithson was four years younger than I was and looked exceptionally fit. Still, I struggled to work out why someone would want to finish almost two hours quicker than I had done.

My pre-race plan had been to finish in 13.5 hours on Day One but the course had dictated a much slower opening time than I had thought realistic and achievable.

A few weeks earlier, I had spotted a report on the internet outlining what experience each competitor had in their locker. It showed that Smithson, a professional triathlon coach from West Yorkshire, had completed four iron distance triathlons. Perhaps the one that stood out most was the Norseman event in Scandinavia. Known as a gruelling iron distance course, competitors began the day by being thrown off a Norwegian car ferry trawler into a cold North Sea.

After the 2.4 mile swim (3.8km), competitors had to cycle 112 miles (180km), the first 25 miles (40km) of which was all uphill. The marathon run had a flat first 15.5 miles (25km) before competitors were required to finish the distance by climbing the 'Gaustatoppen' mountain, 1880m above sea-level. Toby had finished high up in that field so he obviously had a good pedigree. Notwithstanding that, I wondered was such a pace really wise on Day One? Not only was this not a one-day event, just like the Norseman, this course was a beast.

Toby had considerable experience before he arrived at the deca though and had eight years of triathlon experience all told. He was on a journey to find out what was the hardest event in the sport.

Toby

'My first Ironman opened up a whole new world of challenges. People were saying this is a tough event, this is hard, this is impossible, etc. It struck me that no-one could decide which event was the hardest – so I set about doing all the tough events that existed so I could find out for myself.'

He had prepared as well as anyone.

Toby

'My plan had been put together based on my experience, asking people, internet research, ultra running, cycling stage racing. I knew I'd be comfortable with the swimming. As well as sessions getting longer, I did lots of bricks (two different disciplines back-to-back) and back-to-back days. The main training block was a week's camping in Wales where I did at least a half-iron distance triathlon every day and then tapered from this.'

He had arrived...

Toby

'...with a mix of trepidation and excitement. I felt confident that I had done the training I needed to do and I arrived well rested, without injury and ready to go.'

The second man home had crossed the line in a time of 13:48.14. Impressive as well but on Day Two he didn't show. I had finished in fourth place and was quietly chuffed. I knew I'd paced as cautiously as my competitive streak would allow.

Already some looked more tired than others. The final finisher Keith Laing had crossed the finish line at 1:37am. That was less than four and a half hours before he had to do it again. The only lady in the field Monique Hollinshead, had finished just nine

'DON'T WE ALL HAVE A WAKE-UP MOMENT SOME TIME IN OUR LIVES?'

FORE! This picture of me with my sporting hero Seve Ballesteros in 1995 was my wake-up moment. I was overweight, unfit and unhappy. My new story began there...

FOREST FAN: Training for the Deca pushed me further than ever before including four half iron distance sessions in four consecutive days. The third morning saw me in Mullaghmeen forest (above) at 6:30am having already cycled 35 miles to get there. I was determined to do whatever it took.

THE CREW 'TO ACHIEVE ANY MAJOR GOAL WE NEED TO SURROUND OURSELVES WITH GREAT PEOPLE...'

JACINTA O'NEILL

BRENDAN DOYLE

KEN WHITELAW

DOUGLAS BATES

JARLETH MAHON

DOROTHY DUFFY

ENDA MUNNELLY

ALAN MAYE

BARRY WHITELAW

THE TOWN I NOW KNOW SO WELL: The village of Burley in Hampshire, England played host to the deca... It was full of ice-cream parlours and horses.

'NO HIDING PLACE' THE MEN IN CHARGE PROMISED. AND THEY WERE RIGHT... EVERY QUESTION WOULD BE ASKED

EVENT ORGANISERS STEVE HAYWOOD, DAN EARTHQUAKE AND EDDIE ETTE

FEATURED COMPETITORS

EDWARD PAGE

MONIQUE HOLLINSHEAD

MARK PADLEY

MIKE TREW

TONY RAYNOR

TOBY SMITHSON

HANNO NICKAU

AND THE DOCTOR WHO WATCHED OVER US...

DR LEIGH COWLING

DAY 1
03.06.2011

'VERY PENSIVE, VERY NERVOUS, VERY RESPECTFUL OF WHAT LIES AHEAD...'

LIGHT, CAMERA, ACTION... Dawn breaks in The New Forest on Day One.

HERE COMES OZZY: Having Brendan there was like having Clint Eastwood as my co-pilot.

KEEN AS MUSTARD: Walking down to the lake on Day One was a surreal experience. Until I saw this picture I didn't realise I was first into the water.

IN AT THE DEEP END: We had to swim 295 metres 13 times a day. Accurate counting ensured we all swam every metre.

VILLAGE PEOPLE: Burley was full of magic and ice-cream

THE LEADING MAN: Englishman Toby Smithson got off to a flyer, finishing in 12 hours and 53 minutes, almost an hour ahead of the field.

TUCKING IN: Tony Raynor fuels to start his first marathon of ten

'FIRST DAY ENTHUSIASM HAD ALREADY DISAPPEARED'

HEAD DOWN: In the early days my swim stroke actually started to improve with all of the practice.

HORSES FOR COURSES: As well as having to obey the rules of the road, we also have to give way to the horses.

MOUNTAIN TO DESCEND: This 10-metre stretch put fear into my legs almost every day. By the tenth day it took me over a minute-and-a-half to get down. After that descent, we immediately then had to duck underneath these overhanging trees.

'IT WAS HARD TO COMPREHEND THAT IN A WEEK'S TIME WE WOULD STILL BE HERE'

OUR HOUSE: Our camper was a luxury relative to sleeping in a tent. There was little wardrobe space though.

CEREAL EATER: Every morning I ate some cereal after lap one of the bike. The crew drank the coffee.

IF THE CAP FITS: No pain, no dry hair in the lake

FOREST TRAIL: The organisers had offered a beautiful but very challenging running environment

THREE DOWN... Back in the camper with Jacinta and Brendan.

MISTER FLASH: Ken, a keen photographer, got unique pictures of the lights emanating from the head torches of the competitors as they ran through the forest.

'BY NOW I WAS IN SECOND PLACE. I DIDN'T REALISE IT AT THE TIME'

HEAD DOWN BUT WATCHING AHEAD: On Days Three and Four Toby's demeanour seemed different. Something was up.

HELPING HANDS: By now Jacinta, Brendan and Doug were operating like a professional Formula One pit crew.

HOW ARE YOU DOING LOVE? Jacinta walks to the bike with me.

BYE GERRY: Jacinta and Brendan bid farewell on Day Four

HAMSTER IN A TURNING WHEEL: We had to complete 262 laps of the run course.

DAN THE MAN: Mr Earthquake and I share a moment after four in four.

COOL RUNNING: Every night I headed back to the cold water in the lake to help soothe and heap recovery into my leg muscles. I am certain it helped.

'IF WE FINISH TODAY, WE WILL HAVE REACHED AN IMPORTANT MILESTONE'

LEFT: Big Ted brushes his teeth during a break. During the event we did not have a spare minute.

ABOVE: I was in charge of the smoothies, protested Doug. Putting up the tent was Ken's job.

OUCH: 7pm on Day Five. Maybe the injury was starting even before I first consciously noticed it on Day Six.

DIN-DINS: Mark Padley and Big Ted stopped for dinner every night. I preferred to keep moving. We all had different strategies.

minutes before Keith. That meant at best Monique had got four hours continuous sleep. A week later she and I met up briefly on the bike course. I told her then that she was the greatest sportswoman I had ever had the privilege to meet. My reasons for making this statement will emerge as you travel this journey with me.

As Day Two had dawned, I was awoken by my crew member gently stroking my forehead. It was a few minutes before 5am. I grasped the hand warmly, keen to embrace the compassion. The touch was comforting. Human contact can mean so much. By now you are thinking that either Brendan Doyle was taking this crewing a little serious or else he and I were getting on very well. Well it was neither, wash out your mind. Jacinta had arrived in late on Friday night.

The records from Day One indicate I had finished in 14 hours, 41 minutes and 14 seconds. This was more than an hour beyond my already cautious first day strategy. Yes, it did concern me. It meant I was already down on sleep and I knew I was unlikely to get any faster. I was already tired and sore and within a few minutes I had to do it all over again.

Monique Hollinshead

'I think we were all shocked about how demanding the course was. All of us took longer than expected and all of us felt worse than we had anticipated. After Day One I had to re-adjust my expectations. You can't enter a race thinking you won't finish but after Day One I thought precisely that. Paradoxically, this made it easier. I wasn't worrying anymore about how I would feel on days 3, 4, 5 and 6 etc as I was unlikely to make those days. Instead it became a case of seeing if I could walk in the morning. If I can get up, I'll head down to the lake.

This was a trip into the unknown, a new event on a new course. I realised that I had treated it all wrong – this wasn't about doing an iron distance each day an hour or two slower than my stand-alone time and then getting a full night's sleep – this was about eating enough during the day to fuel for the present and the following day.

On Day One I had eaten nowhere near enough while on the bike so I decided to walk the entire first days marathon eating the whole time. It meant a slow time of 19 and a half hours but I would get quicker once I started to run. The course would not bend. The lumps and bumps would be there, so it was up to me to bend.'

As a result of losing valuable time on Day One, Monique decided to develop a strategy whereby she would stop and nap quite often. Her first day's efforts demanded it. Already she probably had not had sufficient recovery time. Each hour's sleep was as valuable to us as a treasure chest bursting with gold. Unless she managed somehow to recover it during the day, it would have serious consequences further down the line. On Day Two, that was already evident as she finished just six minutes faster than her first.

Big Ted perhaps best summed up the mood.

Big Ted
'What the hell was going on? These incredible, experienced and well-trained athletes were talking so negatively. Few seemed happy.'

The average finishing time on Day One had been 16 hours and 20 minutes

Day Two would take me 15 hours and 21 minutes or 40 minutes longer than it had on Day One. Were I to continue to slow at this rate of decline, then at some stage I might struggle to make the cut-off. That had never entered my head in advance of the event.

My audio diary later that night pulled no punches. Listening back, I could actually sense the exhaustion creeping quietly into my voice. My breathing too, sounds laboured.

AUDIO DIARY (AT THE END OF DAY TWO)

'If I thought yesterday was hard, today was even harder. Left arm stiffer in swim. Run was just horrendous'.

That is the printable part of the audio as I replayed it. My opening three words are unprintable. It was recorded a little after 10pm. Sixteen hours earlier we had gathered at the lakeshore a few minutes later than the opening morning. First day enthusiasm had already totally disappeared.

At the lake Steve went through the entire list of 20 names as he had done 24 hours before. This time only 16 people responded to the names being called out. Reasons for this spread like a virus. One had a genuine family reason for withdrawal (Neil Kapoor). The others, we simply didn't know. Was it injury, exhaustion, ability related? Rumour had it that one competitor had simply commented that 'this isn't for me' after he crossed the finish line. Well at least that's honesty.

Nobody seemed overly-enthused to get into the water much before 6:00am. The opening day had offered a very hot 27 degrees Celsius (80.6°F). Perhaps that had also affected our performances. Day Two would be a few degrees cooler but still warm nonetheless.

My second swim just like the first, was uneventful. I emerged three minutes slower but already I'd lost interest in even knowing that fact. It was what it was. I knew it was somewhat similar to the first swim and in the overall scheme of things a few minutes here or there in the water hardly mattered. I was pacing myself.

My only change from Day One saw me eat my second breakfast of the day immediately after the swim. Over two hours earlier, I had eaten my first when Brendan prepared organic porridge, honey and various milled seeds made with water and milk. It was my foundation meal every morning.

Immediately after changing into my bike kit, I sat down in the breakfast marquee and sampled the talents of the chef. Before me was scrambled egg for protein and sausages for their high fat content. The toast was simply for carbohydrates. I ate the egg and meat slowly as I was keen to digest it properly. My crew of Jacinta, Brendan and a first cousin from London who was on a two day visit, Padraig Sherry, hovered over me as if I was a protected species. If I stuffed it down my throat I knew I'd be reprimanded, so I indulged them by sitting for a brief two minute period.

As soon as I had it swallowed I rose to my feet carrying the toast in my hand, eating it slowly as I made my way to my bike. My brain was razor sharp. I wasn't keen on wasting time which is why I consumed the toast as I walked. I was learning to put the inches together while I ate, slept or exercised. I knew at the end of the 10 days they would add up to something pretty big. By the time I climbed aboard the bike it was 7:30am. For the second day in a row, I was first out onto the bike.

Early on Day Two some extra tests sprang up. The first was the wind. We had experienced quite a breeze on the first day but that was hardly a shock. This was not the south of France. As soon as I turned out of the estate it hit me in the face. All day long it blew. It wasn't overly challenging and certainly nothing that I wasn't used too. It just sapped a little extra energy as we all had to pedal a fraction harder.

On lap six of the bike a day earlier, I had felt a piercing pain in two of the toes on my right foot. In all my years of cycling I'd never felt such discomfort. I convinced myself that it was a one-off and I tried to forget about it. The first few hours of the cycle on Day Two were uneventful but as I climbed the long drag at the end of lap six (70 miles/112km), I let out a sharp yelp as the pain returned. It was like an unexpected injection jab. Again it was centred on the same two adjoining toes and was extremely painful.

Immediately I took my foot out of the clipped-in-shoe and repositioned it on top of the shoe itself which was clipped into the pedal. This made pedalling quite awkward but mercifully the pain disappeared. I was only a few minutes from home so I stopped to update Brendan. I asked him to have a think about it to see if he could come up with a diagnosis. For the next 10 miles (16km) with my foot back in the shoe, the pain disappeared, only to come back again as I climbed the same hill. I'd no option but to cycle the next 20 miles (32 km) with my right foot on top of the shoe again. With about 25 miles (40km) remaining I put the foot back into the shoe to test it. This time it was fine. I'd plenty of time to consider what might be causing it. It seemed obvious – the shoes. I'd only broken in a new pair a month before. Before that I'd worn the same pair for four years. They were in the camper and for sure would be on my feet the next day.

My average lap time on Day One on the bike had been just shy of 49 minutes. This included transitions and quite a few food breaks. On Day Two it was 52 minutes. I don't put this down to exhaustion. I had a slower swim to bike transition because of the breakfast stop (nine minutes longer) but that would be negated by not having to walk to the marquee after lap one like I had the day before. Perhaps it was the stronger wind and having to cycle more than 20 miles (32km) with the aid of only one shoe clipped in. Overall I was 40 minutes slower, covering the 116 miles (186km) in 8 hours and 44 minutes, a sizeable drop. I couldn't dwell on it though as I still had 26.2 miles (42.2km) to run before bedtime.

As I dismounted, Brendan told me Toby Smithson had only got off his bike 25 minutes before me. The day before he had been one hour and 20 mins faster. That was quite a drop. Perhaps he had deliberately slowed down.

> **Toby**
> 'My strategy was simple... to win and I wanted to win every day. Day One was interesting. I raced hard (especially in that heat, which people seem to forget) to see who would come with me, knowing that I would bank time against the

more experienced athletes because they would take it easy and play the long game. I took it easier the next day as the event became more organised and we fine-tuned our processes. Everyone was learning how to do this.'

By now I was starting to formulate a few personal strategies myself. I'd asked Jacinta and Brendan to have my run gear ready at the bike finish so that I could commence the marathon without undue delay. On that turnaround alone I made up over 12 minutes on Toby. It wasn't that I was trying to catch him. In my eyes this event could not be raced in the sense of absolute speed.

I felt I needed to exercise caution and discipline this early on. I was also very conscious that on days six, seven and beyond, my body was going to ask me many questions. How did you look after me in the early days Gerry? Did you feed me well Gerry? Did you pace me well Gerry? Did you rest me? Did you get me a massage? Cool me down in the lake? Fuel me to finish not two or three days but ten?

That is why at all times I tried to move competitively but within myself. This was all about finishing 10 days.

Another strategy I decided on was not wasting precious minutes chatting to anyone. Starting at 4:05pm, I still had a marathon to run to complete Day Two. I felt that the transition should never have needed any more than a minute or two. Out of the bike gear and into the run kit. Simple. Others felt differently and that was their right. Maybe they wanted to stretch, to eat, to sleep for a few minutes or to chat to their crew. I just wanted to get each day done as quickly as possible and within the pace I had set down.

My strategy was to bank all those precious five minute breaks or 10/15 minute rest periods that others were taking, so that by the end of the day I would finish an hour or more earlier than I might have. By doing so, I felt I would add an extra hour or more to a single bout of continuous sleep and recovery.

The run route was unique at every turn. Our final test every day was to complete it 26 times. The first 80 metres of it was the same climb that we had to do on the bike. Here the bike and run route ran parallel for a few short seconds. At the top though, we took a 90 degree turn to the right to begin a 300 metre descent. That might sound comforting. It was exactly the opposite. Any runner will tell you that overworked muscles do not like running downhill. It's a killer on the quadricep muscles. On Day One I was stunned at how angry my quads were here. Having pain that early into this challenge really took me by surprise. Day Two was no different. The surface here was also littered with small rocks which ensured that every metre was uncomfortable. Walking it with Brendan a few days earlier I'd hardly noticed them.

At the bottom of this hill we took a sharp turn to the left and entered a covered forested area that meandered through a myriad of tree species like spruce, ash and beech and over some small man-made sleeper bridges that assisted us over gaps in the topography. A significant part of the challenge of this 150 metre section was the angle of the terrain and the requirement to continually switch direction every five metres or so. Much of it had a 15 or 20 degree slope to the right meaning you had to run sideways in parts. The continuous repetitive impact that this would have on one of my legs would only become apparent the further I got into the event.

The complete loop was one big circle with the exception of a small digression in the centre. Midway through this bottom section of the course we encountered what for me would emerge as the most difficult part of the entire run loop. Just before turning at the bottom of the circle, there was a significant drop in the terrain, perhaps three metres over a mere 10 metres. That might not sound challenging in a regular afternoon stroll, but this was far from a stroll. That drop was littered with tree-roots that whilst offering tiny ledges to assist our descent, also presented a very undesirable test on every lap. It wasn't the severity of the drop.

A three-year-old could manage it. It was the fact that we had to do it so often.

> **Monique**
> 'It was a short but sharp slope where you felt that no matter how carefully you took it you were bound to trip and fall.'

Even at this early stage I was already beginning to dread this section. On top of the fact that it slowed my momentum almost to a walk. Every metre of descent, hurt. I was determined to run as much as 90 per cent of every marathon but here I had no option but to slow down. That deceleration put an extra 10-20 seconds to every lap and added 6-8 minutes onto each marathon.

That second marathon took me 5:18:52. I crossed the finish line a half an hour before nightfall.

It was 9:22pm.

STANDINGS AFTER DAY TWO

Competitor	Cumulative Race Position	Day One	Day Two	Cumulative Total
Toby Smithson	1	12:53:33	15:12:30	28:05:03
Gerry Duffy	2	14:41:07	15:22:12	30:03:19
Hanno Nickau	3	14:16:25	16:33:11	30:47:36
Andy Kemp	4	15:39:39	17:14:05	32:53:14
Roderick Elder	5	16:25:49	17:11:33	33:37:22
Mark Padley	6	16:51:49	17:16:45	34:08:34
Mike Trew	7	16:57:45	17:15:34	34:13:19
Tony Fisher	8	16:34:58	17:38:23	34:13:21
Richard Ginn	9	16:38:51	17:45:44	34:24:35
Tony Raynor	10	16:41:06	18:19:58	35:01:04
Russell Clarke	11	15:17:11	20:28:48	35:45:59
Mick Barnes	12	17:46:47	19:27:11	37:13:58
Andrew Moore	13	18:17:38	20:16:14	38:33:52
Monique Hollinshead	14	19:28:49	19:23:00	38:51:49
Edward Page	15	18:11:34	21:19:14	39:30:48
Keith Laing	16	19:37:26	21:19:13	40:56:39

CHAPTER SEVENTEEN

Backroom Team
Take Centre Stage

By the beginning of Day Three Jacinta and Brendan were operating like a professional Formula One pit crew. Having my cousin Padraig arrive unexpectedly also generated new energy into the team. Padraig had a lot of marathons in his legs so he knew the importance of focussing on the job. Jacinta and Brendan had both crewed together with Ken and I in the summer of 2010 as we had visited every county in Ireland. They were very experienced.

A crew's labour was already as trying and even more demanding timewise than for the athletes. Given the length of each day's on-course activity, sleep for them was very scarce. They had to rise 15 minutes before we awoke. They had to prepare our kit and meals for the next day long after we would close our eyes. They had to be positive and sometimes lie through their teeth telling us how well we looked, when in reality we looked like we had been run over by a charging rhinoceros.

Astonishingly some competitors had arrived without a crew. That made no sense to me. To achieve any big goal you need to surround yourself with great people. Brendan and Jacinta took up the mantle of cheering every competitor, happy to give them all a boost. If anybody else wanted something they obliged as did some other crews. One thing about this event was that the camaraderie was palpable. Everybody was rooting for everyone.

A hundred metres to the left of that 80 metre climb that we had at the beginning of each bike loop was where our camper van and sleeping quarters were located (*see maps, pages 12-15*). Brendan saw the pointlessness of travelling down to the bottom of the hill to meet me between laps and instead set up camp (a chair) at the top of the hill. This meant he was only 15 seconds from the camper as I returned after each bike lap. Several times I would shout out what I needed and he would run and get it while I descended the hill to finish a loop and climb it seconds later to begin the next. The timing always worked. On meal stops I'd step off the bike and sit for a few minutes in the chair. I never asked where he got it but it certainly didn't come in my luggage.

That second night I recall Brendan confessing to falling asleep earlier in the camper in between laps three and four of the cycle. When he woke up, he was completely oblivious as to how long he had slept. As it transpired I was crossing the final speed bump and re-entering the estate as he raced down to the chair. For all he knew I could have done three laps. I didn't know about his siesta and he didn't make me any the wiser at the time. After the event, he denied it had ever happened. Perhaps his memory faded under the workload.

Once Jacinta arrived, she immediately began from where she had left off a year earlier. The truth is she had been doing it throughout my training period as well. Her attention to detail was exceptional. Jacinta becomes incredibly focussed in a mission and isn't afraid to give me a stiff lecture when it is called for. She arrived in late Friday night on a flight from Dublin having finished work at 3pm. One of the first duties she carried out was a late night massage of the legs. It felt like heaven and a reward for my hard efforts earlier that day. She knew I had a low threshold for pain after race exertions and only applied pressure on my legs to a level I could tolerate.

On Day Two amongst the hundreds of tasks she carried out and assumed authority over, was the making a post race 'smoothie drink'. This for me, was a vital recovery strategy. I learned this tactic from the wisdom of a food scientist in 2010. Back then, the advice I received was about the importance of food recovery and of giving the body every opportunity to repair itself for the next day by consuming muscle repairing nutrition.

"The quicker you can get it into you, Gerry, the faster the body will begin to repair itself," was the voice I kept hearing as I consumed its qualities.

This 1,000ml blended concoction typically consisted of a natural whey protein, orange juice, a mixture of fruits or berries combined with honey, sea-salt and water. To get to the end of Day Ten was going to put every small part of my strategy under examination.

I knew that every question whether physical, mental or nutritional would be asked at some point. Already many tests had appeared. The shock of my slow time on Day One, the pain in my toes and the difficulty my leg muscles experienced on the marathon every night. I had become more adept in later years of expecting the unexpected and then dealing with it. Getting the right food at the right times was also key.

A few final words to close out on food. For the duration I had to eat 'normal' food. Much of it would not usually be on my menu in everyday life but now I had no choice. Here is a sample of the type and quantities I was consuming in the opening three days. This was what I ate on Day Two.

BREAKFASTS
- A large bowl of organic porridge mixed with lots of milled seeds, milled nuts, goji berries, honey and a cup of tea
- Large portion of scrambled egg
- Two sausages
- Two slices of buttered white toast
- One bowl of Special K

LUNCHES
- Two large dessert bowl portions of chicken and wheat free pasta (after laps two and four)

DINNERS
- Steak sandwich (lap 2 of the run)

- Scrambled egg sandwich (lap 10 of the run)
- Chicken, potatoes, spinach, sweet peas and potato salad (lap 20 of the run)

POST RACE
- Smoothie full of fruits, orange juice, sea salt, and honey
- Large bowl of Special K cereal and tea (yes Kellogg's!)

MISCELLANEOUS ITEMS DURING THE DAY
- Three bananas
- Three Ma Baker bars (c.470 calories each)
- One Mars bar
- Regular citrus flavour energy drink (5 litres)
- Three cans of Coke
- Regular Dioralyte (rehydration salt taken in water)

DAY THREE

CHAPTER EIGHTEEN

SUNDAY 5TH JUNE, 2011

Today was our first Sunday. It was hard to comprehend that in a week's time we would still be here.

The first Sunday began like any other with 13 laps of the lake. By now I could actually feel my swim stroke starting to improve. I had nothing to measure this by. I simply felt I was moving at a similar pace but with less effort. I looked forward to the swim. The thought alone soothed some of my aches and pains.

Up to now the swim was always unexciting which was a relief. Each morning we were submerged in it from 6am until we had completed 13 laps. The lake was unattractive, pitch black beneath and much of it was covered in lily pads.

By now an early pattern was emerging every morning sometime around 7.10am or thereabouts, whereupon Mike Trew came out first. On Day Three he exited a full five minutes ahead of yours truly.

A married father of three from nearby Poole (10 miles away) Mike was amongst other things, a long-distance swimmer. His list of achievements in sport also included completing one iron distance triathlon, two double irons and a triple distance as well. His CV didn't stop there. It was also propped up by more than 40 marathons and 20 ultra marathons. Before the event his plan was to complete each day in approximately 14 hours and then drive home to sleep in his own bed. After the wake-up call which the course gave all of us on the first day – 17 hours for him – he erected a tent less than 50 metres from the lakeshore and slept there instead. By then he already knew the importance of energy conservation.

I was second out on Day Three in 1:15:21. The top five usually read Mike, Toby, Mark Padley, Hanno Nickau and myself. Not that it mattered this early, but that was how it was.

Today we had two more casualties who didn't appear for the swim. Russell Clarke added a 2:28am or 20 hr 28 min day to a

9:27pm (15hr 27min) first day finish. There simply wasn't enough time for Russell to recover. Likewise Andrew Moore had burned way beyond the midnight oil and he too did not show. This meant we were down to 14.

Monique however was aiming to prove that you could finish late and still recover in time. On the second night she finished at 1:23am, a time very consistent with her first but surely not a good omen this early. People were now already concerned for her and others. She was getting to bed at 2am and was back up a little after 5am to do it again. The reality was that nobody was getting faster.

Monique seemed to pace herself very cautiously and particularly on the bike leg. It's not that she couldn't go faster. Monique had finished one place ahead of me in an event in 2009. She simply was working off a different strategy to mine. Her's involved stopping quite often to eat slowly and to have short power naps during the daytime.

> **Monique**
> 'After a few days I found I needed to go for a sleep after the swim, otherwise I was nodding off on the bike. Power naps and a sleep after breakfast were added in but they contributed to the lengthening time out on the course meaning less time in bed.'

On lap six of the cycle, again the same pain in my right foot returned. It also surfaced in my left as well. This really baffled me as by now I was wearing my old shoes. Maybe there was more to this than I had thought. I'd no option but to regularly cycle with both feet out of the shoes. 'Do whatever it takes. Just keep moving forward' I thought to myself.

At least 40 miles (65km) on the third day was done using this method. It was awkward but I had no option. As soon as I took my feet out of the shoes, the pain instantly disappeared. Sometimes I would do a lap and then put the shoes back on. Ten or 11 miles might pass before it returned again. Each time it was excruciating. I am a low-tolerance patient at the best of times. For sure I love the pain of endurance, but this was different.

On a scale of one to 10, the pain was close to a nine. Often I couldn't get my foot out of the shoe quickly enough. Sometimes I screamed loudly but I was alone so I didn't care. I knew though that it wasn't practical to have to cycle significant portions of the remaining 850 or more miles (1360km) with my feet out of the shoes. But what could I do?

I also had another concern. For 14 or 15 hours every day I had a lot of time to think. I am somebody whose brain is normally going at 100 miles an hour. Now all of a sudden, all I had to do was swim, cycle and run all day long. Apart from that, I had no jobs, tasks or errands to run. Just lots of time to think – and about nothing in particular. Sometimes that can be a good thing but now it allowed time for negative thoughts to pay a visit. Hitting some low mental moments during an event of this magnitude was perhaps inevitable. But not every day. On each of the first two days and now again on Day Three it happened.

I pride myself on having a strong mind. It wasn't always the case. I was the opposite at one time when I doubted myself at every turn. Now I rarely do.

So much of what can be achieved lies in our mindsets. That is something I feel I've learned to tap into. A chance meeting with a supporter and crew member at a double iron event back in 2009 had taught me a lot. Low mental moments in events such as this are sent to test us. As Thomas Fuller said in a proverb: *'It is always darkest before the dawn'.*

Back in 2009, I had learned a valuable lesson about what to do when you are hit head on by a low moment or a state of mental anxiety. In August of that year I was competing in a double iron distance event in Litchfield, just a few miles north of Birmingham.

Having started at 9.30am on a Saturday morning, by 2am the next morning I had already swum 4.8 miles (7.6km) and cycled 178 miles (286km) of the 224 miles (360km) required.

At that unearthly hour the temperature had dropped and a fog was not helping my mood or indeed my navigation. As I sat and ate at the bike turnaround, I was very low. Just then a lady called Sally Robinson who was crewing for her partner Graham came over and had a quiet word in my ear. She suggested that in just a few hours the sun would come up both literally and indeed metaphorically and that I should simply keep going even though I was doubting myself. At the time that she said it, I was in a very negative state of mind but due to her timely advice and encouragement I got back on my bike at 2am.

As a result of her intervention, by the time the sun emerged to herald a new day, my mood had indeed come full circle and nothing would have stopped me from finishing the remaining 52.4 mile (84km) run that we were required to do. For the entire nine hour duration of the run, my mood was positive. The entire event took me 28 hours and 41 minutes.

The experience taught me a lot and I never forgot it. I'm not saying it comes naturally or that it's easy to keep going all of the time. What I have learned is that very often we can choose when to be at our strongest. Whenever something happens in everyday life or in an event, I always try to be watching out for the warning signals, so as to be ready for it. I need to be consciously ready so as to be able to put a positive spin on it. Sally and Graham appeared again at the deca on Day Three simply to lend their support. Their cheering and enthusiasm gave several competitors a timely boost.

I always tap into gratitude for the fact that I've never had to complete a real challenge. Big ambitions and big goals, yes. But never real challenges in the strictest definition of the word. So many others are not so lucky. That is the first thing I did when this low returned. I reminded myself how lucky I was to be out there doing things I like to do. I was here by ambition. I didn't have to do this event. I had signed up for it voluntarily. Therefore I got to do it.

Given the magnitude of the journey I had in front of me, however, I knew I had to dig even deeper. For some reason over the first three days, on lap six of the cycle I became consumed by negativity. It was that moment or time when one really doubts ones ability or loses the desire to keep going. As I had all the time in the world to think about it, I soon diagnosed the problem.

My brain was saying to me: 'Gerry, it's one pm (or thereabouts). We have already swum for over an hour and we have been cycling for over four hours. We still have at least four more hours of cycling to do and then you want me to run a marathon. And tomorrow you want me to do it again.'

You wouldn't be human if you didn't have low moments I guess. It was always going to happen. I knew it. I expected it. But not every day.

It was hard to self-administer mental medication but I knew I had to as so much of this challenge lay in the mind. I said earlier that both physical and mental energy would help me achieve my goal. I know there is nothing new in that. But to be consciously aware and to be ready for it is the secret. You can only physically prepare for so much.

For an hour or more I was low. Still though, I was conscious of it and the need to find a solution. Given the mileage we had to cover, I had plenty of time to think. Then it hit me and a mental trick was hatched in my brain.

It immediately lifted my spirits and I've since brought it into everyday life a hundred times or more. I realised that this event was all about the number 10. Ten laps of a bike course by coincidence every day and 10 days to be done.

I needed a mental trigger to jolt me from the negativity one part of my brain was determined to go into each lunchtime. When the mind is in negative space, it needs to come up with a trigger to shock itself back into focus.

W Clement Stone, Businessman, Philanthropist and Self-help Author
'Everyone who achieves success in a great venture solves each problem as they come to it. They help themselves. And they are helped through powers known and unknown to them at the time they set out on their voyage. They keep going regardless of the obstacles they meet'.

My learning was uncomplicated but magnificent. I am so glad this happened now because I conceived a solution of which I am immensely proud. It's so simple and it since then it has helped me achieve many other non-sporting goals.

My Eureka moment is that you cannot get to 10 without passing through six. It is impossible. All I was doing was passing through. If I kept moving, barring injury or withdrawal I would be guaranteed to reach 10. This low was an invisible force trying to knock me out. I had to be strong. I was travelling a journey that had a certain number of boxes to be ticked. I realised that unexpected obstacles would arrive along the way. And that is what makes it such a challenge. This is when I would find out what I was really made of.

Six had to be ticked as did Seven, Eight, Nine and Ten. If I skipped Six then I would only complete Nine. Once I kept pedalling, kept swimming and kept running, then sooner or later I would pass through all these numbers. Only then would I reach that Holy Grail. Simple I know, but so simple I had never used its logic as a motivation before.

This applied every day for 13 laps of the lake, 10 laps on the bike, for 26 laps on the run and for 10 consecutive days. All I was doing was passing through them all.

I have since harnessed this trigger into many other aspects of life. In business for example, if I am let down on something, I remind myself that my business year has 12 months in it, not 10 or 11. It can't all be good days and plain sailing.

In previous events I had learned how obstacles are sent to test our mettle. This mental test was just that. This was a sneaky question that formed part of the exam paper whether I liked it or not. How tough are you, Gerry? Have you got what it takes, Gerry? You do know this is a physical and a mental test, don't you, Gerry?

This is when I would find out if I had what it took. This new mind trick worked instantly and immediately lifted my mood. Lap six was ticked off and I came in for a fuel stop. With food in my belly and a bout of camaraderie with my crew, I went out and completed laps seven, eight, nine and 10.

By the time I finished the bike in a time of 8:24, my legs were tired. A few heavy showers and a blustery wind on the bike course had demanded the withdrawal of an extra portion of energy from my tank.

That evening the sun came out which helped lift everyone's spirits. Not only that, but close friends in the shape of Brian and Caroline Boyle, along with their two children Hannah and Daniel, had arrived from London to cheer me on. Also due to arrive following a lunchtime flight from Ireland, were two of my crew Ken Whitelaw and Douglas Bates. Months before I had planned the rota of crew with precision and a built-in crossover. It was important that each new crew member should spend time watching how the outgoing crew were working through each day.

Ken and Doug would need at least 24 hours to learn the ropes before going in the deep end. This event was a learning curve for us all. Ken was due to stay until Wednesday and Doug one day longer. It was great to see them both.

Both men watched Brendan and Jacinta on that first evening as they responded to the events many demands. It was rare that the crew had a spare five minutes from before dawn until way beyond dusk, with Brendan's alleged siesta a rare exception.

Ken Whitelaw

'Doug and I were anxious to get chatting to Brendan to find out what we what we needed to know so we started to pick his brains between his shuttle runs back and forth to Gerry as he ran his 26 loops. We watched what Brendan was doing, what Gerry was drinking (lots of coke), what he was eating and listened to the conversations they were having.'

The marathon each day began at the precise spot where you got off your bike. Because this exact point was actually midway through the run loop, the first run lap was always a short one and finished back down in the main field (see run map). Thus it was mentally a boost to realise that we were on lap two of the run before we knew it. That first lap was perhaps half a mile in distance. Each of the remaining 25 laps were then measured from the actual marathon finish line back to the same point. The first short lap on the run each day began with that 80 metres climb which was also the starting point for the bike loop, followed by a descent of that difficult 300 metres drop section.

For the first three laps I actually felt very strong. I looked forward to getting off the bike and connecting with terra firma every day. By this stage I was in uncharted territory because I'd never done more than two iron distances consecutively before. That thought alone injected fresh confidence and energy.

Over the first eight laps or approximately eight miles (13km), I consistently hammered out laps over a minute quicker than on the opening two days. That wasn't a strategy. In fact, I didn't even realise it at the time. I just felt good. There was a three minute slow down on lap nine as I walked briefly while eating the first of two dinners during the marathon. I had quickly changed my first day strategy of going into the marquee for dinner. On that first night my leg muscles immediately stiffened up and I really struggled for momentum when I had returned to the course. It was like starting a car in third gear.

I decided I would be better off walking and eating. Not only would I be more patient with consuming the food, I would also be eating into the mileage as I did so.

All these tiny learnings were now serving me well. I was willing to admit my errors and was prepared to adapt as I went along. The breakfast strategy after the swim, the chair at the bike turnaround and now a new adaptation for the marathon. It felt that as a team, we were all growing nicely into the event and were moving forward.

Dinner that evening consisted of scrambled eggs on brown bread. My breakfast 10 hours earlier had been exactly the same. I ate every morsel and wiped my crumb-covered lips into my running shirt. Once I finished, I picked back up the pace to the previous level I had churned out. By the half marathon mark, I began to feel it both physically and mentally. Thirty minutes later, as I was on mile 16 (26km), my head was struggling. The severity of the terrain beneath me was extracting a fee. That physical toll turned to my mind for sympathy.

Spontaneously I said aloud the number '16'.

Then I repeated it. '16, 16, 16.'

I continued saying it and must have said it 100 times over the next eight or nine minutes until I changed it to 17. I was doing it to inject some fresh mental stimulation.

'17, 17, 17.'

As I travelled that lap I continuously repeated the number 17 aloud. Pretty soon it became a must, I had to say it out loud and repeatedly. It was part mental stimulation, part security.

As we passed the finish line at the end of each lap, often the timing stewards would shout out how many laps we had completed. They didn't have to. It was simply done it in solidarity with the athletes. We were all part of a special journey, organisers, competitors, crew, marshalls and timing marshalls. It probably helped alleviate some of their own boredom as well. Their days were equally long.

Thankfully, they always confirmed the number I had in my head. Once or twice I would hear a fellow competitor query what they were being told. Perhaps that is why I began counting. Imagine if you felt you had done 19 only for them to say; 'well done, Gerry, that's 17 done'. That is what I meant by security. To have the number conflict negatively with what you believed you had done might play havoc with your mood. I didn't know anyone who wanted to do more than 26 laps.

On lap 19 I spotted Monique. I had earlier seen her dismounting from her bike so I knew she was several hours behind me. As I referred to earlier, Monique's tactic each day was to pace and power nap often. Even though that was her strategy, I still felt for her. By now she was at least 10 miles (16km) or more behind me.

This 44-year-old theatre and tv costume designer had a strong pedigree before she arrived in the New Forest. Like me, Monique had taking up running in her twenties. Originally from Cheshire, she had moved to Leeds in 1990 where she spent the next 20 years.

Monique

'I got into running through boxing which I'd done for three years in my early twenties. I had enjoyed the running part of training for that sport even though others used to moan about it. Within a short period I entered my first race of seven miles. Then I joined my local running club who were into long distance events.

Six months later I was up to running 17 miles (27km) but I got injured with a stress fracture. At the start of my running phase I read an article about a deca and for some reason I cut it out and kept it. It must have appealed, although I never imagined I would actually attempt one.'

Monique's idea back in the late 1990s was to run a marathon, tick it off her 'to do' list and then stop running so she entered one. In fact she entered several but all in the same race. In April 2000, she appeared at the starting line of the infamous challenge called Marathon Des Sables (MDS), a 156 miles (251km) race over six days in the Sahara Desert. On Day One alone competitors were required to complete 45 miles (72.4km) in the searing heat.

Monique
'In the MDS event I developed every ailment known to the human race; heat problems, swollen legs, diarrhoea, throwing up, the lot. I couldn't run in the heat and eventually only acclimatised on the penultimate day.'

It is fair to say that Monique was not afraid when confronted with a sporting challenge. In that race 11 years earlier, she had ingrained invaluable experience into her mind and her body. Her final words illustrate just how hard that race had been.

Monique
'I seemed to spend my whole time convinced I was going to die.'

Personally I was always keen to hear the number of laps officially confirmed each time I passed the timekeepers hut. Monique had a different take on it.

Monique
'I told the timekeepers not to tell me what lap I was on and forbade anyone else as well. Instead I decided to count people that I passed. I set myself a target of 50. This meant passing the same people several times as there were only a small number in the race. It was a number I pulled out of the air and with no scientific basis, but it gave me something to aim for.'

As evening slowly turned to night, Monique innovated further.

> **Monique**
> 'By then the tedium of multiple laps was starting to take a hold so I occupied myself devising a thousand square snakes and ladders game, based on the ups and downs of the deca.'

At 21 miles (33.8km), I ate again. Turkey, parsnips, three small potatoes and a portion of carrots. The organisers provided three official meals per day and thankfully the chef was nothing if not varied in his menus. Anything new brought fresh mental stimulation as well.

Despite pains in both quads late in the run, I was actually 16 minutes quicker on Day Three than the day before, crossing the line after 15 hours and 6 minutes. Such an improvement might have been a variation in the wind or the fact that the first eight laps were a minute or two faster. To delve any deeper at that time in order to offer a diagnosis, would have used up mental energy I could ill-afford to squander.

STANDINGS AFTER DAY THREE

Competitor	Cumulative Race Position	Day One	Day Two	Day Three	Cumulative Total
Toby Smithson	1	12:53:33	15:12:30	14:29:19	42:34:22
Gerry Duffy	2	14:41:07	15:22:12	15:06:49	45:09:08
Hanno Nickau	3	14:16:25	16:33:11	17:13:00	48:02:36
Roderick Elder	4	16:25:49	17:11:33	17:32:33	51:08:55
Mark Padley	5	16:51:49	17:16:45	17:13:52	51:20:26
Tony Fisher	6	16:34:58	17:38:23	17:33:54	51:45:15
Mike Trew	7	16:57:45	17:15:34	18:00:58	52:12:17
Richard Ginn	8	16:38:51	17:45:44	18:36:07	53:00:42
Andy Kemp	9	15:39:39	17:14:05	20:52:19	53:45:03
Tony Raynor	10	16:41:06	18:19:58	19:03:47	54:03:41
Mick Barnes	11	17:46:47	19:27:11	18:05:38	55:18:36
Monique Hollinshead	12	19:28:49	19:23:00	20:29:56	59:20:45
Edward Page	13	18:11:34	21:19:14	21:39:45	61:09:33
Keith Laing	14	19:37:26	21:19:13	21:30:15	62:01:00

CHAPTER NINETEEN

Pain, Pain Go Away

After Day One I was sore. By the end of Day Three, I was feeling it even more so. A complete ache was slowly spreading through my body like lava down a mountainside. As soon as I crossed the finish line at the end of the third day, my leg muscles started to tighten.

It is remarkable what we value and appreciate when normal living standards and regular comforts are not as readily available. All day long I dreamt about the 'luxury' of showering and saw it as a priceless reward for my efforts. By chance we had set up our sleeping accommodation just 150 metres from the camp site washing facility which proved a Godsend.

Overall, looking back on what was working for me during the event, was the fact that my crew and I were so conscious of what we needed to be doing at all times. It has always intrigued me why competitors in a marathon or in a similar type endurance challenge are always stiff for days after. I am not saying that I have a truly unique solution but I feel the following tactic I employ, helps me to recover that tiny bit quicker.

Earlier I spoke about the importance of rebuilding your body using food. Nutrition is of paramount importance. That's why I always had a recovering protein smoothie just after I finished. I knew the sooner I consumed it, the quicker it would begin rebuilding my muscles.

Two more tactics I benefit from, include something I did in the final 300 metres or so of each night's marathon. I was keen on running at least 90 per cent of the time. The only two periods I wished to walk were when I was eating each of the two dinners I consumed during each run. Most nights I ate them at mile 10 and mile 20 or thereabouts.

My strategy was to briskly walk the final metres of each

marathon. Perhaps this added two or three minutes to my finishing times but I knew the wisdom of it in the grander scheme of things. This allowed my leg muscles to enjoy a gentle stretch prior to finishing, which meant I was already thinking of the next day. I now employ this tactic at the end of most long training runs as well. It helps me recover a shade quicker than I used to.

Another technique I employed was to do what I call a micro stretch after I finished. For the deca this was done while in the shower. On Day Three my upper leg muscles and particularly my right quad muscle had tightened as hard as a clenched fist. On the first two nights in the shower, I employed a strategy of raising each knee to waist height in particular to stretch the quads.

I am always intrigued when I see some marathon runners literally stop after they cross the finish line. Yes, the goal is achieved but this is a time when we have a great opportunity to give ourselves an immediate chance to begin a slow recovery. The recuperation might be difficult but why not try and help it on its way.

I believe this can be as easy as a few simple knee raises and continuing to walk for a good five or 10 minute period at a slow to medium pace as we go to rendezvous with family or friends. It's the last thing we might wish to do but therein lies the crux. It is partly because we stop moving or walking that our muscles seize. Instead of stopping and starting, sitting and resting, we can use that walk as an immediate recovery tactic to help us feel at least one per cent better the next day.

Another thing I do is climb the stairs when I go home. I'm not suggesting we run up and down or take two steps at a time. I go up and down it two or three times at a slow pace. This helps recovery in the legs and especially the calf muscles. The next day I try to resist the temptation to spend the entire day or evening on the couch. I might go for a gentle five or 10 minute walk as I find it helps me to recover faster.

After any marathon or indeed iron distance triathlon naturally all your muscles want to do is go into hibernation. I didn't have that luxury available to me. In a matter of a few hours, I had to do it all over again. I was exhausted and all I wanted to do were simple things that required minimum effort. That involved washing the dirt and sweat that my body had accumulated and then walking that final 150 metres back to the sanctuary of the camper. Once there, I wanted to climb into the sleeping bag as every minute of sleep was a gold bar lodged in my body bank.

That night I stood in the shower and reflected on what had been another demanding day. As the hot water poured over my body, I began my night-time ritual. I was weak and tired but I knew another micro workout would have my body thanking me the next morning.

I was conscious of needing to do a quick knee-raise exercises. I knew my muscles would hate me at first but would acknowledge this wisdom over time. The left leg took a little bit of work. Trying to raise your leg after 15 hours of endurance in a day or a cumulative 45 hours in the previous three days was hard. Still, after a minute or more, the left was starting to feel a good bit better. One down, one to go. It is when I went to lift the right that I hit a brick wall.

It was just under an hour since I had finished. My right foot must have felt its work was done because it was stuck to the ground. Its weight felt as heavy as a ship's anchor. I tried to send a message from my brain to my leg muscles but it fell on deaf ears.

I immediately became concerned. What if it was like this in the morning? What if that leg said: 'Leave me in the camper. I am done with this'. What if the rest of my body felt ok but this right leg remained uncooperative and stubborn?

Then I realised the wisdom of why I did this in the first place. What was happening was one of the most significant lessons I would learn over the entire 10 days. I needed these right leg muscles to remain cooperative. In six or seven hours' time I would be asking those same leg muscles to power me through another 15 hour day or more.

During this event every brain cell and every muscle would question the logic of what I was trying to do. Many unexpected questions were being asked. To be successful I realised I had to answer all of the exam questions well.

Even when I didn't want to, these were other exams I had to sit. This was just a harder question. An unexpected but compulsory one nonetheless. If I got a poor mark or made a bad attempt this early on, I could fail. During the 10 days, I had many defining moments. On reflection I now realise the significance of when and why they presented themselves. This was one of those moments.

I resolved that I wouldn't leave the shower block until I could raise that right knee to 90 degrees from my hip joint. No matter how long it would take and even if the hot water ran out, I would stay. My crew waited anxiously outside. I shouted at them that I was fine and that I was going to be a little longer than usual.

At first I simply tried to raise the back of my foot to 45 degrees from the ground, akin to a bedroom crawl before a 5k run. I really had to work hard, continuously sending messages down to the base of my leg and foot. Tiny lifts at first, then slightly bigger ones. After a few minutes I was able to lift the sole of my foot into the air. Then slowly I inched my leg further and further. After three minutes or so I had my foot about 10 inches off the ground. Even my quad seemed surprised.

The pain was slowly easing. I'm not saying it left entirely because it didn't but I knew that if I didn't do this now, tomorrow it would be far worse.

The entire routine took more than five minutes but by the end of it I could raise the knee comfortably to 90 degrees.

DAY FOUR

CHAPTER TWENTY

MONDAY 6TH JUNE, 2011

Today was always going to be hard. Both Jacinta and Brendan had to return home. I would miss them both and for different reasons. Thankfully their flight was not until late afternoon, so they would stay with us until lunchtime.

Not only were we losing Brendan and my partner, we would shortly lose another competitor, Andy Kemp. A one-time relay member of a cycle team who had completed the massive 3000 mile (4800km) cycle race across America (The RAM), Andy would withdraw on Day Four after just one mile of the marathon due to injury. This meant that only 12 of the initial 20 entrants would continue.

As Doug and I walked down to the lake at 5:45am, he informed me that Ken had been deputised the night before to pitch the tent he had brought over for me to change in after the swim. What Doug didn't realise was that Ken had never been a boy scout as a youth and had never pitched a tent before.

'It's over there somewhere,' Doug said proudly as we travelled down through the tented area to begin the swim.

I scanned the busy campsite spotting more than 20 tents. All of the ones I saw at first were superbly erected and standing rigidly in readiness for any inclement weather conditions that might visit.

Then I spotted one that was a different standard; one that looked like it had been erected by someone who had been both handcuffed and blindfolded during the task. Furthermore, the tent fabric that was meant to protect from the elements, buffeted like a kite in what was a very light breeze.

Doug couldn't evict the words from his mouth quick enough: 'Eh, Ken pitched it, I was doing your smoothie last night when he took charge of it.'

We both laughed as we passed it, but we never told Ken. By the time I emerged from the lake it was beginning to resemble something close to the picture on the holdall that it had arrived in.

One man going strong despite not getting much continuous sleep was Big Ted. The times it took him to finish the first three days however, resembled a night-time train schedule from Waterloo, 18:11 (18 hours and 11 minutes), 21:19 and 21:39. That meant close to a 4am finish on Day Three.

As far back as April, Ted had outlined on his personal blog his reasons for entering.

> **Big Ted's training diary (Sunday April 3 2011)**
> 'I just want to see how many I can do. I believe I could do an Iron distance tomorrow. Pretty sure I could do two in two days. I believe also that three is possible on the basis that I did the Triple in 2010. If I remain uninjured and train well for the next six weeks or so then I'd like to think four would be possible. Somewhere beyond that, if I can start Day Five, lies my limit and that's the objective – to find my limit.'

Now in his own words, three days into the event, exhaustion had set in. Ted knew he wasn't getting sufficient time to recover. This man was as hard as nails though. That triple event I've mentioned had taken him 56 hours to complete. On the first day of the deca he had finished just after midnight. Now he was getting progressively slower like we all were and he was conscious of it. Similarly, he was trying to adapt as he went through each day to give himself the best opportunity to continue.

> **Big Ted**
> 'On Day Three even in a state of utter exhaustion, I could still think straight. Something needed to change. It was time to start running more. Just enough to get my lap times

> down by a minute or two. I knew I needed to get more
> sleep.'

Up to this he had paced himself cautiously on the run. On many miles as I passed him, he was walking. It was part weariness and part strategy.

By now I was in second place. I didn't realise it at the time. Nobody told me. I was glad. This early on I didn't need to know. Why on earth would it concern me? My crew and I had enough to do with managing my needs and the thousands of demands that each day brought. Jacinta joked that she had plenty of practice doing this over the preceding two years of our relationship. The reality though is we had only ticked three of ten very large boxes. Only 30 percent was done. Still a long way short of half way.

By now I had settled into something of a regular routine. Each morning, I would open my eyes at 4:55am usually by the sound of someone turning on the stove to cook porridge.

The first few minutes were spent monitoring my body for feedback as to how it was dealing with the demands placed on it the day before. Over a breakfast of porridge and tea, the mental motivation was worked on to lift my spirits and energy to harness my body both physically and mentally to carry me through the next 15 or 16 hours. Then at 6am, we would enter the lake and begin that day's exam.

Every morning when we arrived there we were met by both Steve and Dan Earthquake. An accomplished channel swimmer, Dan was always very encouraging. Regularly we could hear him shouting support in our direction as we passed to confirm our race numbers with the lap counters.

'Four', I would scream every five minutes or so as I passed through the funnelled pontoon area that brought us close enough for clarity. It was a clever idea. After all, each of the competitors looked almost identical when mostly submerged and hidden underneath a cap and swim goggles.

'Four,' they would shout in reply, indicating they had correctly recorded my progress and ticked off another lap.

It was always easy to spot Dan as we front crawled around the lake every morning. Just like each of the competitors, he wore a wetsuit – for two reasons. The first was because he had to swim out at 5.30am and position the buoys at exact points to ensure the accuracy of the course. During the day, the lake was an amenity used by other groups who were lodging on the grounds. The second reason was to be immediately available should anyone get into difficulty. As he sat at the side of the lake he also proudly wore a large bowler hat. A beard, a wetsuit and a black bowler hat meant that he certainly stood out each time we swam passed.

On the fourth day I was third out of the water in a time of 1:16:46. Mike Trew was as consistent as ever finishing first in 1:13:18. A competitor whom I hadn't noticed up to this point was an Englishman from Grimsby. Mark Padley (35) was quietly going about his business. He appeared calm and very focussed and as the event unfolded I would begin to see more and more of him.

Also that day I spotted another competitor – Tony Raynor. That might sound strange but a lot of the time we were gone off on a bike course where you might not see another competitor from one lap to the next. Only at the turnaround point might you see someone as they ate a meal or chatted to their crew.

Like Mark, Raynor was a similar age and also hailed from Grimsby, the great east of England fishing port. A physical training instructor in the British Army, Tony was responsible for the selection of new recruits and had 12 years served. Having done his first triathlon at the age of just 13 he waited 12 more years to do his second. Now in his thirties he was into extreme triathlons.

Back in his early triathlon days he was unable to front crawl so he had completed his first half ironman distance swim by breast-stroking the 1.2 mile (1.9km) distance. After that he taught himself to master the front crawl and had completed 15 full iron distances triathlons spread over a multitude of single, double and triple events.

On top of that he also had a quite a number of individual one off marathons in his arsenal. At 5' 10" in height, this 35-year-old Englishman was making quiet progress each day.

Tony's finishing times were always on the other side of midnight. Perhaps he was tapping into some army training techniques to ensure progress was made. I later learned that he had prepared well and had centred much of his training, like me, around the middle discipline of cycling.

Tony
'In the months of preparation, I was doing about 500-600 miles a month on the bike alone with 1,100 miles as my highest. Over a six month period I racked up over 3500 miles.'

On Day Four, Tony swam the 2.4 miles (3.8km) in 1:32:00. A good time for the distance considering that this was his fourth such swim in as many days. On top of that Tony had only closed his eyes from the previous days labours four hours earlier.

Tony
'I figured I could live without sleep. Just get it done. I could sleep for the rest of my life.

Day Three had taken him 19 hours and 3 minutes. By then he was already starting to have some tough questions asked.

Tony
'My biggest problem was blisters every day. Usually it would take 30 minutes to sort my feet out before the run but then the pain for the first five or six miles was

unbelievable. After that I got into a rhythm and the pain would ease. I just had to get on with it. Then on the third day I got tendonitis in my ankle.'

For Raynor, this translated into a 1:03am finishing time. What I noticed about Tony when I spotted him after lap three of the bike was the exhaustion on his face but also the fact that he was smiling through it. I wonder if I would have been as content had I only had three and a half hours of recovery. I had slept for over five.

Tony
'Sometimes I would stop for a 20 minute sleep during the bike but only if I felt really really tired.'

Something else I noticed that day on the bike was a difference in the physiology of Toby Smithson. On the first few days, Toby had his head down, was completely focussed at all times and was keen to move as swiftly as possible.

By the end of Day Three though, he had certainly reigned in the horses after his first day sprint. By now he was slowing and coming back to the field. He finished the third day just 37 minutes ahead of me in a time of 14:29:19.

After 23 miles (37km) of cycling I stopped briefly at the turn-around area and noticed he was sitting on the grass and resting against a wall. He was eating a meal of sorts but his demeanour seemed different. Surely he didn't need to rest this early in the day? Certainly he hadn't done it before. What's more, he looked to be in no hurry. That second lap had taken him one hour and 26 minutes. It should have only taken about half that time. Something was up.

By 10:35 am I'd cycled four of the 10 laps required, with almost 50 miles (80km) covered. I sat briefly with Jacinta and Brendan

and ate a chicken pasta brunch, washing it down with salt rehydration and water. While we were chatting, Doug joined the conversation.

'Ray D'Arcy wants to interview you,' he interjected.

'What?' I exclaimed. I knew the significance.

Ray and his show had been brilliant to Ken and I in raising awareness of the 32 marathon challenge. Back in 2010 not only had D'Arcy mentioned our event as we travelled the country, he interviewed us on his show during it as well. On our 30th consecutive marathon he also came and ran 13.1 miles with us.

'Yeah', Doug continued in his strong Dublin brogue. 'His researcher called. They want to talk to you after the 11am morning news.'

I looked at him in bewilderment. For sure, I thought they might be interested in how I was getting on and that listeners might want updates but doing a live interview during the event had never entered my head. Under normal circumstances I would have been delighted to do it. I had been in the studio just a month before. But now I had no desire.

It's not that I didn't want to oblige, it's just that I was trying so hard to stay focussed on my job. I was engrossed in the greatest sporting ambition of my life and therefore didn't welcome any outside interferences. I had enough to think about. On top of that they wanted to determine the time? I realised they might not be aware of the difficulties this posed so I turned to Doug and Ken who was beside him.

'Can one of you do it? I'd prefer not to'.

Ken disappeared into the hedgerow to call the researcher and to ask if this would be acceptable. I understood the significance and what it would do for the profile of the challenge and for the charity, but I just wanted to compete. That was my job. Let the crew take care of it.

Ken came back 90 seconds later. 'They really want you, will you do it?' He held the phone pointing at it to indicate the researcher was listening to the conversation.

'Ok,' I said rather reluctantly.

I immediately realised that just after 11am, I would be somewhere mid-lap but that would hardly matter. The only challenge would be listening out for the phone to ring. Given the wind that was blowing and the speed I was travelling, it would take concentration. The interview was important, I knew that. The charity would certainly benefit as long as I didn't come across as completely crazy in doing what I was doing or accidently swear over the airwaves.

Over the next 25 minutes I kept checking the time. At 11am I took out the phone and clasped it between my right hand and the handlebar of the bike but by 11:05am it had yet to ring. I looked down at the phone and saw I had no signal. That part of the course had no coverage. I realised the futility of stressing about it so I just kept turning the pedals.

Five minutes later and still there was no signal so I went to put the phone away. What could I do? Then just as I began to put it out of my mind, it sprang to life. I pulled over to the side of the road and pressed the incoming call button. D'Arcy's voice was immediately recognisable. It was the first of three interviews I would do over the next number of days, his listeners keen for progress updates and insights into what I was going through.

'Concentrate Gerry. Mention the charity website Gerry,' I thought to myself as Ray informed me we would be going live in less than 10 seconds.

He immediately asked a litany of questions. I enjoyed talking to him, although as I spoke, I became aware of the bizarreness of my surroundings and circumstance. A wind was whistling around me and so the line was not good. I was all alone in the middle of the English countryside, having a conversation with one man on a dodgy phone line while one in every 15 people in Ireland listened in on the call. A large black and white Friesian cow was breathing heavily from two flared nostrils just inches from my face and its body odour wasn't to appealing, or was that me?

Just then Monique appeared from nowhere drawing up alongside me and staring into my face.

'Are you ok, Gerry?' she shouted loudly, trying to be heard above the wind.

I gave her a thumbs up, anxious not to begin a second conversation whilst still conducting the first.

A few seconds later, Ray wished me well. With that he went back to his listeners and I said goodbye to the cow.

By mid-morning I had cycled five of the required 10 laps. Only 58 miles (93km) left to go. Earlier a few issues had arisen. On lap one of the cycle I got a very unexpected and very sharp sciatic pain in my left glute (buttock). It was not something I experienced before and at the time I was taken aback at its severity. As quick as it arrived though, it disappeared and never returned.

For the first time on the bike I also felt a little sleepy as I began what would be an 8 hours and 40 minute cycle ride. At one point I even contemplated climbing into a ditch but I was afraid that if I did, I would sleep for hours and that it might take all the kings horses and all of his men to put me back up on my bike again.

By 11:45am I had stopped twice. The first was after lap one for a bowl of cereal and again on lap four for a chicken pasta dish. As we approached midday I felt the urge to stop for a very quick toilet break. I dismounted, handing the bike to Ken as I did so and headed behind a nearby hedgerow. A minute later as I remounted, Ken spoke to me in a tone that had a headmaster's pitch.

'You're not eating enough food,' he said in a non-negotiating voice.

'What?' I said somewhat in disbelief. 'I'm fine,'.

'You're not'. He repeated in a tone of entrenchment.

I struggled to take him seriously. I had enough to deal with. I felt I was eating plenty. If you don't believe me go back and see what I ate on Day Two .

Perhaps his logic was that I had earlier expressed the fact that I was starving. As I descended the hill at the exit of the estate, I was upset by the conversation. Cycling through Burley 10 minutes later it had grown to annoyance. If I didn't have so much time on my hands, I'd have dismissed his opinion from my mind but I still had more than four hours to go on the bike so I thought a lot about what he had said.

The more I considered it, the more I realised what he said made sense. Steve Haywood, the race director had warned us to eat proper food and to eat as much as an army regiment. He suggested that a barometer of how well we had monitored our food intake should see us maintaining our body weight for the duration of the 10 days. The truth is I was starting to feel a little thinner as each day passed.

Back in 2010 in the 32 marathon challenge, for a time Ken had to slow to a snail's pace because of injury. As a result he was spending twice as long on the course as I was. One thing I recalled was the additional food he forced himself to eat. Afterwards as we had talked about it, he equated it very simply – as he was spending much longer on his feet than me, he needed to eat a lot more.

Ken had come back as strong as a Roman gladiator and it now dawned on me that food played a part in his recovery. In my case, fatigue was invading my body. Perhaps I should heed the advice of someone completely clear in his thoughts and on the outside looking in.

From here on I was sure to get slower. That would mean I'd be on the course for 30 minutes to an hour longer each day, maybe more. Even if he was wrong, what harm would extra nutrition do. I decided to heed his advice.

Ken Whitelaw
'From my perspective on the sidelines during those few

hours it became clear he was burning far more calories than he was ingesting and if he kept it up, his already lean body was going to run out of fuel before the end of the challenge. Having spent so many training hours together with Gerry, I know what he can be like; he can be very persuasive and convincing. And so it was that he had convinced Brendan that he was eating enough.'

By coincidence I was actually starving at this time. Doug decided to give me something different and I was handed the first of two tuna pasta dishes. Maybe it was the variety or maybe it was the fish oil. It was like having fuel injection inserted into my engine as I felt a surge in my energy levels for the next two laps.

By one o'clock, Brendan and Jacinta had positioned their luggage next to the 'chair', 150 metres from the turnaround area and close to the camper. This was lap eight. I was due another meal break so I sat and we chatted for a time.

Jacinta
'I hated leaving but I had to return to work. I knew going back home I would be thinking about what he was going through almost every minute. Not being there to help would make that even harder. Waiting to come back four days later would feel like a decade.'

As they departed, so did I. They had to travel 22 miles (35.5km) to the airport. I'd a similar distance left to cycle.

That was hard. I thought about them both. Over eight months of training never once had Jacinta complained when I disappeared at 5:30am or before, morning after morning for a workout. Now in the event itself, if she wasn't massaging my legs as I slept, she was preparing one of the eight or nine meals I was eating. In between she would cheer me at every passing with great enthusiasm.

I began the marathon run on Day Four at 3:55pm. That Monday afternoon as I started, the sun was a welcome companion. Earlier we had a few heavy showers but now it was warm and calm. Before arriving in England, I'd questioned how difficult it might be to pick myself up to begin a marathon in the mid-to-late afternoon having swum and cycled such distances. I felt I would need to draw on a lot of what I had learned.

The mindset that I tapped into during each run was straightforward. The first thing as I have already mentioned was gratitude. I reminded myself day after day how lucky I was to be out there doing something I loved to do.

Secondly I was ticking another of those 30 boxes. By the time Day Four finished, I'd have 12 boxes out of the 30 ticked off.

Another technique I used was to project forward to when I had the marathon finished. I'd plenty of time to calculate an approximate finishing time. A hypnotist had once taught me to project myself beyond a goal to a time when I would have it accomplished. He suggested that no matter how challenging a time you had in between, the universe would ensure that the time you were now focussing on would eventually arrive.

As I ran, I projected my mind to 11pm and created an image in my mind of what I would be doing around that time. A vision of my crew and myself eating cereal and drinking tea in the sanctuary of the camper appeared. These were things that in the normal world I took for granted. Now they seemed like a priceless incentive.

Midway through the marathon word filtered through that the event organisers were sending out a clear message that every athlete was being watched. Safety was paramount and anybody deemed a danger to themselves would be withdrawn. We didn't realise it then, but for one competitor, that threat would become a reality in a few days time.

It wasn't Toby who would be withdrawn without his consent but it was obvious by now that something was seriously wrong with him. Not only had he taken over 37 minutes in transition from bike to run, by mile 15 of the run I was passing him with ease. Toby always displayed a poker face exterior and gave nothing away. I didn't realise it at the time but earlier that morning he had woken up in terrible pain. On Day Four his finishing time would plummet to 19 hours and 22 minutes.

Toby
'When I woke on Day Four, my right Achilles was very painful. Towards the end of the bike I was in agony.'

(The Achilles is a tough sinew that attaches the calf-muscle to the back of the heel bone.)

As for Big Ted, three iron distances was his previous limit so completing Day Four was in his own words 'critical'. Finishing it would see him stretch his limit by 25 per cent.

Big Ted
'My mindset was simple. Complete Day Four and if the mind hasn't closed off, the deca is mine for the taking. This was further than I had ever been. I was breaking new ground.'

In terms of this kind of challenge, I myself was in unfamiliar territory since the start of Day Three. It wouldn't be easy for either of us. Ted was tired having only got 12 hours of sleep in the previous three nights. Like Monique, he was power-napping during the day, but walking most of the marathons was doing him no favours for an early bedtime.

Ted had exited the swim on the fourth day in 1:48:25. In the marquee over breakfast his confidence was not helped by the sight of another competitor announcing his withdrawal. Ted couldn't be blamed for feeling deflated, particularly when you realise he had done the graveyard shift with Keith Laing the night before. Both finished just after 3:30am.

Big Ted

'Keith's a great athlete. He finished just ahead of me at the triple in 2010. Seeing him stop, as well as others who had now retired, made me doubt myself.'

On top of that, Ted's wife, Marie, also had to leave for home on Day Four. Emotionally Ted felt there would be an impact. Taking over the crewing though was a friend who himself had completed a deca. This new crew member had been kept up to date on Ted's times and his strategies, which would soon have to change. Despite having developed an Achilles problem, Ted knew he had to throw caution to the wind. Finishing well past midnight day after day was not allowing him sufficient recovery time. He would have to gamble and hope that the injury got no worse. On top of that he was urged to take less rest times during the bike. He realised he was stopping far too often.

Even as he got off the bike at 5:40 pm, his energy and motivation was flagging as loneliness set in.

Big Ted

'It was a combination of Marie leaving, sleep deprivation and physical exhaustion.'

As he began his first lap of the marathon he asked to see the medic. A little breathlessness was concerning him.

Big Ted

'Given my desire to go to the edge, I felt it was a sensible move. I knew if I kept her informed, she would spot any warning signals.'

By 15 miles (24km), Ted had made up ground on his originally anticipated finishing time but then a calf muscle injury flared up. Realising his legs were cold, he stopped to put on a pair of leggings. The length of the day and a sore leg ensured it was a slow final 10 miles (16km) and he crossed the line at 2:45am.

> **Big Ted**
> 'I went to bed having gone further than ever before and having covered over 100 miles on foot in four days. The mind hadn't given away. I was up for Day Five. And although I was tired, my overriding emotion was anger. Anger with A.T. (Avon Tyrell, the location for the event). Anger with myself.
>
> Well f*** you AT, because I will be back for another go at you tomorrow.'

STANDINGS AFTER DAY FOUR

Competitor	Cumulative Race Position	Day One	Day Two	Day Three	Day Four	Cumulative Total
Gerry Duffy	1	14:41:07	15:22:12	15:06:49	15:31:04	60:41:42
Toby Smithson	2	12:53:33	15:12:30	14:29:19	19:22:54	61:58:16
Hanno Nickau	3	14:16:25	16:33:11	17:13:00	18:41:43	66:44:19
Mark Padley	4	16:51:49	17:16:45	17:13:52	17:02:06	68:24:32
Roderick Elder	5	16:25:49	17:11:33	17:32:33	18:10:07	69:20:02
Tony Fisher	6	16:34:58	17:38:23	17:33:54	18:27:21	70:14:36
Mike Trew	7	16:57:45	17:15:34	18:00:58	18:12:28	70:26:45
Mick Barnes	8	17:46:47	19:27:11	18:05:38	17:50:25	73:10:01
Tony Raynor	9	16:41:06	18:19:58	19:03:47	19:37:47	73:24:05
Richard Ginn	10	16:38:51	17:45:44	18:36:07	20:23:23	73:42:38
Monique Hollinshead	11	19:28:49	19:23:00	20:29:56	19:51:12	79:12:57
Edward Page	12	18:11:34	21:19:14	21:39:45	20:43:18	81:53:51

DAY FIVE

CHAPTER TWENTY-ONE

TUESDAY 7TH JUNE, 2011

Since Day Two, each morning as I opened the sleeping bag and descended the six rungs of the ladder from the top bunk, I was monitoring my body for feedback. I had chosen to sleep there rather than the bottom. It was a strategy on my part as each climb and descent would gently stretch my calf muscles last thing at night and first thing each morning.

I suppose it was inevitable. Almost every morning, it was like someone had evenly spread the weight of another full sandbag throughout my body as I felt a few pounds or two heavier each time I climbed down.

I don't mean like regular weight gain. Rather it was just that every day my body felt heavier as I carried it down to the lake. Each morning it ached a little more.

Overnight it was if a cement mixer had pulled up and inserted a hose into my body and poured cement into my bloodstream. Every night in the darkness another bagful was silently being added. Perhaps that is why I looked forward to the swim so much every morning. It soothed the throbbing ache that was rising and spreading with the passing of time.

As I walked down to the lake on the fifth morning, I monitored how I was feeling physically and how the other remaining competitors looked as well.

Perhaps I was looking for solidarity that I wasn't alone. By now most were beginning to look as if they were on round seven of a 15 round boxing bout with the former heavyweight boxing champion Muhammad Ali. Battered, bruised and exhausted all, but still none of those remaining wanted to throw in the towel.

Most were beginning to look like test patients in a sleep deprivation clinic. If a bed salesman had been passing, he would have been confident of sales.

Ken

'I'll always remember that daily five minute walk to the start of the swim as it was like a re-enactment of Michael Jackson's 'Thriller' music video. Bodies back from the dead were crouched over in stiffness and pain. Haggard and weary souls, slowly, sleepily, awkwardly, pulling themselves out of their tents and campervans, their oh-so-tired eyes fixated on the small area where the race was set to restart for another day. You couldn't but admire them.'

We all knew the significance of completing Day Five from a mental standpoint. Going beyond halfway might ignite new fires. As Steve spoke loudly, 12 voices confirmed their attendance.

Big Ted

'If we finish today, we will have reached an important milestone.'

It's unlikely that any of us were confident that we would still be here to the end. In my Monday night recording, I had confessed as much.

AUDIO DIARY

'I hope I can look back some day having finished this event because at this stage I genuinely have no idea if I will.'

By now, I was in totally uncharted waters. If I was looking for security in numbers, Tuesday would do nothing to inject hope. It became a day when three of the 12 would make the decision to stop the next day. Perhaps some of them already knew it or perhaps not.

Those three would start the following day but would do so with no intentions of finishing it. That mightn't make sense at first reading but their reasons for entering the lake a day later was related to a rumour in circulation. The word was the record books would not allow them the honour of being recognised as having done a 'quintuple' iron distance triathlon (5 in 5 days) if they didn't swim at least 10 metres on Day Six. It was an incorrect rumour that deserved no wind.

Sixteen hours later and a few minutes after I finished Day Five, Doug handed me the audio recording device. Having carried out the nightly cool down in the lake after the marathon, we had passed the medical tent a little after 10pm. As we did so, we noticed the doctor's treatment bench wasn't being used. The air inside the tent was warm so was a very suitable location for a lower leg massage. My legs were in dire need but even the light rub that Doug applied had me biting my arm a little.

The few stationary minutes provided me with a chance to record my thoughts.

AUDIO DIARY

'Swim felt lovely today. Got a lovely stroke going. Think I was out in 1:10.'

This was consistent with how I had felt on the first four days. The swim refreshed my aching 43-year-old frame. The 1:10 refers to my swim time but it was actually 1:12:51. I must have glanced at my watch as I had exited the water and before I had crossed the timing mat.

AUDIO DIARY

'Got quite cold coming out of the lake.'

I didn't realise it at the time but this was very significant, as it was the first signal that my immune system was showing signs of weakening. On the audio I sound almost dismissive of the fact. Until then, cold or heat had never been an issue. Sure, the first day had been very hot but I would take that over the cold anytime.

Day Five would also be my slowest marathon to date. It took me 5:50:51.

Possible reasons? Well, firstly, it was Day Five. I was gradually getting slower whether I liked it or not. Secondly, in this event, at times a metre could feel as distant as 100 metres. On some nights, 26.2 miles felt like a trek to Everest base camp.

In the audio I also commented that I had pushed too hard on the bike. Even a half a mile per hour in terms of effort over eight or nine hours of cycling, could wreak havoc on your ability to run a marathon later the same day. On Day Five I was guilty of such a misdemeanour.

Given the sheer length of each day, it was only natural that we would have highs and lows. At times during each day you might feel a surge of energy. Other times you were only moving forward because of a will to continue.

Today I had felt strong on the bike and I pushed a fraction too hard. It was silly. I wasn't as disciplined as I should have been and rather unnecessarily used some energy that I would need in a few days time.

Despite my time being almost identical to the previous day (one minute slower) this does not take into account the fact that we were now a day further into the challenge. That audio was my confession box as to how my body was dealing with it and also to how I was reacting. I knew I had pushed harder. My penance for my bike exertion was a hard evening and night-time run.

Earlier on the first of the cycle loops I had a very brief panic attack. As I descended the giant hill at the beginning of the route I was approaching 40 miles per hour (65km) as I reached the midway part of the descent. Out of nowhere the back wheel began shaking uncontrollably. Given my speed, I was somewhat powerless to prevent anything happening anyway. It was either going to bid me farewell or it wasn't.

At that precise moment I was not in control and I had cars all around. I had a chicane just ahead through which to navigate. I was going faster than was safe so I had no option but to wait until I descended further. I decided to push on and pray that I was imagining it. It turned out I was. When I got to the bottom, I glanced beneath to diagnose the cause. There was nothing out of place at all. It must have been just a combination of wind forces coming at me from all angles and combined with the speed and the exposed height. Or perhaps it was entirely in my mind. The truth is, I was starting to feel quite tired and perhaps a little paranoid.

> **Ken**
> 'I remember one pit stop on the second day; as Gerry was leaving to head off on another lap he mentioned that he was nervous about the bike. 'Oh bugger,' we thought, as we looked over at the spare bike, still in pieces in a brown cardboard box underneath the campervan. We had never thought to put the spare together .
> Forty-five minutes of mechanical panic ensued as we looked for tools, put pedals, handle bars, saddle on, tweaked the gears, tightened the brakes, pumped the two tyres... and made his dinner. When he reappeared again we were at our station, sweat dripping from our brows, but trying to seem in control. Thankfully he didn't need to change... but it was a close call.'

On lap five I was hurtling down the same hill but this time I had to jam on the brakes. Two horses had appeared from behind a bush and must have been in a hurry to get to a local equestrian gathering as they crossed the road without even looking. The cheek.

> **AUDIO DIARY**
> 'Lap six of the cycle was very hard mentally. I don't know why but it was.'

I can only assume this was one of those lows that come after a high.

AUDIO DIARY

'On the last two and a half bike laps I had to take my right foot out of the shoes completely and on the last lap the left foot was seizing up too.'

Old news I know.

AUDIO DIARY

'Thai Curry and salad, chicken and garlic with mushroom with wheat free pasta, lots and lots of chocolate, two mars bars, a snickers and a few bags of M&Ms (both chocolate) less dioralyte than usual (salt rehydration) and four cans of coke'.

That is what I ate and drank on the run. Earlier I had consumed my usual two breakfasts of porridge with milled seeds and nuts and a cup of tea together with my daily ritual of scrambled egg, two sausages and a slice of toast.

On the bike I ate a bowl of Kellogg's Special K after lap one – a personal favourite I looked forward to each morning. Funny as I don't eat it normally. In fact 80 per cent of what I ate, was not in my usual diet.

After completing 23 miles (37km) and again after 70 miles (112km), I ate two bowls of chicken pasta. At 93 miles (150km) Ken had prepared a bacon, egg and sausage roll and two cans of Red Bull as I felt in need of a pickup (maybe that had something to do with the bike speed).

I also drank some energy drinks and water and a few mars bars. Later in the comfort and reward of my sleeping bag, I ate two more bowls of Special K cereal and some toast washed down with a cup of tea.

AUDIO DIARY

'Mile 23 of the marathon was brutal.'

Is it any wonder, I hear you cry, given how much food you were eating!

The truth is I have never had difficulty eating and moving forward at the same time. It's an acquired ability. An insatiable appetite is a great assist.

Fortunately my concern over the tree cones snagging in my shoes never came to pass. Funny that, as it happened repeatedly when Brendan and I had walked the course before the event began. Perhaps I was concentrating now on avoiding them a little more.

Ken

'As the marathon wore on I could see that Gerry was tiring which was to be expected. As I witnessed quite a few times during our 32 marathons in 32 days adventure, his head drops a few degrees, the smiles melt away and he become intensely focussed on his goal for the day – reaching the finish line.

That night verbal interactions went from full chats at the start of the run to short one-line directives from Gerry as the miles wore on. In those tough and sore last few miles when the pain had fully absorbed him, it took all his energy just to avoid the tree roots. By now the spoken word was deemed to require an unwarranted output of energy and it became our job to interpret as best we could his nods, head shakes and hand signals.'

By the fifth day that 10 metre descent at the bottom of the run course was starting to put the fear of God into me.

Sometimes it took an age to descend what was in reality barely the length of a bus. Often at the top, I would stop deliberately so as to plot a routing that would offer the least amount of pain. For some of those times I had to adopt a mindset of a soldier plotting a passage across a minefield. Any momentum on that lap was temporarily brought to a standstill. To amuse myself, I calculated on one occasion that night that I only had to do it 133 more times.

After the descent we were hit by a brief ambush of rocky and undulating ground for about 20 metres. Anyone taller than 5'5 (all of us) then had to duck under some extensive overhanging foliage where we were plunged briefly into darkness. By now we were at the rear of the lake and at the lowest point of the entire run course. From here we had to ascend 100 feet or more to reach the highest point. Whilst it was graded, it still sapped energy from every competitor.

One positive feature of the route was the immediate access to three separate toilets which were on the course itself and which were used often. I will save you any more detail on this except to say that one of these was a permanent ecological toilet which we passed every 11 to 15 minutes. If the door was open I would have sprinted half a mile to avoid hitting the odour that it emitted.

From there the climb back to the top section was slow. Half way up, there was a brief diversion where we had to cross over the finish line and onwards to the grassy terrain I mentioned before. That was a tough section as it began with a two foot uphill step. From there the jagged, hardened and broken ground of about 60 metres was as welcoming on our limbs as a butcher's knife.

AUDIO DIARY

'Toby is falling behind. There's a good chance three or four of them mightn't start tomorrow. It looks like Hanno is one of those.'

Every day injuries dictated that some competitors withdrew and this was a fear that we all had in the back of our minds. Every competitor was well prepared coming into the event but the only thing that might be beyond our control was injury. It might be a mistake we made or perhaps lady luck not shining in our direction.

Unbeknownst to me, Toby Smithson was by now in serious trouble with his right Achilles and would soon bow out.

Toby
'It was all going very well for me until the morning of Day Four. I knew I was in trouble but you just hope it's going to go away. The medic advised that it could rupture and permanent damage could occur if I continued. I was gutted but agreed with Rachael (girlfriend and crew) that I was going to try to finish five as part of the Quintuple event. It then became a case of damage limitation.'

For Toby it was devastating news. Sadly he had fallen from an opening day that took 12 hrs 53 mins to over 19 hours three days later.

Toby
'It was a typical overuse injury. I've a number of theories that may or may not have contributed. Not enough trail running in my preparation given the surface of the run course. Also, when I returned to London I noticed my saddle was tilted downward by an inch or two. I am not sure when this happened but I would regularly check the bike in future.'

A year later, his thoughts on withdrawing were philosophical.

Toby
'It's strange. On the one hand it was quite straight forward. I was injured. If I didn't stop I might do myself permanent

damage. So, it's a case of perspective and remembering that there is more to life than this.

On the other hand it was one of the hardest things I've ever had to face. I'd created a lot of pressure for myself. I received a lot of support from friends and family in the lead up and on every day of the event. Many of them took time out to come down to cheer me on.

I was doing the event in support of children's charity, 'Right To Play.' People had made very generous donations and I had appeared on regional television and in the local press. The months after were tough but friends and family were very supportive. It's hard for people to understand as its not something many people have been through and I'm still coming to terms with some of it even to this day.

It was however, one of the greatest experiences of my life.'

On Day One, Toby's physical appearance illustrated utter professionalism and proper preparation. He was strong and fit and no doubt had the ability to finish. This event was truly unforgiving though in asking a thousand questions about the participants preparation and strategies as well as the mental state of mind. So much of the ability to finish lay in there. At least 50 per cent, maybe more.

A clear indication of Toby's physical distress was illustrated by his 2:55am finishing time on the fifth day. He had entered the lake 21 hours earlier.

Another man who looked immeasurably strong but would soon bow out as well was Hanno Nickau, the tall athletic German. Previously Hanno had completed a sub-10 hour iron distance triathlon in 2005 as well as a double in '08 and a successful treble iron distance in 2010. A treble required competitors to complete a 7.2 mile (11.4 km) swim, a 336 mile (540 km) cycle and a 78.6 mile (126.6km) continuous run. Also about to head back to normal life was my stable mate and previous deca finisher Tony Fisher.

By now I felt a bond with almost everyone. It is not that we were spending a lot of time together but we were on one level. Usually it was just a word of acknowledgement as we passed. A bond does not have to be through physical interaction. It can sometimes be simply out of respect for mutual endeavour. Often it was a smile or a glance of empathy that signified we simply knew what the other was going through.

AUDIO DIARY

'My sole objective every day is to be one of the lucky ones whose name is called out the next morning and that I will be there to respond to it.'

That in itself would signify progress. There could be no greater measure. Tony Raynor had an identical goal.

Tony

'I just had a goal to make the swim everyday and then start the process all over again.'

As long as we achieved that, it meant we were getting there. A vision of entering the water the next morning became on occasion my one and only focus. I knew that thinking about Sunday was pointless. This was only Tuesday. For now, it was as far away as a pot of gold at the end of a rainbow. I needed something more tangible, so it seemed a good ploy.

Every day I had hours and hours to think. Every day I doubted my ability. It was partly human nature but also strangely, partly a strategy. I didn't want to take success for granted. My 'go to' strategy in my mind 50 times a day was always this. Be one of the lucky ones who is there at the lake tomorrow morning to hear your name called out. That is all.

A second Ultra Triathlon event would shortly commence. On

our sixth day we would be joined by five who had signed up to attempt five iron distances over the remaining five days. They included Ian Walsh, an Irishman from County Waterford. Having been sent details in advance, we both knew the other was taking part. As I emerged from the forest down at the lake on one of the run laps, I spotted him as he arrived to set up camp. We said a brief hello and wished each other well. Our common nationality harnessing a bond of sorts.

At around 7pm, I felt a pain starting to develop on the side of my right foot. It was a blister but thankfully after putting a Compeed on (blister remedy product), it began to ease. I only mention this because remarkably this was my first ever blister in all my years of running.

Day Five took me 15:42:57 to complete of which 5:50:51 of that time was spent running or at least imitating running. I had tried to run virtually every metre but still it took that long. At times I must have appeared to be slower that a snail. I was moving though and that is all that mattered.

Big Ted was also working hard but he was on a different strategy to me. We all had our strengths. Mine was in running. Ted was very strong on the bike. It was his favourite discipline and he had a wealth of experience.

Ted was the Bear Grylls (survival expert) of cycling, having been known to be able to extract a tyre's tube using only his hands and a twig as a lever. One of the many bikes in his garage had journeyed over 11,000 miles (17,000 km) with him. The opening four days had been a roller-coaster for most and Ted was no different. Now he was immersed in Day Five, well beyond his previous limit. He was shattered and experiencing exhaustion like never before.

In his own words Day Five for Big Ted was "a major struggle". It started with his slowest swim to date. His time of 1:55:47 for the 2.4 miles (3.8km) swim was seven minutes slower than the day before.

Big Ted

'Having eaten and changed after the swim, I hit the bike late. Given my problems already with the cut offs, this annoyed me.

'The first lap felt terrible and the next. I was getting irritated. I ate some food and felt it sticking to my teeth. I meant to brush my teeth earlier but had forgotten. They felt disgusting. On top of that, I hadn't showered in five days.'

Small things can make a huge difference in an event such as this. Stopping at the end of a lap to wash his teeth, Ted climbed back on the bike feeling 'refreshed'. Still though his legs felt like they were immersed in treacle. Given his pace and his body's condition, he calculated that missing the night's cut off was now a distinct possibility.

Big Ted

'I was getting nowhere and feeling lonely, sleepy, frustrated and mad. Just before 2pm, I got to the end of lap six (70 miles/112km). Mark Padley's mum, Ange, or his dad, John, I don't remember, pulled a chair up for me. I sat there staring at my feet. Someone asked if I was ok. "We've got you some food Ted. Is everything ok?"

I stared at my feet shaking my head slowly. Then the medic came over.

"Ted, are you alright?"

I put my hands on my head and squeezed my fingertips hard into my scalp, my elbows resting on my thighs. I was in utter despair.

"This is hard, this is so hard."

I squeezed my fingertips harder into my scalp. Someone began rubbing my back in sympathy. Maybe they had their arm around me?

"This is just so....."

With that, tears began to flow. I was emotionally in tatters.

"This is just so hard," I kept repeating. The medic knelt down to talk to me asking if I was missing Marie. I can't remember what I said. Probably that I missed my two little girls too. I felt lonely.

I was crying and I didn't care who saw me. My mind was giving up. And these are the moments. The moments I do this for. Never experienced this before. There are those who bend and break, I'm the other kind, aren't I?

I was passed some food and I start to eat. While still crying, I looked at my watch. Eddie Ette came over and suggested I take a power nap, that it was doing the other athletes a lot of good. I want to tell him to f*** off, that I'm not other athletes. The difference is they're talented. They have experience. I don't have time to sleep.

I looked at my watch but was told to stop. Sleep is more important right now. I finished up my food, stopped crying and went for a lie down in the transition area.'

As hard as he tried, Ted was unable to sleep.

Big Ted

'For 20 minutes I tried. I felt the mind briefly flirt with it but it didn't happen. I got up and I think the medic commented that I'd got up early. But now I was angry. Not emotional. Not lonely. Just really angry. I was screwed for the cut-off and I just wasted 20 minutes trying to sleep. Oh and I still felt like s***.

I got on the bike and Eddie wished me well. Everyone around clapped and shouted for me. Awesome people. I may have been in tatters but I still appreciated every time they clapped or said "well done" or "Go on, Ted!"

In anger, I pushed hard up the little hill out of the transition area. But within a few hundred yards I was labouring again. Nothing in the legs. It was slipping away. There were four laps to go on the bike on Day Five and it was slipping away from me.

Soon Gerry Duffy passed me and said some kindly words. Then Mick Barnes sailed past me. And that really cheesed me off.

Mick was a bit faster than me on the bike but when he had caught me on the bike in previous days, I'd tried to stay with him so that I could focus on getting the lap done. To see him just sail past me like that and for me not to have any response was just horrible. Gerry was now a few hundred yards ahead as was Mick.

AND THEN I JUST CRACKED.

It wasn't anger so much. I think it was a case of if I didn't do something I knew the cut-off would disappear. So although Mick was way up the road, I resolved that I would allow him to move no further away. I had no choice.

Before long I had Mick back in my sights. As I caught him I asked if I could ride alongside to prevent me losing focus and keep my speed up. Mick was fine with that. But I had caught Mick just as the road started to go downhill and the adrenaline was flowing.

I left Mick for dead and saw Eddie at the side of the road who, given my emotional breakdown earlier, had come to check that I was ok. I gave him the thumbs up. No smiles though. I wasn't for smiling now. I realised that I needed to play to my strengths. Big guys like me are good at one thing on a bike, time trialling. It was time to do what I was best at.

Within another mile or so I flew past Gerry who along with Mick must have been wondering what the hell was going on. Ten minutes before I had been going under

10mph struggling to keep the pedals turning. Now it was in my head to time trial for the next 40 miles.

I continued to push the pace and record something like a 43 min lap. I flew into transition, stopped the bike, took my jacket off (I was hot from the effort at last) and sped away again. Eddie was there with a huge smile on his face, saying what an amazing lap that was. Well, it was probably over 25 minutes quicker than the last one.

And off I went again. I was worried that the legs might die. But they didn't. On the next lap I'd hit the nasty, steep, twisty little rise just outside Burley. On that hill I'd power past Rod Elder, a far stronger cyclist than me. He'd later comment on how strong I looked.

Still I pushed on.

I caught and passed Monique. I felt bad for tearing past her like that.

As I approached transition again I was not stopping this time. I screamed at the timing people "last lap split for number 15" at the top of my voice. (My race number)

Someone shouted; "eight laps done, Ted".

"No, I need the time, the time. "Last lap time for number 15."

My voice was loud. It was clear. The words were well put together and clearly communicated. I had my mind back. I was in control again. Someone shouted 42 minutes just as I was leaving transition.

"Thank you," I shouted as I powered up the rise out of the saddle. I wasn't ready to slow down yet.

It was joked about how the normally mild-mannered and ever gracious Ted had become a monster all of a sudden as he screamed (in a nice way) at everyone in transition.

But I was saving my race. Doing what I had to do.

There are those who bend and break, I'm the other kind.

The next two laps were very similar, probably a little slower at 44/45 minutes, but in essence I had made back an hour and half, probably more compared to how things were looking only three hours before.

It was approaching 6pm as I put my run shoes on. The cut off was unlikely to take me now.'

As I ran through the bike turnaround point later that evening, I spotted Big Ted dismounting from his bike. He was hard to miss. Ted was taller than our camper van and had the chest of an American footballer. A 38-year-old company director from North Lincolnshire in England, Ted had completed just one iron distance event before but that triple iron success demonstrated what exceptional ability he possessed. That event saw him cross the line after 56 hours of non-stop effort. Big Ted had excellent credentials.

In the lead-in, his training had not gone as well as planned. At times he questioned both his preparation and his participation, having experienced many highs and lows along the way.

Training, working and raising a family of two young children meant every hour had to be utilised. At times he was simply unable to train as he might have wanted. But still he remained resolute.

Given his afternoon revival, this 14 and a half stone gentle giant was now safely back on target to make the cut off. Making it was one thing. Having less than two hours to recover and a requirement to do it all over again the next day however, didn't augur well for his continued participation.

As I continued on with the miles, Ted closed his eyes for a quick power nap. By now the adrenalin had fallen and so a quick siesta seemed timely and tactical for him. In that afternoon he had experienced more highs and lows than a theme park rollercoaster. Now he had finished that discipline but in triathlon there are three.

Twenty-five minutes after closing his eyes he opened them again, changed out of his bike kit and started his fifth marathon in as many days.

For the first few miles of the run he was strong, but soon he began to wane. Picking up that adrenalin rush when his body was beyond exhaustion was proving difficult. Still he ticked off one lap after another. Hours later as darkness took over the forest, he put on a pair of leggings to avoid the same chill he had felt the night before. By 11pm he was climbing into the higher miles. 14, 15, 18, 20.

Big Ted

'And then tiredness kicked in. I mean really, really kicked in. I don't think I've ever felt so drained. I was struggling to move forward again. I wanted to sleep on my feet.

I stopped for a short rest. Either Rob (crew) or the medic suggested another power nap. Otherwise I would go outside the cut off if I carried on like this. The anger welled up inside again. Which bit of "I don't need sleep" do these people not understand? But the desire to sleep was just too great. I made a mess of my nutrition and Rob got me through that. So I did as I was told. I got into the sleeping bag and fell asleep immediately.

Rob woke me 20 minutes later. I have never felt so rejuvenated in all my life. I did a couple of laps and the cut off looked far less scary. I wanted to run on but Rob told me to stay in the present. He was right of course. It's not over until it's over. I was doing fine. I was exhausted. I had hit a serious limit that night. A few of the other guys who were still out on the course after more than 20 hours, had planned to quit the next day. I discovered the true meaning of one foot in front of the other. I was completely exhausted. I had so little left to give. It was time to quit. I felt I probably wouldn't do anymore after this.

Richard Ginn caught up with me on my last lap. He was

on his last lap as well and asked me to run into the finish with him. Richard was making Day Five his last day. Rob was with me. I asked him if that would be ok.

"No, just walk," Rob said. Stay in the present. He was right and so I didn't. After a couple more minutes, I jogged the last 100 yards or so to the finishing chute with Richard. We crossed the line together that night and embraced. It is probably my favourite memory of the event. Richard was in a celebratory mood and it rubbed off on me.

Having learnt the true meaning of staying in the present, I resolved that I would just wake up in a couple of hours and see how I felt. But I probably wouldn't carry on.

As I laid my head down I wasn't sure if my alarm was set properly or not. As my eyes closed I reasoned that if I overslept it didn't matter. I'd done what I came here to do. I was happy at last and if I wanted, I could retire gracefully.

STANDINGS AFTER DAY FIVE

Competitor	Cumulative Race Position	Day One	Day Two	Day Three	Day Four	Day Five
Gerry Duffy	1	14:41:07	15:22:12	15:06:49	15:31:04	15:42:57
Toby Smithson	2	12:53:33	15:12:30	14:29:19	19:22:54	20:55:07
Mark Padley	3	16:51:49	17:16:45	17:13:52	17:02:06	17:04:42
Roderick Elder	4	16:25:49	17:11:33	17:32:33	18:10:07	17:59:33
Mike Trew	5	16:57:45	17:15:34	18:00:58	18:12:28	18:08:08
Hanno Nickau	6	14:16:25	16:33:11	17:13:00	18:41:43	21:51:24
Tony Fisher	7	16:34:58	17:38:23	17:33:54	18:27:21	20:26:30
Mick Barnes	8	17:46:47	19:27:11	18:05:38	17:50:25	18:04:36
Tony Raynor	9	16:41:06	18:19:58	19:03:47	19:37:47	18:58:44
Richard Ginn	10	16:38:51	17:45:44	18:36:07	20:23:23	21:27:43
Monique Hollinshead	11	19:28:49	19:23:00	20:29:56	19:51:12	20:28:52
Edward Page	12	18:11:34	21:19:14	21:39:45	20:43:18	21:27:44

Competitor	Cumulative Total
Gerry Duffy	76:24:39
Toby Smithson	82:53:23
Mark Padley	85:29:14
Robert Elder	87:19:354
Mike Trew	88:34:53
Hanno Nickau	88:35:22
Tony Fisher	90:41:06
Mick Barnes	91:14:37
Tony Raynor	92:41:22
Richard Ginn	94:51:48
Monique Hollinshead	99:41:49
Edward Page	103:21:35

CHAPTER TWENTY-TWO

Ticking Boxes
To Keep Going

I spoke earlier about the many strategies that I felt might assist me in my quest to achieve this huge goal. There were the months of training and surrounding myself with a great crew. There was bringing over the best equipment I could afford. And sponsorship. A superb AR4 FELT bike, my most prized possession, was very generously provided by a business acquaintance Aidan Duff of Eurotrek, a bike distribution company in Ireland.

I was very fortunate to have access to the best contacts in the business through Dor who had her own multi-sports and triathlon store called 'Tri and Run'. A Blue 70 wetsuit, Mizuno shoewear as well as 'Look' bike clothing from their distributor in Ireland (Cycle Superstore) had also been stowed into my luggage.

In addition to the equipment, other important approaches included preparing and executing as best I could my nutrition and pace. I had to be conscious of these at all times. That also included being open to the idea of adapting and changing as the event progressed, such as when Ken had pinned me against that verbal wall on Day Four.

Three other boxes ticked every day included drinking a finish line recovery smoothie, a late night ritual of climbing back into the lake to cool, soothe and partially rebuild my leg muscles ahead of the next day's labour and a short five minute massage by a crew member. No other competitor seemed to share these tactics.

To be fair some were finishing so late, an extra 15 minutes of sleep was of greater value to them. It's difficult for me to prove that the late night water immersion worked, but I'm certain it did for me. Even as the crew were lifting me out, I was already feeling its benefits.

As I spoke into the audio and Doug massaged my legs in the medics tent, I felt like dozing but my body started to shiver. I longed to close my eyes. My mind was fine but I was physically drained. It was almost 11pm.

My walk back to the shower block and then to bed was slow as my leg muscles had cramped a little. As I crossed over the run course. I passed two athletes. It was pitch dark so I had no clue as to their identity. Hopefully though we would all be fit enough to be back at the lake in just a few short hours.

DAY SIX

CHAPTER TWENTY-THREE

'Every step is a step towards home'
Author unknown

WEDNESDAY 8TH JUNE, 2011

At 5:55am we got word that Toby was out. By the end of the sixth swim, he would be joined by two more. By 9am there would be another withdrawal, leaving only eight competitors in the field.

> **Toby**
> 'The hardest moment was waking up on that sixth day. Unbeknown to me, Rachael had written to a lot of my friends and sporting idols asking for them to send words of support. Each morning she would pick one and read it out to inspire me for the day.
>
> As I lay there listening to those left in the event walking down to the swim start and to the sound of Steve calling out my name, Rachael read out a letter from Chrissie Wellington (four time World Ironman Triathlon Champion) and I just lost it. Staying in the tent was one of the hardest things, but also one of the most sensible things I've ever done.

As a result of the rumour that had spread about having to get into the lake on Day Six, two others were determined to start the swim but they didn't have the ambition to finish it.

After the swim and before we mounted our bikes, Hanno Nickau and my camping neighbour Tony Fisher had bowed out. A short while later they would be joined by Richard Ginn who retired from the event before 9am. All had proudly finished a quintuple iron distance triathlon, an exceptional feat in its own right.

The night before, Tony Fisher had been the earliest of the latest retirees to finish, crossing the line at 2:26am. Toby Smithson's day didn't end until 2:55am, Richard Ginn at 3:27am and Hanno Nickau 3:51am or just nine minutes inside the cut off.

Later I chatted briefly to Tony Fisher during a food stop. Having already completed a deca before he was very happy with his performance and very philosophical. A measure of the man saw him stay for a few more days to support the remaining competitors.

Big Ted had earlier awoken at 4:45am. He had only been asleep for about an hour but now he couldn't sleep. In some ways he had already achieved more than he had thought possible.

> **Big Ted**
> 'I just lay there with the thought of quitting in my head. I was tired, my eyelids heavy but I couldn't sleep. My mind though was uneasy with the notion of quitting. On reflection it was making me reconsider. This was getting ridiculous. How much more could I take? Had they retired me medically that morning, I think I would have accepted it graciously.'

But he refused to give in. At 5:50am he was back out of his tent again and donning his wetsuit for a sixth time before climbing back into the lake once more.

By 8:17am I had the swim completed and 11.6 miles (18.6km) or one lap of the cycle finished. With five hours unbroken sleep secured the night before, I'd started the first few miles of the cycle in a good place. This was Day Six and I was one of the lucky eight. If I needed to harness any positive energy from somewhere I just reminded myself of that fact. Sixty per cent of the field were gone and we had only reached half way.

As I sat in the chair eating a bowl of breakfast cereal, I reflected on who was left. All that remained were Mark Padley, Tony Raynor, Monique Hollinshead, Edward Page, Mick Barnes, Roderick Elder, Mike Trew and myself.

I will shortly pay a tribute to Mike Trew for in less than 24 hours he too would bow out. His exit would not be ability related. He had plenty of fight left in him. He would though suffer a late night fall on Day Six. His reaction in spite of what had happened and in trying to continue, would beggar belief.

Mark Padley was someone I was now starting to notice a lot more. In the autumn of 2010, he had committed to his entry.

Mark Padley

'When I first read about it, I dismissed it. I felt that nobody in their right mind would be daft enough to take it on. I didn't realise that I was that man. It took over three months of contemplation and acceptance of the task in hand before I told anybody.'

Every morning, Mark and I seemed to exit the swim within a minute or two of each other. Usually he was marginally ahead but today I was out in 1:12:38, pipping him by a whopping 20 seconds. Mike exited first as he usually did in a time of 1:11:49 although both Mark and myself were narrowing that daily gap.

Mark was a strong cyclist. He and I were well-matched and usually came in close to each other. Mark also had a superb crew managing his every need. It was interesting that we seemed to share a similar strategy, that of only stopping when absolutely necessary.

Doug Bates

'Just like Gerry, Mark never stopped except for the briefest of requirements. His crew were brilliant at managing his needs and he never had to leave the course for more than a minute or two.'

As I sat there eating, Mark headed to the turnaround point for the final few metres of his first bike lap of the day. His parents, as well as two friends Rob and Rich, were crewing for him. By Wednesday, they all looked as tired as he did. I saw his father John quite often and he always gave me a big cheer.

I'd just finished my pit stop and was remounting as Mark passed to start his second lap. On several occasions he would finish the bike five or 10 minutes ahead, but faster transitions and the fact that running was my strongest discipline, meant that by the start of Day Six, I was over seven hours ahead of him. Roderick Elder was almost two hours further back again. The significance was that we now filled the top three places in overall classification.

At the time I wasn't sure that I was leading. Yes, I had a vague idea that I was towards the top of the leader board but no one told me I had passed out Toby as race leader after the fourth day. As I sat in the chair on Day Six, I overheard Ken on the phone give someone an update.

'Yeah, he's in front by over seven hours.'

With the exception of Toby, the updates about the people who had withdrawn earlier that day had yet to register with me. Even at the lakeshore I wasn't paying too much attention, because to me it was still early days.

When Steve was calling out the names, I was really only interested in hearing my own name and responding accordingly. Other than that, I was busy trying to insert my body into the wetsuit and at the same time avoid a raw chaffing wound just below my neck that the wetsuit was intent on aggravating every day. That is why I turned to Ken when he finished that conversation and asked, 'Who is in front?'

He simply smiled, almost childishly continuing to conceal the fact from me. I later found out that the crew had decided against telling me as a tactic.

I hadn't known that it had taken Toby over 19 hours to finish Day Four. Nor did I really realise when he withdrew, who was lying where or how long it had taken them. The enormity of the challenge didn't allow time for much questioning. There was simply too much going on for us to investigate how anyone else was faring.

Any information I was computing was simply through observation and simple calculation. Every day just demanded so much out of us. There were 11 or 12 meals a day that had to be eaten as well as snacks and continuous hydration and rehydration. There were the many changes of clothing, the massage, the lake cool-down and the night-time shower ritual. Not to mention the matter of the swim, the cycle and the run. The truth is I had never thought of myself as being in a competitive race. I was there to participate and to finish. Once I finished Day Ten, I had done what I went there to do.

Now the prospect of winning was suddenly weighing heavily and the truth is I didn't welcome it. I had enough of a physical and mental load to concern myself with. This event was designed to extract every ounce of energy we possessed. Certainly a lead of an hour or two with a day to go would have been welcome, but now suddenly I was up there as a target and we were only at the half way stage. Toby's two and a half hour lead after Day Three had been obliterated in one fell swoop when he took over 19 hours to finish the fourth day.

I decided to put it completely out of my head, convincing myself quite rightly that at this stage it was irrelevant. I needed to focus all of my energy and concentration into simply finishing Day Six.

AUDIO DIARY

'My sole objective every day is to be one of the lucky ones whose name is called out the next morning and that I will be there to hear it.'

Competitors were falling faster than shares on a bad day in Wall

Street so concentration and focus were of paramount importance. On the bike we had hours and hours to think. It meant I was constantly having to work hard to ensure my mental state remained resolute. As I began my second lap, I was a little down. Apart from the 'burden' of being in front, I knew the mental and physical magnitude of what lay ahead between now and 3:30pm or thereabouts when I would have to cycle the remaining 104 miles (167km).

Time and time again I reminded myself that I couldn't get to Day Ten without passing through Day Six. All I was doing every day was passing through on the way to deca. This morning I had felt a little cold as I began the cycle. For the first time I had to put on a hat and gloves and they stayed on for the first four hours.

At this stage into the event I had broken the cycle loops into several smaller stages. I had to, otherwise it would have engulfed me. Stage one for me was from the turning circle to the bottom of the giant descent. That drop was my favourite. It offered the first of only two opportunities to make progress without actually pedalling. A brief 30 or 40 seconds of ecstasy. On Day Six however the wind direction changed so it was less favourable.

From here we had approximately two miles (3.2km) until we hit Burley. I found this section hard. Here the terrain offered no assistance and you had to work for every metre. I knew as well that so much of the lap was still to be cycled. The landscape was not mentally stimulating either and it had those nine chicanes through which we had to navigate, which took constant decision-making and concentration. Then we would arrive into the village.

By 10am most mornings Burley was as busy as a bee-hive. After five days I knew every junction, road sign, pot-hole, shop name and was on first name terms with many of the areas equine inhabitants.

The main route through the village was very narrow and was pedestrianised in everything but law. Given the many recreational cyclists around in June, it was assumed we were in no hurry. As a result, while beautiful and distracting, Burley was always frustrating because of its traffic and the constant requirement to slow down. We also had to watch everyone eating ice-cream. At times that was proving harder than the deca.

As soon as we left Burley we had two climbs. The first was quite short, about 75 metres in distance and the second a half a mile further on, was maybe 200 metres all told. I had long since designated this point as the beginning of the centre piece of the bike loop. With those short climbs behind us we were now firmly back out in the quiet of the English countryside. Here, we were amused by lush greenery and a road surface and direction that changed repeatedly.

In the middle of this segment we passed the second of two cattle grids. Earlier in the week I had conceived a mind trick when crossing them. Each time I passed over one, I subtracted this from the overall requirement to cross 200 grids in that 10 day period. Having the number dwindle every day was mentally very encouraging. As I had crossed the first of them on lap one, I quickly calculated that I had only 99 remaining. Psychologically just entering into double digits rather than treble was like scoring a goal in an All Ireland or an FA Cup final.

By now we were on the back end of the course where it was much quieter. The lower elevation also meant less wind. To begin with, there was a fast but brief downhill section where we gained free momentum for 300 metres. There were a few junctions where we had to give way and exercise caution. Indeed the detail on the many signposts I passed, could now form my 'chosen subject' were I to appear on the 'Mastermind' tv programme. By Day Six I had long since memorised them all.

Here we were offered gorgeous lush countryside but given the low elevation we never could see much apart from the many green hedgerows. As a result, this section became very monotonous at times and I found I had to continually keep my mind alert to the job as we ate into the higher miles each afternoon.

Having travelled approximately 10 miles (16 km) of each cycle lap, we arrived at a left hand turn to begin the climb back to the turnaround point. An illustration of just how tired we were starting to feel occurred when Big Ted actually missed this turn, even though he had already taken it over 50 times. Imagine the mental slump that hit him when he realised it.

> **Big Ted**
> 'As I continued my eyes got really very droopy. At some point the roads and hedgerows began to look unfamiliar. I continued, assuming that I was noticing different buildings for the first time. Soon after, I entered Bransgore. Then I thought to myself,
>
> "Don't remember that from previous days".
>
> And then, belatedly it hit me. You never get to Bransgore on the route. You turn back up Braggers lane before you get to Bransgore.
>
> S***, I've missed the turn off – and I must be at least a mile and a half past it.
>
> I turned the bike around, very, very angry and riding as fast as I could. I was now desperate to see the turn off. In my sleep-deprived state I wasn't entirely sure where I was, but thankfully I found the turn. I assume that I must have fallen asleep on the bike and missed the huge neon signs that pointed us towards the race village.'

Earlier as I turned to climb back up the hill at the rear of the course on lap six, I got a bit of a shock myself. Why was it always lap six that something happened ?

There to greet me was a giant Irish flag with two friends from home, hidden behind the Irish tricolour. I cannot begin to tell you what a lift I got when I found out that Colm Connaughton and Paul McDermott had arrived for a brief four-hour stopover to lend their support. Their contribution occupied my mind for hours.

Although the final climb back to the race headquarters was tough and slow, I welcomed it as it was a sign that we had ticked another box. Immediately we turned off the Burley to Bransgore road, we were hit by a continuing drag of about 300 metres. Then we needed to get out of the saddle for the next 100 or so (*see map, pages 12&13*). By now we only had another 400/500 metres to climb. The average gradient over this entire section was approximately four or five metres for every 100 metres progressed. By Day Six I could have cycled it blindfolded. We had to be careful because motorists coming in the opposite direction had no knowledge that there were tired, wandering cyclists approaching from below.

Out of the 100 bike loops we had to cycle over the 10 days, it was mentally stimulating and uplifting to subtract each one from the overall target. By midday on Day Six, I had now climbed it 55 times.

Toby

'The amount of laps was a huge mental challenge. It was like going around a hamster's wheel. But, a short course was good for friends and family, crew and medical support and to chat with fellow competitors.'

From here we knew that we were just minutes away from human contact, interaction, music, camaraderie, food, bike maintenance, medical attention and mental energy from our crews and the organisers. It was a very special bond that everyone shared and a unique journey that the few remaining were immersed within. This event was very special, a challenge in the extreme to find out what our bodies could do. Whatever number were left by way of competitors, crew and organisers, around 25 in total, we were all rooting for each other.

My cycle lap times on Day Six were making grim reading in terms of the direction they were headed. All bar one was over 50 minutes – a best time of 48:57 on lap two and a low of 57:25 on lap five. On Day One my fastest lap had taken 43:53. Almost a week later a fast lap was almost five minutes slower. Perhaps it was inevitable.

On lap six, I had to evict my right foot from my bike shoe once again. On the final loop, both feet needed daylight so I positioned them on top of the shoes for the last 11 miles (18km). Dismounting at 4:09pm it had been my slowest cycle to date. Just three minutes shy of nine hours in the saddle.

In the pre-event rota both Ken and Doug were due to return home after Day Six. This meant Jarlath Mahon would be crewing solo for most of Thursday and all of Friday. I now realised that having two crew members there made a huge difference and where possible was a must. The crews labour was far greater than we had all anticipated.

On Day Six I asked Doug to stay an extra day. The only issue was the fact that we knew we had to pay his wife the courtesy of an enquiry to clear the way.

'I have a plan,' I smirked.

Earlier that day Sharon Bates, Doug's wife, had gone into work to run her busy barber's shop which she did six days a week. Sharon was into triathlon and was obviously into Doug. After all she married him. As I was one of her barber clients, I also knew she was an avid listener of a certain radio programme that I was about to be interviewed on (The Ray D'Arcy show).

I sent a plea out over the airwaves to allow Doug to stay an extra day and apparently Sharon nearly sliced the head off the poor guy in her barber's chair when she heard her name mentioned. It all ended in smiles though and Doug got his extension for the crew rota. Apparently the whole shop had gone quiet for the interview, erupting into a cheer when Sharon's name was mentioned. Jarlath was perhaps the only one more relieved than the poor guy in the barber's chair, as it meant Doug would continue to crew with him.

With the beginning of the other quintuple race, having five new faces on the course had offered some fresh mental stimulation. Anything new in fact stood out. We were in a cocoon shielded from anything that was happening outside. These new competitors offered a connection akin to a prison visit where new information was relayed from the outside world. Early on in the evening marathon I bumped into Ian Walsh, one of the five, and we chatted briefly.

Close examination of my run lap times shows better consistency than other days. On Day Six I was almost always between 12 and 13 minutes. I must have eaten on lap eleven as my time fell by over four minutes to 17:45. My strategy of walking and eating at the same time was now routine.

Strangely, on days five and six, I felt my body was now becoming accustomed to the daily ritual. That is not to say I was finding it easy because I wasn't. Nor am I saying that I was no longer exhausted as I crossed the finish line in a time of 15:48:16, because I was. It's just that I felt things had levelled off a little. It was almost as if there were no more sand bags left to attach themselves to me but those that were already attached were still there.

What crept up unnoticed was a niggle that at first I barely took in. As Ken interviewed me on video while I was cooling down in the lake, I mentioned this new problem with my right shin. In the swim that Wednesday it had felt a little tight. On the bike I hadn't noticed it but on the run it played up just a little.

Soon a little would become a lot.

Soon after 11pm, I climbed into the sleeping bag and called Jacinta. I wanted to talk to her before I closed my eyes. Over a brief call I expressed how tired I felt with four more days still to do. Perhaps I was looking for sympathy. I'm not sure.

"How does your car registration finish?" Jacinta asked.

"What?"

"How does your car registration finish?" she repeated

"What do you mean?" I asked, without the faintest idea of where she was going with her questioning. I was tired but I still had firm hold of my faculties. 'Just call it out', she persisted.

"4, 3, 2, 1," I replied.

"Now repeat it ," she requested.

"4, 3, 2 ,1," I replied a second time.

"There, see how fast you can say it", she summarised. "Say it again."

"4, 3, 2, 1," I repeated even faster on the third occasion.

"See how it only takes you a split second to say that," she continued. "Just keep repeating that to yourself tomorrow. That is all you have left. Four days. Then three days, then two and one. 4, 3, 2, 1. Look how quickly you can say it. It will pass that quickly and will be over before you know it."

This would prove to be a very empowering mind trick for me in the days ahead. In its simplicity it was brilliant. I planted it firmly in my brain and decided to try it the next day. Over the remaining days, I would repeat it a thousand times.

With that I said goodbye to Jacinta and closed my eyes.

"4, 3, 2, 1,

4, 3, 2...

4, 3..."

What seemed like a minute later, I opened them again.

It was 5am.

STANDINGS AFTER DAY SIX

Competitor	Cumulative Race Position	Day One	Day Two	Day Three	Day Four	Day Five
Gerry Duffy	1	14:41:07	15:22:12	15:06:49	15:31:04	15:42:57
Mark Padley	2	16:51:49	17:16:45	17:13:52	17:02:06	17:04:42
Roderick Elder	3	16:25:49	17:11:33	17:32:33	18:10:07	17:59:33
Mike Trew	4	16:57:45	17:15:34	18:00:58	18:12:28	18:08:08
Mick Barnes	5	17:46:47	19:27:11	18:05:38	17:50:25	18:04:36
Tony Raynor	6	16:41:06	18:19:58	19:03:47	19:37:47	18:58:44
Monique Hollinshead	7	19:28:49	19:23:00	20:29:56	19:51:12	20:28:52
Edward Page	8	18:11:34	21:19:14	21:39:45	20:43:18	21:27:44

Competitor	Day Six	Average Per Day	Cumulative Total
Gerry Duffy	15:48:16	15:22:09	92:12:55
Mark Padley	17:12:41	17:06:59	102:41:55
Roderick Elder	18:54:39	17:42:22	106:14:14
Mike Trew	18:59:56	17:55:48	107:34:49
Mick Barnes	18:07:59	18:13:46	109:22:36
Tony Raynor	19:40:43	18:43:41	112:22:05
Monique Hollinshead	21:26:13	20:11:20	128:08:02
Edward Page	21:49:14	20:51:49	125:10:45

DAY SEVEN

CHAPTER TWENTY-FOUR

'One man's meat, is another man's poison'.
Lucretius, First Century BC Latin Writer

THURSDAY 9TH JUNE, 2011

I described in my recording the seventh day lake experience as a 'dream swim'. It was definitely my most memorable of the entire event. It felt effortless and for several reasons.

It was soothing on my aching body and felt like massage oil being rubbed into every muscle. As the swim was non-weight bearing, I was also ticking another box with modest impact. The cycle and the run was a daily battle but my seventh swim was enjoyable and helped de-stress my body just a little.

Given all the practice, my swim technique and efficiency in the water was actually improving. It was the last time however it would feel that way. From there on, the swim also became a major challenge where my thermal defences were tested to the limit. Friday would definitely be different.

In terms of withdrawals Thursday morning was ruthless on the competitors list. For Mike Trew, Mick Barnes and Big Ted it was a morning to forget. All three had the ability to finish, but sadly destiny dictated it wouldn't happen in 2011. All of these men would soon depart and not all by their own decision. First to withdraw was Mick Barnes.

Mick was a good swimmer. His strategy afterward was always to go conservatively on the bike and then run as fast as he could. On each of the first four marathons he was the only one of us to get faster each day. He was an exceptional competitor with whom I enjoyed a lot of banter. For some reason I rarely saw him on the bike but I did meet him every night on the run. He had a cheery disposition and a word of encouragement for me every time we met up.

When he emerged from his camper on Thursday morning, Mick

knew that he was in trouble. A voluntary visit to the medical tent to check his body temperature confirmed what he already suspected. The advice was to stop. Mick accepted it. Later that morning I spotted him at the bike turnaround point surrounded by more blankets to keep him warm than found in a boarding school dormitory. He sat there for hours cheering all of the remaining competitors.

For Mike Trew, my 'dream swim' in the lake was for him a swim too far.

Just hours earlier and towards the end of his sixth day, Mike was trundling through mile 16 (26 km) of his marathon with a head-torch illuminating the path ahead. It was only for a split second that fatigue forced him to lose concentration, but it would have devastating consequences. Tree roots at times could take on the appearance of show jumping fences. Mike hit a root and fell heavily.

> **Mike**
> 'I landed hard and I knew I'd done some damage to my side.'

He had no idea just how serious it was.

> **Mike**
> 'I told Dan (crew) that it was not going to stop me from completing the marathon. So I kept going.'

For the last 10 miles (16km) or so Mike was slower than a tortoise but he completed it because he had the heart of a lion. As an illustration of how much this injury slowed him, he completed the last few hours at a speed of just 2.5 miles per hour.

Sometime after 1:00 am he quietly withdrew into his two-man tent. By now he was utterly spent and in a lot of pain but he still sought no outside assistance. It would have been a fruitless exercise. Perhaps he knew that his race was almost at an end.

Four hours later at 5:00am, he was roused by his son who was crewing for him. Under the camouflage of the tent, Mike monitored his body for damage. Overnight the pain had worsened. Mike, a foundry maintenance supervisor by day, gently manoeuvred the wetsuit around his body. Given the level of physical pain he was now in, it took an eternity. An hour later he got back into the lake and tried to swim but after just 80 metres he knew he was facing an uphill battle.

Mike
'The injury was painful but not enough to stop the run. The swim though was like being stabbed with every stroke.'

What he didn't realise was the extent of his injury. Nobody did. He had two broken ribs.

Mike
'I didn't tell anybody at the start of the swim just in case they didn't let me start. I swam a loop with my left arm only. I am right-handed, so this was not good.'

For over 800 metres of the swim he fought, but most of the time he was just making circles. He stopped to rest before trying to swim again but by then he realised it was futile. He climbed slowly and agonisingly out of the lake before heading to 'confess' all in the medical tent.

His race was over.

Even before the swim had started, it was over for Big Ted as well. I only found out mid-morning. Everyone was upset when they heard about Edward Page and particularly because of how it had happened.

As the roll-call was being called at the lakeshore, we knew he was close by. We assumed that he was about to get into the water with the rest of us. Just minutes earlier I'd spotted him getting out of his tent. As we put on our goggles, we didn't know what was happening just metres away.

As he came out of his tent at 5:50am, his crew returned with a message that the medic wanted to run some tests on him just to check he was ok.

> **Big Ted**
>
> 'The medic sat me down and hooked me up to an ECG (electrocardiograph) Everyone else was about 75 yards away waiting to get into the water. I don't recall what she said to me or why she said she needed to test me. I already knew I was being pulled from the race. I didn't understand it but I knew. And I hadn't even been tested yet.
>
> The medic fiddled with the machine and jotted down some notes. Probably took my blood pressure too. Then she took my core temperature and looked at me with a glum expression.
>
> "Ted your core temperature is down to 35.2. I cannot let you continue," she uttered.'

His premonition was accurate. Immediately his 125 hours of effort over six days had ground to a halt. His ambition and dream over.

Big Ted is a larger-than-life character. Now though he was temporarily broken. Just like Samson when he lost his hair, Ted now had all his powers stripped. His hands went on top of his head and his fingertips pressed into his scalp just like they had when he was enduring a tough afternoon two days before. The white towel was thrown in without his consent.

Then the tears came.

> **Big Ted**
>
> 'I didn't understand all of this. Why were they doing this to me? What had I done wrong? The medic said something comforting but I don't recall what it was.'

A year later he shared with me that this was the first day he had actually woken up thinking he would finish. Everyone felt for him. If we could have sacrificed a degree of our own body temperature to assist him we would have queued to donate. Everyone else who had retired had made the decision for themselves. Perhaps that is why an extra cloud of sadness hung around for most of that day.

Leigh Cowling (Doctor)
'Ted's main issues were due to sleep deprivation/exhaustion as well as the trauma each competitor was putting their body through. He was losing hours each day and coming in later and later, which meant he was getting less and less sleep. Consequently his times were getting slower and slower, a vicious cycle. This was having the well-documented effects that sleep deprivation has in combination with the stresses of an iron distance a day (There is a reason it is used as a torture).'

His decision making process was becoming impaired.

There were numerous reports of him being asleep on the roadside during the bicycle ride, a fact which concerned me both in terms of his safety, his temperature (it wasn't the nicest of weather) and his tiredness whilst cycling on public roads. Steve Haywood followed him in the car and reported swerving and erratic cycling.

He was feeling nauseous, which meant his fuel and fluid intake was suffering. When pushing your body to its limit, adequate energy and nutrition is key. On his final day when he came out of the lake, all of these factors were going through my mind.

When I found out about Ted, I knew it could just as easily have been me in that medical tent. Perhaps not for core body temperature reasons at that precise moment, but any minute I could be hit with an injury. Lady Luck owed me nothing. I was one of the lucky five still going, still allowed to continue, and still injury free. I was being left out there for whatever reason. Ted had more training done than I. He retired to his tent temporarily broken.

I found out later that shortly after, he went back to see the medic.

Big Ted

'Anger raged. Deep, deep fury. Could I have taken one more stroke in that water? Yes. I asked for an explanation. I said I wanted to understand what had happened earlier. I wanted to know where I failed so that I could learn from it. The medic told me that I hadn't failed, that I shouldn't see it like that.

I sat in the tent getting mad at the world. I was alone in my thoughts. I was furious. I was paranoid. I guess the mind was playing tricks with me.'

Leigh Cowling

'On his final day when he came out of the lake all of these factors I have outlined were going through my mind. When I did basic obs on him (blood pressure, heart rate, oxygen sats, resp rate, gcs, temp) and chatting to ascertain his safety and give a subjective measurement of health, his temperature came back as around 35 degrees Celsius (normal being 37-37.5).

This was somewhat unsurprising to me as he has been subjected to numerous causes of hypothermia (wet, cold, wind, prolonged coldness, sleep deprivation, physical exhaustion) and he was also exhibiting the "umbles" of symptoms shown in hypothermia – stumbles, mumbles, fumbles and grumbles. This alluded to the progressively impaired functions caused by hypothermia. In fact temperatures of below 35 are often referred to the 'I don't care' attitude as there is a loss of emotional cognition.

At this point I did an ECG, as hypothermia can cause changes in electrical conduction in the heart. Fortunately this was normal sinus rhythm. However by this point I had a comprehensive picture in my mind (from spectator reports, the medical observations and questioning of Ted) and I did not feel that it would be safe for him to continue.'

As time passed, Big Ted's anger subsided and gave way to considered reflection on what had happened.

Big Ted

'This wonderful lady (Leigh) had patched up my feet, taken an interest in how I was feeling, helped me out and kept me in the race for six days. It wasn't her fault but for a few days it was.'

Perhaps a fitting tribute to Big Ted would be to reprint an oft-used quote attributed to Theodore Roosevelt, the 26th President of the United States.

I have included it for two reasons. The first is that it feels entirely fitting to be positioned here in tribute not just to Ted but to all of the 20 starters. Secondly, I have since learned, it is a personal favourite of Big Ted's as well.

Theodore Roosevelt

'It is not the critic who counts; not the man who points out how the strong man stumbles, or where the doer of deeds could have done them better. The credit belongs to the man who is actually in the arena, whose face is marred by dust and sweat and blood; who strives valiantly; who errs, who comes short again and again, because there is no effort without error and shortcoming; but who does actually strive to do the deeds; who knows great enthusiasms, the great devotions; who spends himself in a worthy cause; who at the best knows in the end the triumph of high achievement, and who at the worst, if he fails, at least fails while daring greatly, so that his place shall never be with those cold and timid souls who neither know victory nor defeat.'

Big Ted

'Once the event was over, I returned home and began to see what I had achieved. I realised also that it was my responsibility not to get cold. It was my responsibility not to get into an exhausted state in the first place. The other thing I accepted is that race organisers care about the athletes and sometimes they have to make decisions when the athlete is in no fit state to think for themselves.'

A few weeks after, he shared his final thoughts.

Big Ted

'The deca iron at Avon Tyrell doesn't take you early. She lets you build your confidence. And then only then, does she take you out. Because that hurts the athlete more. That course is brutal, utterly relentless. And if you get the details wrong, you will be punished.'

As Ted's dream was fading, I had unexcitedly exited the swim in exactly 1:12:00. On the bike though it would be the opposite. Nothing mechanical or to do with injury, but soon some unexpected visitors on the roadside would appear, and I'd also have an unexpected request.

DAY 6
08.06.2011

'IF A BED SALESMAN HAD BEEN PASSING, HE WOULD HAVE BEEN CONFIDENT OF SALES'

SNAP SHOTS: Mike Trew was as strong as an ox; even someone's birthday didn't go unmissed; and Big Ted had to grit his teeth to get through Day Six.

WELL DONE MATE: Steve Haywood (right) congratulates German Hannau Nickau on finishing five in five. His desire to do a sixth swim was in response to a misguided rumour.

HUNGRY HEADS: Doug's culinary talents are keenly studied and commented on by Jarlath.

THE JOY OF SIX: One of my favourite pictures., taken at at the Day Six finish line. Included are co-organisers Steve and Eddie as well as co-crew members Doug (centre) and Jarlath (extreme right).

'ONE MAN'S MEAT IS ANOTHER MAN'S POISON'

TED'S GONE: Big Ted's expression summed up the cloud of sadness that hung around all day.

HAND IT TO THEM: Competitor Mick Barnes knew how cold he was when he woke on Day Seven. Dr Leigh Cowling confirmed it and along with Dan Watford offers assistance.

FOOT LOOSE: Ken gives my feet the once-over while I tuck into my third lunch.

FOOT DOCTOR: Tony Raynor had blisters almost every day.

LATE NIGHT: Dan embraces Monique after she had finished Day Seven at 3.15am.

'THE EIGHTH MARATHON WOULD SOON UNMASK THESE ENEMIES'

FAR FROM TICKER TAPE: Like almost every competitor, I needed Dr Leigh Cowling's medical expertise from Day Eight onwards. Here she applied some kinesiology tape to my foot.

2, 1: Eight down, two to go but by now I was shattered.

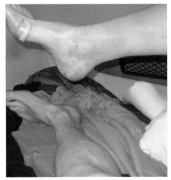

TAKING ITS TOLL: Cellulitis and a stress fracture ensured I would be asked every question.

'BY DAY NINE, I WISHED THE SWIM WOULD HURRY THE F*** UP'

YOU RAISE ME UP: For the last three days I was unable to get out of the lake without assistance. Here the two Dans (Watford and Earthquake) make it easier.

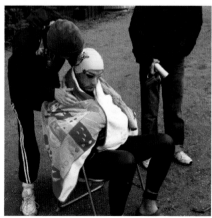

ARE YOU ALRIGHT, SON? Mark's Mum offers encouragement before he gets into the lake.

WHAT A MESS: Not sure who was on cleaning duties on Day Nine...

 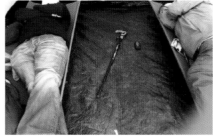

FATHERS AND SONS: Mark Padley's Dad tries to steal some sleep as they climb to transition (above left), while my Dad and my brother Tom (above right) grab 40 winks as I finished the ninth cycle.

A PROTECTED SPECIES: By Day Nine I had to stop repeatedly to apply ice packs and kt tape. Here Jacinta and Enda watch over me while Dorothy and Leigh stand guard.

DIFFERENT DIRECTIONS: On Day Nine Monique would need 12 hours to recover whilst Tony Raynor lived to fight one more day.

'NOTHING WORTHWHILE COMES EASY'

BIG HUG: Dorothy wishes me well on the morning of Day Ten. Mark Padley's Dad John encouraged us in

OH CAPTAIN, MY CAPTAIN: Enda assumed control of my swimwear on the final two days when my immune system was at its weakest.

TWO'S COMPANY: Fello from the lake alongside his

ROUND TEN: I was frozen and headed into the tent to try to warm up. We knew a long day lay ahead so I took a few minutes longer.

is own way.

shman Ian Walsh climbs lfriend Leanne Carberry.

ON YER BIKE: That last cycle needed three clothes changes.

ALMOST THERE: By 6pm I knew I would make it. Despite the pain in my legs, I was as warm as toast in a bin liner for the final run.

DAY
10
12.06.2011

I WAS HORRENDOUSLY SLOW BUT I DIDN'T CARE...'

THE LAST STEP: Jacinta to my left and co-organiser Steve Haywood (centre) are there at the finish. The time was 11:59pm.

FINISHING LINES: Tony Raynor and Mark Padley celebrate success.

FAMILY AFFAIR: With Dad and my brother Tom.

COUNT THEM: Ten fingers, ten days. The shower block was a happy place on Day Ten.

SEALED WITH A LOVING KISS: I wanted to share this moment with Jacinta more than anyone in the world. Inset: Brian O'Connell interviews me at the finish. It made the lunchtime and 6pm television news the following day back home in Ireland.

'THE DISTRACTION OF SUCCESS CAN BE A POWERFUL ANAESTHETIC'

EARLY RISE: The phone was hopping from early morning. On the phone here to Ray D'Arcy.

TRIUMPHANT TRIO: Day Eleven thankfully and in celebratory mode with Mark and Tony,

TEAM EFFORT: We did it. With the people who made it happen. From left to right. Douglas, Brendan, Jacinta, myself, Ken, Enda, Jarlath and Dor.

WELCOME HOME: A huge crowd of well wishers made the trip to Dublin airport.

ON CAMERA: Jacinta and I are spotted sharing a moment.

ON THE AIR: Appearing on The Ray D'Arcy Show two days after finishing.

IF MY STORY PROVES ANYTHING, IT IS THAT YOU TOO CAN ACHIEVE YOUR OWN DREAM OR AMBITION IN LIFE

HOW THE 20 DECA COMPETITORS FARED...

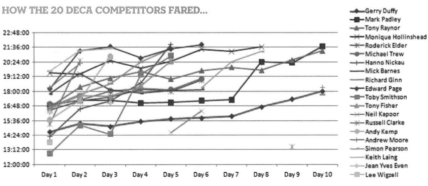

Just like every other day we would continue to pedal another 116 miles (186km). On Thursday, from 8:30am until 1:00pm, I experienced a low mood. The camaraderie with Jarlath and Doug as I returned after each lap was welcome but in between it was a long period of just 'thinking'. Sometimes that could be my friend. Sometimes I was happy to be all alone. Other times it could be my enemy, when no matter how hard I tried, the enormity of it all tried to smother me like a blanket. On Day Three, I had used the time well, coming up with a mental trick to lift my sometimes fragile mood.

'I cannot get to 10 without passing through six. All I'm doing is passing through.'

On Day Seven, I had to fight it as I felt low for much of it. Heavy rain didn't help. I was having to work hard to keep positive thoughts flowing. I felt I was within touching distance of potentially finishing this event but that in itself was starting to make me very nervous. By now I was over 10 hours in front. If I didn't make it through days 7, 8, 9 and 10 though, then all the hours I was in front would count for nothing.

I had heard other competitors periodically talk about wanting to sleep during the day. On Day Seven it arrived at my front wheel. By mid-morning my eyes started to droop. I'd experienced a small amount of this the day before, but now the temptation to stop and climb into a ditch was almost intoxicating. Several times I had to shout aloud just to stay awake.

"4, 3, 2, 1." I whispered, spoke aloud and sometimes screamed repeatedly. A passerby might have thought me delirious.

Other times I would sing at the top of my voice. Katie Perry's 'Firework' was riding high in the charts at the time. The fact that the single was written for a female soprano rather than a male tenor like myself is my defence for scaring much of the local wildlife.

Sometimes to relieve the boredom or to relieve the pain in my glutes (backside) I'd stand up out of the saddle and stretch. Most of the time I didn't need to. In the preceding eight months I had spent more time in the saddle than John Wayne had during his entire film career. It was just something to do.

Anything to stave off the lure of simply closing my eyes. As afternoon approached it got harder. Drinking some Red Bull helped but I had to be careful not to become reliant on such intoxication.

After 70 miles (113 km), one of the event team stopped me at the turnaround. What he said didn't help my fragile and exhausting temperament.

'A chap called Brian O'Connell has contacted us. He wants permission to come down and film you over the weekend. Is that ok?'

I was immediately grateful for the courtesy he had shown to seek my permission but I was also annoyed. Not by what it meant. It was an indicator of potential success.

Brian O'Connell was then the London Editor for Radio Telefís Eireann (RTE) the Irish Radio and Television broadcasting service. Word had spread to the national broadcaster back home that there was an Irishman doing well in a significant sporting event in the UK. O'Connell was a man whose face I regularly saw on my television screen. Usually he was reporting from Downing Street or the Houses of Parliament in London. If there was big news happening in the UK that might interest Irish viewers or listeners, O'Connell was the person who relayed the information.

Earlier that morning at 5am, the crew had taken a call from RTE and I had carried out a pre-recorded radio interview while eating my porridge. This was later broadcast on morning sports bulletins in Ireland.

The 'Morning Ireland' radio programme (between 7am to 9am) is a current affairs show with a listenership hovering around the 440,000 mark. When added to the listeners on the other radio station hosted by Ray D'Arcy, it meant that somewhere close to three quarters of a million people were now aware of the story back home. When you consider that Ireland has a population of just four million you get an idea of how much awareness there was in what I was doing and how I was getting on.

I found out several weeks later that Des Cahill, the RTE radio interviewer who had called at 5am and who is very widely-known and respected in sport's circles in Ireland, had opened the interview by saying: "And now to the man I am suggesting has to be a contender for the title, Ireland's most Remarkable Sportsman".

That comment from him brought great awareness, respect and a huge spotlight to what was going on 600 miles away in another land. That interview, in addition to the updates from the Ray D'Arcy Show, would have a huge domino effect in terms of consciousness that would only become apparent to me in the weeks and months afterwards.

This event was happening on O'Connell's patch and so he had been requested to go down and interview this sole Irish entrant. His enquiry to come down from London didn't annoy me at all. I was annoyed because of a further comment made when I asked the messenger why O'Connell had been in touch. Of course, I should have worked it out for myself but I had long since lost the ability to concentrate to a meaningful degree on anything except triathlon, eating and sleeping.

My annoyance came when the messenger replied that I was a 'shoo in' for victory. He meant well but I took it badly. What's more, I wanted to be annoyed. I needed to be. I kept this annoyance between my ears but if I explain why, you might be able to understand my thinking at the time.

It was out of respect for the event, the enormity of the challenge and the fact that I had still had 35 per cent of it still to complete. Not only was I not a 'shoo in' to win, there was a good chance that none of us would finish. At that time, I still had over seven miles (11km) of swimming to do, over 400 miles (644km) to cycle and four more marathons still to run. I was absolutely exhausted and I was really starting to feel that pressure.

Anything could go wrong. Injury, illness, hypothermia, a mechanical or digestion problem or just complete exhaustion. We were sitting a masters degree in endurance. It was only Thursday. No matter how fast we went, we would still be here until late on Sunday night, if we were lucky.

Today had already taken out Mick Barnes, Edward Page and Mike Trew. A day earlier, Trew had no injuries to concern him and was at that time as strong as anyone in the field.

If I wanted any more evidence to reinforce my argument, Roderick Elder provided it. By early evening he too would withdraw. It happened on mile 10 (16km) of the run. Rod had been dogged by injuries. How he made it as far as he did was exceptional. I needed to be vigilant or otherwise I might be next. On Day Seven alone 20 per cent of the original field of 20 were wiped out. That was why I needed to be annoyed.

Back to Brian O'Connell's request. I nodded my agreement. I would not have said no. One part of me was very happy. It was a sign of potential success and would create awareness and perhaps realise more funds for my chosen charity.

2:10PM

It was something I had never experienced before but now it was happening in broad daylight.

That enquiry about Brian O'Connell had happened at the end of the sixth lap. It was on the eight that some unexpected visitors appeared. Sure, I had read about it happening to other competitors in other extreme events but never to me. An overcast Thursday in early June on a quiet secondary road somewhere in Hampshire in the south of England was not a time or a place that I had expected it. This was early afternoon. That sort of thing happened in the dead of night, if at all, didn't it?

After I left Burley, a spell of heavy rain came down. I am not normally fond of rain when cycling but now it was a crumb of new mental stimulus. At that exact moment it was a sweet and welcome opportunity for my mind to digest something different and a welcome contrast to the hourly and daily routine that had been my life on those first seven days. A chance for the left side of my brain to chat deliriously with my right to kill a few miles of terrain.

It hadn't rained an awful lot up to that day. Everything else had been thrown at us in the first six days but not an awful lot of rain. Sure we had the odd heavy shower on a few occasions but it had been sporadic. This was a downpour.

And then they appeared in broad daylight right in front of my eyes. There were two of them, I think. At first I squeezed my eyes firmly shut but when I re-opened them they were still there. In fact they had increased in number. Now there were three.

They were in a puddle, a roadside bath, all three of them playing happily. I stood up and aside on the bike, angling my torso to 45 degrees so as to get the best view of them as I rode past. Within seconds, this show would be behind me.

Then I noticed they were dancing, yes, dancing merrily. They had also brought umbrellas to shield them from the heavy rain. They looked like they were having fun too. All three had broad smiles across their faces. On recollection I think they were possibly ice-skating but then that wouldn't make any sense, would it?

I was hallucinating.

It was a surreal encounter and a bizarre experience. I was imagining it all but I was also conscious of it, so I laughed. One part of my brain was absolutely convinced at that exact moment that I was looking at three rats underneath three umbrellas dancing in a large puddle at the bottom of a road camber that gathered up the rainfall.

By now they were just ten metres from me. No matter how many times I closed my eyes in that brief 20 second experience, every time I reopened them they were there. I don't have any medical qualifications but I have read about this left brain, right brain thing and here I was living and experiencing it like never before.

The other side of my brain began to laugh in an attempt to jolt the other half out of its insanity. That is what made it so bizarre.

As I passed them, I shouted as a tactic to awaken the part of my brain that thought it was seeing this. It was a surreal moment that I actually derived enjoyment from. It was a welcome sideshow and a brief diversion. At all times I felt conscious of it. That heightened the delirium. Yes, I was delirious, but not mad.

It was only lunchtime on Thursday. Over six days done but still three and a half more to go. As the rats disappeared behind me, I was concerned. I needed to be. I realised that I had to focus. I had to jolt myself back to reality. Being sleepy and tired and dreaming of rats in the middle of the afternoon while on a bike is a strange feeling. My body's energy levels were having a conversation with my sleep cells and they were getting on well. Too well in fact.

Utter fatigue was now becoming a fresh battle. I even picked out possible ditches in which to rest. A few were studied with an engineers eye for comfort as I passed. But I never actually did it. I knew I shouldn't and I knew I wouldn't.

I wasn't alone in my hallucinations either. Sometime close to midnight on Day Five, it had happened to Big Ted.

Big Ted

'I wanted to sleep on my feet. The hallucinations were becoming very vivid now. In the forest every twig was a moving worm . Every pine cone a small frog. As I got more and more tired there were hundreds of frogs on the trail. And every so often I swore one of them was real, so I stopped for a look. After a while, not only did they get more real, I thought they were jumping. In the trail were painted pictures of Cowboys and Indians. Chiefs in full Indian head-dress. And as the night went on, the images become demonic. Devil like. It became a little frightening.'

It happened to Monique as well.

Monique

'I remember two tufts of grass around the back of the lake. I was convinced one night they were hedgehogs and spent each lap avoiding treading on them. The following evening on the run just before it got dark, Steve caught me prodding at them.

"What are you doing Mon?" he enquired

"I'm just making sure there aren't any hedgehogs," I said by way of explanation. You can imagine his thoughts given that all he saw was me trying to stab the grass.'

At least my hallucinations were happening in broad daylight. Small consolation but equally bizarre, particularly when one part of my brain was telling me I was imagining it all.

I tried to stay alert. I tried to stay awake and conscious of what was happening around me. I thought of Big Ted, Mike Trew, Mick Barnes and of Toby Smithson too. All heroes. I am firmly of the opinion that everyone who started this event was one. Even to have considered it possible, let alone to have prepared as best you could to complete it, deserved respect.

Anyone endeavouring to reach a goal can only ask one thing of themselves to find out if they have done themselves justice. That is a commitment to do their best. Not an ounce more, nor less. I thought of each of the 15 who sadly for them were back in modern day luxuries. Reasons for not finishing ranged from pure exhaustion, injury, or as in Ted's case, the opinion of a medical expert that it was unsafe to continue. I was one of the five lucky ones who was still in the event. Rod Elder was still competing at that moment. Only later that evening would he be forced to stop. I would continue out of desire to achieve this incredible goal and would stay strong out of respect to those who weren't as lucky.

This event and its unique tests deserved to have some finishers.

MARATHON

I love to run. I have loved it since I first took it up in 1995. In the deca, I was always determined to run – as opposed to walking – as much of each day's marathon distance as my body would allow. Thankfully that remained consistently above 90 per cent. Others mixed their strategy between running and walking.

It's incredible how slow the body becomes in an event like this. Just like the cycle, my marathon times were now taking longer and longer each day.

The marathon route had several steep climbs all relatively short. Most competitors adopted second placed Mark Padley's strategy of running almost as much as their bodies would allow but with a firm strategy to walk the hills. I could totally understand such a tactic. It would also save the legs from the strain.

Monique was the same. She would walk the hills but in between she looked like she was almost sprinting. The reality though for all of us was far removed. It is astounding how deceiving it was to the eye because we were moving considerably slower than we believed we were. Our finishing times offer concrete evidence of this.

My strategy every evening was different to Mark's and indeed to most of the others. Once I was on the run, I felt somewhat at ease. On Day Seven, I was relieved to have completed another day without any technical problems on my bike. Thus far I had not had a single issue mechanically and had successfully cycled 812 miles (1300km).

With that concern behind me for another day, I was now on my favourite of the three disciplines. I didn't find running up the hills overly hard. In fact after a few days into the deca, I derived a somewhat masochistic pleasure from it. It was the long downhill stretch that I found among the hardest.

As well as the drop in elevation, it was almost as if there were tiny invisible creatures lined up on both sides of that long descent with hammers in their hands, all determined to beat my legs relentlessly until I reached the sanctuary of the bottom.

> **Tony**
>
> 'The worst part for me on the run was coming down the stone track. That just killed me every time. My feet were in bits so every little stone felt like a knife. My quads just didn't like that downhill at all. It was like my legs weren't my own, just giving way every now and again.'

Even Ted's diary after Day One illustrated just how hard he had found it...

> **Big Ted**
>
> 'Before the event started, I hadn't been around the run course at all, so I didn't know what I was in for. Well f*** me. Hills, hills and more hills. And the worst part was the downhill that runs from the highest point to the lowest part of the course. If I tried to run or even jog it, I got pains in my ankles. So I had to walk it. Can you imagine the time I was losing on each lap? Over the days this would become a real psychological problem.'

It's hard to quantify just what our bodies were going through. Maybe when comparing it to a stand-alone marathon time might offer an insight into our exam.

My marathon times over the first six days of this event are listed below. Just before you consider them, let me say this. I do feel I am an experienced marathon runner, having covered the distance close to 50 times before this event. My slowest marathon in a previous one-off event was 3:31:40, my fastest is 2:53:08.

The reality is I could not have run the six marathons listed below any faster. I'm happy to admit that from the outset. I was at the limit of my marathon running ability. At all times my goal was to finish these as fast as I could, albeit with a consistent and controlled pacing strategy of sorts. If I had only to complete a one-off iron distance on Day One, then perhaps I could have shaved 75 minutes off that first days marathon. Every day I felt at all times that I was in a minimum of fourth gear and running fast at every mile. Sometimes I felt I was in fifth gear. That is an absolute fact.

Anyway, here are the times.

Day One 5:21:13
Day Two 5:18:52
Day Three 5:26:43
Day Four 5:34:45
Day Five 5:50:51
Day Six 5:38:17

Each day my strategy was always to finish with the minimum of delay so as to get one stretch of continuous sleep. I did at all times feel my pace was pretty consistent. You will notice there is only a gradual decrease in my times.

I feel this was due simply to my body getting a little more tired every day. At times when I would get a sudden burst of energy perhaps after a meal, I felt like I was sprinting. I believe however, that I never ran any faster than a nine minute mile pace at best. Two experienced triathletes who had marshalled for the opening two days had been allowed to compete beside us on Day Three as a reward for their voluntary work (some reward).They both crossed the finish line together in a time of 13:54 with a marathon run of 5:17:16.

I began the marathon on Day Seven at 4:10pm. Earlier I had taken nine hours for the cycle. That in itself warrants examination. It was just three minutes slower than Day Six. It confirmed my theory that because I had remained injury free, my times were more or less consistent but...

AUDIO DIARY

'...with the same level of effort I am getting a little bit slower every day.'

The first four miles of the marathon were a welcome distraction from the sleepiness I had felt in the saddle. I could hardly fall asleep standing up. The opening 60 minutes went fine. Within an hour though, and from lap five through to eight, it felt like someone had a vacuum fixed to my body and was hoovering out any remaining energy molecules.

On one of the early laps that evening I had descended the long 300 metre track and was about to make a left turn at the bottom. Given that we were in an activity centre that had two small lakes, the forest was full of wildlife. As I navigated along the narrow trail a very angry large duck took grave exception to my approach and thought I was coming to steal her young.

As I arrived the four baby ducks were trailing slowly behind and still emerging from the undergrowth. Just then Hanno Nickau who had stayed on for a few days appeared from nowhere. With that the duck went berserk and ran at us both, wings in full flight and quacking loudly. It was a little scary for a split second (honest!). Hannau tried to scare her off and I tried to quicken my pace but given that my limbs were a tad sore, I had no sprinting ability in me. A stand-off ensued until the kids were all safely across and out of harm and then we all went on our way. It added at least two minutes to my finishing time!

I had planned to eat the first of two dinners on lap 10. Doug was about to go and prepare a chicken pasta stir-fry. Just before he left though, I got very weak. I needed fuel and I needed it fast. Doug ran to the camper and lit the stove in haste.

Among his many talents, Doug is a great cook. A painter-decorator by profession, he had taken part in his first triathlon as recently as 2007 signing up for a local cancer charity event in my hometown (Fighting Cancer Tri).

His motivation then was in giving something back after the death of his dad William five years earlier from the disease. Doug's Mum had passed away when he was only eight years old.

Doug

'Coming from a family of 10 children, my Dad felt it a good idea to teach us how to cook and to cook well.'

Before the next lap was finished, I was walking and benefitting from that home nurtured skill, consuming a much needed plateful of energy in the form of garlic chicken with mushrooms combined with a large portion of wheat free pasta. It took it some time to travel into my muscles.

My crew were playing a key role. Much of their time was spent over the gas stove preparing food. On days five through to seven, Doug certainly paid his passage in spades. In addition, along with Ken and Jarlath, they had constant hydration to prepare and had to organise the clothes changes. As if that wasn't enough, on hundreds of occasions each day, they had to administer a blast of positive psychology every time they saw me.

Jarlath

'Thirteen miles in, our man had gone silent. He was suffering badly and looked to be ageing a year on every lap. I believe we could say one sentence to him in this state. He would either mull it over for a mile or two and take encouragement from it or it would take him another five miles to come around by himself. To me the wall we experience in a marathon seems to have no gate.

'I remember Gerry saying that the pain is all relative, that it will end and that these experiences will mean he has really lived his life and experienced all the mind and the body has to offer in terms of a voluntary challenge.'

I was well aware that at times I could submerge into a mood and go very quiet. Sometimes it was due to hitting a low moment in my head, other times it was just to conserve every ounce of energy.

Because of the configuration of the course I was in regular contact with Doug and Jarlath and they kept raising my spirits with words of encouragement. The crew met me at two different points marked x and y on the run map. On virtually every lap each evening, I was handed something there whether an energy drink or rehydration, a sandwich, a dinner, a Mars bar or a can of Coke. Most days I felt I was in consistently good mood but I had peaks and troughs as well. That Thursday night, for a short time, was one of the lowest.

It would be another five miles before I felt any energy return but Doug had saved the day with his cookery skills. By mile 15 (24 km) I felt strong again and was a little over an hour from eating my second meal.

Each night the last 10 miles seemed to take an age. As the course was quiet compared to regular events, we only saw someone every few minutes or so. For long periods during each lap, we were on our own and lost in our thoughts.

Six days into the event I had yet to need a head torch. It was close to the height of an English summer so the evening light only began to fade from about 9:30pm. By 10pm it would be pitch dark. By now I was cutting it fine every night. Usually by the time I was on my last few laps, many had already donned head torches in advance of nightfall. I derived some positive mental energy in the knowledge that I had yet to need one. Some nights it was with minutes to spare, but these tiny empowering thoughts all sent positive signals to my brain.

Before I would finish that nights marathon at 9:43pm and in a time that was just five minutes slower than the day before (5:43:43), I had consumed a plateful of mince with potatoes and tofu, red peppers, two Mars bars, washed down with continued salt replacement in a water solution.

Early in the marathon the right shin pain that had first surfaced a day earlier came back for a second visit. At first it was barely noticeable. In my audio after Day Six, I had mentioned it, but it was only slowly emerging as an adversary. The left leg also began to experience a similar discomfort but nothing compared to what I was starting to feel in my right.

From here on, tiredness would no longer be my biggest concern. As long as I could stay awake, I would cope with that. Over the course of the final 30 per cent of the event, three fresh obstacles would be thrown in my path all of which would test me to my absolute limit.

The double iron distance triathlon in '09 brought me mentally to an edge. I survived that. The 32 marathons in 2010 was a very long month where thankfully I had no major physical tests thrown at me. I did have some hard mental miles back then but that box had also been ticked.

In the deca my mental toughness had been tested as early as lap six of the cycle on Day Three. Fortunately, I had passed that early exam.

What I didn't realise was that with three days to go the event for me was only beginning. Metaphorically I knew I was only at mile 20 or thereabouts of a one-off marathon. So much more of the road was still to be covered. I was about to have some major physical obstacles thrown at me, the like of which I'd never experienced before. This event was about to get a whole lot tougher.

The first of these obstacles emerged as soon as I woke on Friday morning.

"3, 2, 1."

STANDINGS AFTER DAY SEVEN

Competitor	Cumulative Race Position	Day One	Day Two	Day Three	Day Four	Day Five
Gerry Duffy	1	14:41:07	15:22:12	15:06:49	15:31:04	15:42:57
Mark Padley	2	16:51:49	17:16:45	17:13:52	17:02:06	17:04:42
Tony Raynor	3	16:41:06	18:19:58	19:03:47	19:37:47	18:58:44
Monique Hollinshead	4	19:28:49	19:23:00	20:29:56	19:51:12	20:28:52

Competitor	Day Six	Day Seven	Cumulative Total
Gerry Duffy	15:48:16	15:56:08	108:09:03
Mark Padley	17:12:41	17:18:16	120:00:11
Tony Raynor	19:40:43	19:56:46	132:18:51
Monique Hollinshead	21:26:13	21:15:51	142:23:53

DAY EIGHT

CHAPTER TWENTY-FIVE

'The things that go wrong, often make the best memories.'
Gretchen Rubin, Author of 'The Happiness Project'

FRIDAY 10TH JUNE, 2011

AUDIO DIARY, 5:02AM

'Woke up a few minutes ago. Soles of my feet very sore.
Right shin is very sore.'

AUDIO DIARY (20 HOURS LATER)

'The days are so long and getting longer and longer and
longer every day. When I woke up this morning my shin
was very very sore' (voice is raised almost in annoyance
here).
On the swim: 'I didn't enjoy the swim at all. Found it
unbelievably hard. Got very cold at half way. The goggles
played up as well. Getting out of the lake the lads really had
to work to warm me up. I was freezing. Two sets of gloves
and a woolly hat needed on the bike . I never took them off."
On leading: 'I'm finding it very hard to deal with the
pressure of leading and knowing everybody knows so much
about it back home. That's massive pressure but I'm trying
to block it out.'

Even my voice was slurred. The entire transcript is three
minutes in duration and in the final few seconds, my voice has
become garbled with overtiredness.

Every other day the swim had been a tasty starter before having
to consume a mammoth main course. On Day Eight that swim
starter tasted awful. I really struggled to consume it. There was
no gradual decrease in my enjoyment. If Thursday's swim was a
'dream', Friday's was a 'bad dream'.

After about 30 minutes and a little short of halfway through the 13 laps, I experienced a drop in body temperature where I started to get really cold really quickly. For the first time in the event I eagerly started counting down the remaining laps. They couldn't come quick enough. 'Four' and then what seemed like a half an hour later, 'three', then the remainder. On the final 600 metres, I was very anxious just to finish. I had to be helped out, my body stiff and my blood cold.

> **Mark Padley**
> 'The water took its toll from Day Five and six onwards. By then it was a case of who could survive it. My body was cold from an insufficiently short night's sleep. Generally morale was pretty low as well.'

My right leg was very sore as I put pressure on it climbing out of the lake. I needed help just to ascend the two foot exit point and it took two marshalls to assist me. I would have struggled without them. The early shin pain of the previous two days had now spread up and down my leg. Beneath my skin, there were two enemies plotting a revolt. My eight marathon would soon unmask these enemies.

'Be careful, please,' I requested firmly and loudly as they hoisted me out of the water.

I exited in 1 hour, 14 minutes and 16 seconds.

Perhaps I should have known it was going to be a rougher day. Earlier, a mini-wave of panic had set in just after 5:50am at the lakeshore when Doug and Jarlath realised we had left the wetsuit back in the accommodation 700 metres away. Before we had time to diagnose who was responsible, a useless assignment regardless, Jarlath went sprinting up the hill.

Doug cleverly jogged up after him. He knew Jarlath would at

some time run out of steam, so he would meet him somewhere en route to maintain the pace. At 5:57am Doug returned, with an exhausted Jarlath tumbling down the hill in his wake.

It took less than two minutes to insert my frame into the neoprene wetsuit. With 60 seconds to spare, I spat into my goggles having wet my eyes to water temperature and my goggles too. It was a task carried out every morning to avoid the glasses fogging in the water. They would later start to leak for the first time though, so perhaps it was just going to be one of those more demanding days regardless.

> **Jarlath**
> 'With a minute to spare our man was in his wetsuit. Panic over. With that, the race began after which Doug and I laughed long and loud out of pure relief.'

Ken later joked that they had fallen apart once he left.

By mid-morning Doug also had to say farewell. He shared with me afterwards that before coming over to England, he wanted to offer more than he felt he had done two years earlier in the double iron distance event. Back in 2009 he had arrived to crew, transported on a pair of crutches courtesy of a hospital visit earlier in the week. On this occasion, he had one goal coming over.

> **Doug**
> 'At the double iron event in '09, given the fact that I was on crutches, I felt I had little to offer. This time I wanted to make a difference.'

He certainly had done that and much more, even agreeing to stay an extra day when I asked him to do so.

He later confessed to two things.

The first was to shedding a tear in the taxi as he headed back to Southampton. He didn't want to leave. The second was to spending all of the following day on the internet trying to get a flight back to England on Sunday morning so as not to miss the final day. The airfare though was prohibitively expensive.

On Day Eight, the cycle was uneventful, the only highlight was having to consume unhealthy amounts of Red Bull to keep my eyes open. I was exceptionally tired and at a point of sleep deprivation that I had only read about. The non weight bearing effects on the bike meant my body was not impacted with a physical force that I got on the run. As a result, I was really struggling to stay awake.

> **Mark Padley**
> 'Sleep deprivation was noticeable on days seven to nine for me. I had to physically concentrate just to keep my eyes open.'

> **Tony Raynor**
> 'I have never been so tired as I was on the bike, some days to the point of falling off. In fact I fell off twice, the second time was going uphill.

I was also now close to a tipping point. Luckily the rats had disappeared only to be replaced by an image where I imagined that both Steve and Eddie, the event organisers, had turned into two massive trees and were staring at me from a clump of forest. They were easy to spot though as both had orange fluorescent jackets around their trunks.

By now, I was slowing at every revolution of the pedals. We had cycled that loop 70 times, made over 140 cattle grid crossings and had seen more ice-cream consumed in Burley than in the tasting room of a 'Ben and Jerry's' ice-cream factory. We were so near, yet we still had over 50 hours of effort to endure.

> **Monique**
> 'I never thought I'd get this far, people were talking about how near we were to the end but it was still a million miles away.

On the eighth day, I averaged 54:40 for each of the 10 laps of the cycle. On Day One it had been 48:24. Not an alarming drop but it certainly was headed only one way. On our second Friday, of the four remaining competitors, my cycle time of 9:16:18 was the quickest. Because of sleep deprivation and exhaustion, we were all slowing like a piston running out of oil. Mark took 9:44:36 to cover the distance and Tony took 9:48:48. If an elderly grandmother had been spotted passing us out on a skateboard, it might not have been a hallucination.

Earlier Monique had retired to the tent after completing the swim, to sleep for an hour. As a result she lost even more time and only began the second lap at 10:45am. By then the rest of us were already about 25 to 30 miles ahead of her.

> **Monique**
> 'I was getting little sleep at night and consequently playing catch up with power naps during the day. It was an ever decreasing circle."

In the first seven days, Monique's earliest finish had been 1:23am. Who could blame her for stopping and getting some sleep during the day. That was her catching up a little. After all the most she could possibly have slept after completing Day Seven, was a little over two hours. She hadn't finished until 3:15am.

You may recall that the very first day had taken Monique

three hours longer than planned. As a consequence she was always playing catch up. That is why she had to adopt the strategy of grabbing 20 minutes sleep here and there. It was resulting in late night finishes, the very thing she wished to avoid.

On the fourth bike lap, Monique took a 90 minute break for a power nap. It must have worked because by the time she completed her 10th lap, she had reduced the lap time down to 53:09. Her cumulative time in the saddle that day however was over 13 hours.

We were joined on Day Eight by more competitors who were beginning a triple iron distance triathlon where they would complete each of the three disciplines in full, before progressing. By mid-morning we began to see them appear on the cycle loop, a tasty and continuous 348 mile (560km) cycle ahead of them having already swum 7.2 miles (11.6km). The new faces offered us fresh curiosity but very soon the intrigue and the novelty faded.

On one lap I bumped into Anthony Gerundi, the leader of the 'quin' event. On Day One he had finished in 14:11:50. This gave him a 90 minute advantage, a lead he would never relinquish.

'Heard about Sunday?' he questioned.

'No,' I replied.

'Storm,' he added.

'Uh, really?' I replied.

'Yeah, gonna be s***.'

If he was trying to improve my fragile temperament it was a strange tactic. If he was providing me with this news as a result of powers of prediction that he possessed, then he should have pursued it as a career. A storm of almost Biblical proportions was just days away.

RUN

In the swim 10 hours earlier, the shin had made its presence felt a few times, but on the bike the pain subsided. For over nine hours, I only felt the odd twinge.

Once I was on the hard terrain of the run course and with 168 lbs of weight pushing into every metre, it had no hiding place. As soon as I began the run, I was consciously monitoring my legs for warning signs. Well, that and a preoccupation with devouring a mouth-watering sausage and egg sandwich that Jarlath had handed to me moments before. My body craved savoury food and on the run most nights I craved Coke in bucket-loads as well.

Jarlath was now on his own, the one and only day a crew member had to work solo. Doug had already stayed beyond his intended duration. He was already back in Ireland with Sharon and the kids. Jarlath wouldn't have a spare second as I kept demanding so many things, the most important of which was food.

Poor fella, he later confessed to being terrified to being left in charge.

Ken had been so right about not eating enough. By now I was consuming perhaps 25 per cent more every day than in the first few days, but I was still constantly hungry. At one stage on Day Seven I'd eaten six sausage and egg sandwiches in a six-hour window.

At first on the run, my leg seemed ok. The opening five laps of the run were consistent and were completed in 15 minutes and 31 seconds, 11:31, 11:55, 11:47 and 11:43 respectively. The first of these was the one short lap where we arrived in from the bike course and included transition for changing into running gear. By the time I reached the sixth, my right leg was getting very sore. As I hit the long descent it was especially angry. That lap was 30 seconds slower than the previous one and the next was almost identical.

Soon every lap took 14 minutes or more for a distance something close to 1.1 miles (1.77km). I knew then it was going to be a long night. A slightly milder infection had flared up in the left leg too. This played up periodically, but the right leg was much worse. It's normal white complexion having taken on a very strong shade of high blood pressure red.

AUDIO DIARY

'I crawled down the hill on many laps. Leg screamed. It became unbelievably painful.'

After eleven miles (17.7km) I stopped. It was for a pre-arranged meeting with Leigh Cowling, the event doctor. I had requested the appointment when I had dismounted the bike earlier.

Leigh must have had a twin as she seemed to be everywhere. With three different events taking place, her time, her knowledge and the expertise she administered was much in demand.

Mark Padley

'Leigh was the first medical professional I've come across whose main role was to assist athletes to complete their event rather than end it.'

Leigh was a marvel. Our days were long but hers were even longer. Just like all of the athletes, she was surviving on fistfuls of sleep. We met at the finish line area.

This was an area where many chose to stop for a break. Here, there was energising music, the timekeeper's tent, the food marquee and a spectator stand. There was a table too where we could leave energy drinks, food, water, extra clothing etc.

I wanted to stop for the minimum time but Leigh insisted on patience as she was keen on giving my concerns a thorough examination. During that 10 minute stop, I was still conscious of staying focussed on what I had to do, so while Leigh examined my legs, I ate and drank.

The right shin issue was a combination of two things. The first was a cellulitis infection that had crept beneath my skin a few days earlier. Cellulitis is a bacterial infection of the skin tissue just below the surface. I wasn't entirely sure what it was at the time. Only when I returned to Ireland would I get a full diagnosis.

I was fast developing a second difficulty which was equally

painful. It came in the form of a stress fracture in the same leg. A stress fracture is caused by unusual or repeated stress on the bone. Now where might that have happened?

I had cellulitis in both legs but the right leg was more advanced and highly tender even to the faintest contact. The stress fracture was on the fibula on the right half of the lower leg, just below the knee. It was no coincidence that virtually every single turn on the run route was a right hand turn. By now we had run it nearly 200 times, more than enough to give birth to such an injury. Given the fact that the only cure ultimately was rest, there was very little Leigh could do for me. An eight week break was recommended by my own doctor less than a week later.

Leigh suggested some kinesiology tape which is a cotton strip with an acrylic adhesive, that is used for treating athletic injuries (*see picture section*). First used over 30 years ago, this product and its popularity had exploded since it was highlighted in the 2008 Beijing Olympics. Day Eight was the first time I had ever used it in my life. We had no idea if it was going to help or not. In an ideal scenario I would take the weight off it and not exercise until it had recovered completely.

In the research for this book, I spoke at length with Leigh and got her recollection on that night-time meeting.

Leigh Cowling

'Your issues were from the strain you were inflicting on your body on a daily basis. The superficial infection could have been from any number of minor injuries, then exacerbated by the less than hygienic conditions during the race (and in some respects from the sleeping environment) and perpetuated by a lessened immune response secondary to physiological stressors and the hormonal effects from this.'

The stress fracture speaks for itself. In my normal working life the treatment for this would've been rest, ice, compression, elevation and analgesia. However the deca was less than normal conditions and I understood the drive and the need to continue, so my option was to relieve your pain and to strap is up as best as possible; the tape being a poor substitute for the role your body normally plays.

The idea was to protect the stress fracture and give the leg some support with which to carry the shin. Leigh applied it tightly. When I stood up, the tape felt very firm, bordering on painful. Leigh insisted that it needed to be firm for the support. By being rigid, it was taking the strain, weight and slack from the shin. It acted like a crutch in carrying my leg.

By the time Leigh was finished, the tape was mostly hidden from view by the first of many ice-packs that she had taped to my right leg. Soon after, she applied an ice-pack to the left leg as well. This was positioned with care to ease the swelling. The red complexion in the skin was getting stronger by the hour. At first the tape felt very uncomfortable to run on but after about three miles (4.8km) I just tried to put it out of my mind. The pain was not going away so I knew I had to embrace it.

AUDIO DIARY

'Found last seven or eight miles unbelievably hard. Mind was fine. Body was in pieces.'

Most nights the final eight or 10 miles felt like they were taking days to complete. On one lap, Graham Marcussen, the partner of Sally Robinson – who had offered such timely wisdom back in my 2009 double iron event attempt – said just the right thing at just the right time. They make an interesting double act for nuggets of mindset motivation.

Graham
'Good man Gerry, chipping away my son, chipping away.'

It is incredible how I became attached to such words. When the body is at the edge, anything the mind takes on board can be magnified a thousand fold. This might be a thought I captured and where I tried to wring out every drop of its positivity and send it to my brain. Those words from Graham became ingrained into my subconscious and popped into my head at just the right time and on some of the more difficult miles.

> **Jarlath**
> 'With three laps to go it was time for another sprint to the camper to prepare the smoothie. Sprint up, blend all the ingredients, and run down to give him hydration before the second last lap. Back up the hill and finish the smoothie and pour. While there, pick up the kit bag with the towel, shower gel, sandals, etc.

Every night was a long one. Day Eight was also the first night I had to wear a head torch for a prolonged period. I crossed the line in darkness at 10:42pm with the marathon taking 6:12:03. All of this added up to 16 hours and 42 minutes of effort.

That eighth day was 46 minutes slower than the previous day due to a combination of factors. An extra day, a tiring body, two long medical stops and two sore legs (one angry duck couldn't be blamed on this occasion).

A few minutes after finishing as I stood in the lake offering cold water comfort to my leg muscles, I reminded myself that I was one of the lucky ones. Unless I slept through the two alarm clocks, I would shortly be back at this exact spot in a few hours for the ninth roll call. Sleeping it out actually became quite a cause for concern in those final days. Imagine the embarrassment.

'So why didn't you finish, Gerry?'

'Eh, I slept it out.'

'You what?'

Thankfully it never happened.

It took all of Jarlath's strength to lift me from the lake after my cool-down. I was unable to offer much assistance. We headed back up the hill, passing the finish line area as we did so. As I walked in the direction of the shower block I was tired, in pain and feeling really sorry for myself.

Crossing over the run course on our way, we had to give way to an oncoming runner. I couldn't make out who it was. It might have been Monique as she was out there for sure. Tony Raynor also had quite a few miles left to run and he would later finish at 1:42am. For Mark Padley, it was the longest day of the eight, and resulted in a 2:23am finishing time.

We were all feeling it. Already the 'quin' event had lost two of the original field of five. Out of the three remaining in that event, one had finished 13 minutes before me. The other two, David Miles and Ian Walsh from Ireland, had two laps left to complete. It was pitch dark now. Our only warning of oncoming traffic was the beaming headlights from the runners forehead and the noise of runners' feet trampling the forest debris. As I headed to the camper, Monique passed and said 'hi'.

I felt guilty. I was finished, my eighth day done. Yes, I was in pain and filthy from the demands of the course but in less than 45 minutes, I would probably be fast asleep. Monique still had 22 miles (35km) to run. The clock was against her and she knew it.

> **Monique**
> 'On that eighth run I had to disassociate myself to get around, eating regularly, usually rice puddings. My trick on this occasion was to pretend I wasn't human, just mechanical. When any doubts crept in or I started seeing strange things, I could tell myself they were imaginary and machines didn't have an imagination, so therefore they didn't exist. A bit bizarre but it worked.'

It was another horrendously late finish for her, so late in fact she devised a strategy to steal an extra few minutes in her sleeping bag before the Saturday swim. Despite her obvious exhaustion, the following demonstrates just how strong her mind still was.

> **Monique**
> 'Later that night, I lay in the tent shivering with 'flu-like symptoms, freezing cold under two duvets, but pouring with sweat. The last thing I did was put on my wetsuit so I was already prepared for the morning having brushed my teeth whilst on the last lap of the run.'

Jarlath and I had made our way towards the shower block. A hot shower was something I thought a lot about every day. Each day I would remind myself that no matter how tired I was feeling or how low my mood, I would at some point later that night be enjoying the simple but utterly pleasurable sensation of a hot shower pouring over my body. No matter what I went through, as long as I kept moving, that wish would be granted.

As I showered, I shouted to Jarlath to throw my sandals under the door.

There was a delay. 'Eh, they're here somewhere,' he tried to assure me but with a hint of unease in his voice.

I sensed something was up. Under normal conditions it wouldn't warrant a mention. But this was not a normal situation. The distance from the shower block to the camper was 150 metres. That area was littered with forest debris of sharp cones and pine needles. Putting back on my tight fitting running shoes held no appeal. It was hard enough getting them off without having to put them back on. They were tight (lock laces), filthy, smelly, very wet and very unappealing. Coupled with that, 209 miles (336km) of running meant the soles of my feet were in ribbons and littered with cuts and abrasions. The hardened skin at the soles was scorched from battle and as sore as if they had been whipped by a cane.

Jarlath
'His feet looked like something from a horror movie.'

I had no clean socks to put on and so the friction would have meant huge discomfort. I needed those sandals.

"Gerry, I'm sorry. I don't know where they are. I had them but..." Jarlath continued.

I was beyond tired. All I wanted to do was get dressed and go to bed.

'Don't worry, I'll manage', I said calmly. We were in this together. It was nobody's fault.

"You keep showering and I'll retrace our route. Back in two minutes," Jarlath shouted into me, his voice fading as he disappeared from the wash house.

After five minutes and dressing as quickly as my aching frame would allow, I had successfully covered myself in a pair of compression shorts and a hoodie top to keep warm. Once I was ready I had no real option but to stand and wait so I stood there motionless. I expected him back at any moment.

After a while my patience ran out. All I wanted to do was go to bed so I opened the door and began a slow procession. After just 10 metres, the soles of my feet screamed so I returned to the wash house to wait.

Five or six minutes later there was no sign of him. By now I was miserable and totally preoccupied. I had no care for the fact that this close friend had given up three days of his life to help me achieve my goal. It was now after midnight. He had been on the go that day for 20 hours, most of which was spent doing the work of two or three crew. I only wanted him to return so that I could go to sleep.

After 10 minutes I began to shiver. That's when I lost patience. I'm ashamed to admit the following, but it did happen. I screamed aloud my inner frustration.

'Ah come on Jarlath, for f*** sake.'

Immediately the door opened. It was Jarlath. I have never felt so remorseful in my entire life and a bout of guilt for my outburst came over me right away. I was furious with myself. Not because he must have heard me but that I could be that selfish as to be only thinking about myself. I was instantly full of regret. The only person more upset than me at that moment though was Jarlath. He was shoeless.

Wearing my running shoes was out of the question. Now we had no choice but to tread barefoot. I would lean heavily on his shoulder to get there.

Jarlath

'As Gerry was dressing, I sprinted the course with a torch in the hope I would find them. I didn't and so went back to deliver the bad news. Every step he made back to the camper hit me like a slap in the face.

Once back at base, he sat for a while eating a large bowl of cereal and then hit the bed at 1am.'

STANDINGS AFTER DAY EIGHT

Competitor	Cumulative Race Position	Day One	Day Two	Day Three	Day Four	Day Five
Gerry Duffy	1	14:41:07	15:22:12	15:06:49	15:31:04	15:42:57
Mark Padley	2	16:51:49	17:16:45	17:13:52	17:02:06	17:04:42
Tony Raynor	3	16:41:06	18:19:58	19:03:47	19:37:47	18:58:44
Monique Hollinshead	4	19:28:49	19:23:00	20:29:56	19:51:12	20:28:52

Competitor	Day Six	Day Seven	Day Eight	Cumulative Total
Gerry Duffy	15:48:16	15:56:08	16:42:38	124:51:41
Mark Padley	17:12:41	17:18:16	20:23:46	140:23:57
Tony Raynor	19:40:43	19:56:46	19:42:09	152:01:00
Monique Hollinshead	21:26:13	21:15:51	21:38:45	164:02:38-

CHAPTER TWENTY-SIX

Eat And Pace
To End Of Race

With one exception I never had trouble sleeping. That would be the night of Day Eight. Up to this, once I climbed the steps into the top bunk, I closed my eyes almost immediately. Every minute of sleep secured and inserted into my brain cells was a priceless recharge.

That night when I reached the top, I saw a note. It was from Doug. He had left it there many hours before.

Doug's letter

'Well Gerry, another box ticked. I'm sure it wasn't easy (not that any of them are) but you got through it anyway.

I bet when you started you didn't think people would be saying; "well done Gerry, only two to go". I have no doubt you will get there. If you're mind goes to a dark place, think of Rick and Dick Hoyt (more later) and how Rick's Dad felt when he was pushing hard. Hold your head up high and push on through.

Thank you from the bottom of my heart for letting me be a part of it.

Doug.

PS – Eat and pace, eat and pace, eat and pace.

PPS – And drink...'

By now Doug was back home, his sacrifice of time and effort had got me through four more days. He could have done no more for the cause. Jacinta, Dorothy and Enda were due in around midnight to cover the final two days but their flight had been delayed. The shortest day for any crew member had been 19 hours. Jarlath still had another few hours to do before he would sign off. There was much to share and to bring the next rota of crew up to date on.

Over cereal and tea, Jarlath and I had gone through a briefing that he would pass on to Jacinta, Dorothy and Enda who were somewhere on the A35 from Southampton airport to Avon Tyrell.

One request that I passed to him was to get him to ask Jacinta to massage my legs whilst I was asleep. Several times over the next few hours, I would wake up moaning uncontrollably with the pain. My shins were now highly sensitive to the faintest of contact. Even the weight of the material in the sleeping bag was too much so I slept with no cover. The marathon earlier had wreaked havoc. By now my right leg was a sorry mess of pain. If anything touched against it, the pain was horrendous.

Jarlath

'Dorothy, Enda and Jacinta were due to arrive as the fresh crew for the remaining two days. Their flight had been delayed so I decided to clean up. The camper van was a filthy mess. I was shattered, smelly, unshaven and on my last legs by the time they arrived at 2am. I knew Gerry would need the sandals in a few hours time so Enda and I went out to look for them in the darkness. They must have fallen out of the kit bag as I ran down earlier to meet Gerry at the finish line. It was Enda who spotted them in separate parts of the run course. That was a relief.

I showed Enda and Dor the key locations and went through the step by step requirements ahead of the next day. At 3am we all got some rest, but my alarm went off 90 minutes later. On my way to the airport, I was still wound up. I sent Enda a last minute reminder of something a little after 5am.

Enda replied: "Thanks Ja. Get some rest. You need it.

Just look at the text you sent me."

I looked over what I had sent. Not a single word was spelt correctly.

This event not only provided me with a front row seat as to what humans can achieve if they believe in themselves, it also gave me a reminder that even in a solo event you need a team around you.

I got so much out of it. I went back to work and indeed life more confident and more appreciative of what I have, what I can do and what we can all do if we put our minds to it.

As I write this, I can see that this applies to everyday life. Confidence, appreciation, self-belief, positivity, and the value of teamwork.'

At 3am I was half awake, feeling Jacinta's presence near me. I had asked Jarlath to ensure she avoided contact at all costs with the shins of both limbs.

Even while I was sleeping my team were helping me to give my body the best chance to continue. As Jarlath said: 'It is all the little things that make a big difference'.

"2, 1."

DAY NINE

CHAPTER TWENTY-SEVEN

Tony Raynor

'The more the race went on, the more I dreaded getting into that lake every day. It was just getting colder. Towards the end, I was almost frozen getting out.

The crew wrapped me in a sleeping bag as I emerged from the water, put a warm hat on my head and walked me back to my camper which had the heating on for at least 45 minutes.

There, I would sit in a chair and get my wetsuit taken off me.

Until I got in the camper, my whole body shook uncontrollably. Even then it still took a further 10 minutes until it stopped. I was that cold. I have a video which shows me sitting in the chair just shaking.

SATURDAY 11TH JUNE, 2011

If I was hoping for an easier day with my shins, it wouldn't happen. On Day Nine the acute pain in my legs unmasked itself in all its fury. That would be later though.

Climbing out of the swim, I had something else to distract me. Like Tony I was now shivering almost uncontrollably. The cold had entered my veins and was intent on making the start of Day Nine a troubling affair.

Earlier at 5:58am and just as I was about to get into the lake, Enda had placed two extra swim hats into my hand.

'Put these on,' he had said in an authoritative voice.

I had long since stopped making decisions on my own.

'Ok', I replied.

This was two more hats than I had worn any other day but the number I would wear every day were I to do this event again. It is because of moments like these that I had surrounded myself with great people. Enda and I had chatted as we made our way down to the water. I told him about how cold I was getting each morning. He was an international swimmer, having represented Ireland in a master's swimming gala in Italy just three years before. Open water swimming was his speciality. Wetsuits he thought were for softies. I didn't care. I wouldn't have sold mine for all the ice cream in Burley. Every millimetre of lining would be called upon to shield me from the cold I encountered over those final two days.

Later during the swim, I stopped as I passed the lap counters to ask how many of the 13 I had left to do. I was unsure if I had completed 11 or 12.

'That's eight done,' came the reply.

I thought I had misheard.

'Sorry?' I said seeking clarification.

'That's eight done', they repeated.

I stood up momentarily in utter shock. 'EIGHT?' I thought to myself. 'EIGHT?' That meant I had still five left.

I was only unsure of whether I had completed eleven or twelve. They said I had swum eight laps. I wasn't expecting that. Yes, mathematics had been a struggle all through my secondary school years but to be that far wrong?

'Eight?' I questioned again as I lowered my body back down beneath the water.

'Eight,' they replied with a combined air of authority, non-negotiation but also empathy that they were so obviously giving me news that I wasn't expecting.

"F***!" I thought to myself as I continued.

I did think for a split second about questioning it but it would have been pointless. Apart from the fact that they were in charge, they were also in complete control of their faculties. I knew I was tired beyond what was normal and so I reluctantly accepted it and moved on.

By the time nine laps were completed, my fingers were numb. As they entered and exited on every stroke, I felt a chill through each of them. My face was getting colder too. I comforted myself in the knowledge that no matter what, I would be out of the water in less than 20 minutes. Sooner or later, it would arrive. Still though, I wished it would hurry the f*** up.

'Stay focussed,' I whispered to myself. I knew I had to. One arm in. Pull. One arm out. Other arm in. Pull. Other arm out.

Kenny Egan an Irish Olympic Boxing Silver medallist had once given good advice for such a scenario.

'Control the controllables,' he suggested. How appropriate. I had no option but to accept it. I could also choose to embrace it. So I tried.

Every time I passed the gathering of marshals and spectators I turned my face away from them for fear that someone might see me shivering and insist on taking me out to check my temperature.

'Control the controllables.'

For the final 15 minutes my teeth chattered and I groaned continuously like a beached whale. The groan was almost pleasurable and perhaps a sub-conscious diversionary tactic to deflect my brain. I don't know why I did it or to what purpose it served. Ironically it was uncontrollable. It just came out.

I was first out of the water in 1:15:53. Monique was fourth. She had finished the previous day at 3:48am. A little over two hours later she had climbed back into the lake, determined to do another day.

Halfway through the swim she had stood up and announced to those within earshot that she was falling asleep in the lake. Her spirit was willing but her body was not. In the middle of the swim she had had enough and retired to the warmth of her tent, her mind made up that she was finished.

Thirty minutes later after some cajoling from her husband Dave, incredibly she put back on a wetsuit and returned to finish. This lady had more courage than all the lions in the jungle put together.

Monique
'I had been feeling very cold in the swim and was convinced

that I was hypothermic so I got out with about seven laps left. Dave spent half an hour trying to talk me back in. I just wanted to be warm. Eventually I got a dry wetsuit on and swam the remainder.'

Mark Padley was out just behind me in 1:16:48 and Tony Raynor the only other remaining competitor in the deca was out in a consistent 1:31:55. Previous to this, Tony's fastest swim had been 1:23:46. Every other day he was between that and 1:34:10. After the event he confessed that he had actually done very little swimming in preparation, preferring to focus mostly on cycling and running.

Tony
'My swim during the event was consistent every day. Not fast, but I think all the years of doing Ironman events had given me a good swimming base anyway. I remember being really worried about getting pulled out of the swim in the last few days due to hypothermia.'

Tony was experiencing the same hypothermic symptoms that we all were. I thought it was just me. All of us were anxious to get it over with as quickly as possible.

As I walked towards the changing tent and before my second breakfast, Dorothy and Jacinta threw a sleeping bag around me. It was warm and very tempting. To cycle with it around me would have been tricky though so I tossed it aside and with the help of my crew put on my bike gear. It was 7:25am.

For the ninth day in a row, Eddie Ette was there to cheer me on my way. He mightn't have recognised me. By now I had a different appearance to the early days and wore several layers because of the cold I was feeling.

Now I was wrapped up like an Arctic hunter and carried leggings, two pairs of gloves, a hat, a long sleeve top and a jacket.

As I began, I was still exceptionally cold. In fact on the bike that day, I never warmed up and kept those extra layers on for the full duration of 9 hours and 10 minutes of the cycle.

By 9:10am I had stopped for cereal on the first lap and some chicken pasta on the second. An unusual combination I know, but then unusual was imprinted all over this event.

The first three miles (5km) of lap three were negotiated without incident or highlight, but soon I stumbled upon a tale. About a half a mile from Burley and from a distance of about 200 metres, I noticed a fellow cyclist in the distance. It could have been one of a number of people. By now we had the deca, quins and more than a dozen 'triple iron' competitors on the course, so it was even busier than it had been back on the very first day. All I could make out was a yellow jacket and a bike beneath. As I travelled forward, the figure got closer. Whoever the competitor was, was not moving.

I pulled up alongside conscious of the fact that I was on a busy main road with cars whizzing past. My time away from the edge would have to be brief. I strained my neck sideways and as I did, I realised who it was. It was Monique Hollingshead. Having climbed back into the lake earlier, she had by now heroically finished the swim and was on her first bike lap.

When I pulled up alongside, her eyes were closed.

She was fast asleep.

Monique
'My time out of the lake had left me without my sleep-time so once I finished, I had to get straight out onto the bike.'

She was stretched out over the handlebars of an upright bike and totally oblivious to her surroundings. My hunch was that Monique had just stopped for a few seconds of rest but exhaustion had arrived to pack her up and whisk her away. This was broad daylight. It was 9:30am on a busy Saturday morning in the middle of the English countryside and she was fast asleep standing up, with only a bike supporting her.

'Monique,' I asked softly. 'Are you ok?'

She opened her eyes but not in a startled way. She had the appearance, demeanour and tonality of someone that was emerging from an anaesthetic.

'Huh,' she mumbled. 'Oh, hi Gerry. What's the story?' she asked, her voice slurred.

My heart went out to her. I had watched this woman battle through eight days and more. Her quickest finish had been over 19 hours and that was a week ago. Her eyes had bags beneath them that looked like the space rings from Saturn. She looked beyond exhaustion. On at least four occasions I went to bed thinking we had seen the last of Monique. But just like Houdini, every morning at the lake she magically reappeared.

It was going to be mostly a one-way conversation. She looked at me with the eyes of a boxer who had taken a heavy blow. I put an arm of compassion on hers.

'Monique,' I urged. 'You can't stay here. Go into Burley and tell a shopkeeper you are going to sleep outside their shop and to wake you in 20 minutes. Then when you wake up, see how you feel.'

'Yeah, eh, ok Gerry,' she replied in her strong West Yorkshire accent.

'Are you sure you'll be ok?' I asked as I clipped my right foot back into the pedal.

'Uh yeah,' she said without much energy or passion for adopting my idea. I could hardly fault her for that, but it did seem like her only possible remedy.

For sure she had to sleep, but she had to keep going too. The ultimate paradox. She had already taken a break during the swim. Based on yesterday's cycle time, she could ill-afford any more delays. The 22 hours cut off was very strict and she had finished Day Eight with only 12 minutes to spare.

I pedalled towards the village of Burley which was about half a mile away. As I entered the village I got an idea. I crossed over to the other side of the road and shouted into the village's bike shop, the same one that had put my own bike together 11 days earlier. A young sales assistant emerged. I didn't recognise him from before but it hardly mattered. They were well aware of our presence. After all we had cycled continuously through this small village for over a week. The exact magnitude of the event, was unlikely to have registered however.

'Hi, I'm in the cycle race,' I said.

There was no time or any point in trying to explain the background.

'There is a cyclist in a yellow jacket right behind me,' I continued. 'She is exhausted and is going to stop and sleep. Can you encourage her to stop outside your shop and can you wake her after 20 minutes?'

'Eh sure,' he replied, but with a puzzled expression.

Poor Monique. This lady had the heart of an army battalion. Were Julius Cesar short of a successor to inherit Rome, he might have considered her. We read about sporting role models all the time. Many justify the tag. It has taken me six months of writing to arrive at the opportunity to type these few paragraphs in tribute to this one. She is the greatest sportswoman I have ever had the privilege to meet.

Never mind the sink, Monique had the entire kitchen thrown at her. From a first day miscalculation and the three hours she had lost. The fact that she was usually one of the last competitors to close her eyes each night. The fact that she always blitzed the run. Partly because she was a superb runner but also critically to ensure she made the cut off. Her absolute ability to motivate herself day after day despite her incredibly long days. And her encouragement to others despite her state of constant fatigue, and her consistent sense of humour.

In the first eight days Monique swam, cycled and ran for over 164 hours. Without question she had the ability to finish this event. Her only shortcoming was she couldn't keep her eyes open long enough to see it through.

When I came around on the next lap and about four miles further (6.4km), Dan Earthquake was chatting to Monique at the back end of the course. I later found out she had taken my advice. She had slept, she had been re-awakened and she had remounted. By then she was operating on automatic pilot and was no longer in control. The organisers were at all times monitoring us and they pulled alongside, eager to ensure her safety.

> **Monique**
>
> 'Dan came past and stopped and I pulled over and made the decision to stop. If I took the two hours of sleep I knew I needed, I wasn't going to make the cut off. There was nothing wrong with me that a night's sleep wouldn't cure but I didn't have even an hour.
>
> I considered my decision. I was very conscious of how many times it would have been easy, tempting and desirable to ditch out. Was this one of those times? The answer is no. I made the decision. It wasn't taken out of my hands by injury, ill-health or cut offs. But the alternative would have been to get into some kind of accident on the bike and it wasn't fair to involve someone else in my stubbornness.'

By mid-morning Monique became a reluctant spectator. She would later sleep for 12 hours. We were down to three.

By now I was just grinding down the last couple of hundred miles of cycling we had still to do. I was shattered and having to constantly fight just to keep my eyes open. Such was the volume of energy drink I was taking on board, I was only short of consuming Red Bull intravenously. Previously my consumption was carefully measured. Now that was overridden by an insatiable and non-negotiating thirst.

Just like the story from last night concerning Jarlath, I'm not proud to admit the next one either but it is important I share it because it happened. Utter exhaustion is my rather lame excuse.

After finishing lap nine of the cycle (104 miles), I returned to base as I had done 89 times before. With one lap to go, I wanted to take more nutrition on board ahead of the run. As I entered the gate I could see our personal HQ from a distance (the chair). Normally I could always spot the crew from a distance of 100 metres as I navigated the final speed bump. As I passed the chair, there was no sign of anyone. That had never happened before. I was annoyed. Where were they, I wondered? I was very hungry. Surely they must have known I would be back by now.

It was only when I descended the hill at the turnaround that I spotted them. For some reason Dor was holding my running gear but I couldn't see any food. What was going on?

'Why are you not up there?' I asked in frustration. I hadn't spotted the food in her other hand. Dor held out the runners and went to take the bike from me.

'Well done, you're finished,' she said encouragingly.

'No I'm not.' I replied in a tone that suggested that she should have known better. I was tired for sure but I was certain I only had nine laps done.

Dorothy had earlier been informed by a trusted source that I was on my last lap. For a few seconds confusion reigned.

"But I have only done nine laps," I replied.

'Well, we have been told that you've enough done'.

Quite rightly she assumed the information she had been given was correct.

'Well it was 10 laps every other day', I snapped back in response.

With hindsight it was a simple piece of misinformation that the crew took to be accurate and certainly wasn't deserving of my snarling retort. I had bitten an entirely innocent party whose presence in England was solely to help me achieve a goal.

'Can you go back and check. I know I have only nine done'.

Dor ran the 20 metres to the timing tent as I waited impatiently. I was cold, tired, in a fragile mental state and very self-indulgent. All I wanted to do was continue on and finish the 10th lap.

I could see the timing tent from a distance and my sister courteously demand an instant and accurate update. They typed a few buttons and awaited a reply. It seemed to take an age.

'Yeah, you're right,' Dor shouted over the short distance. 'You have one to go.'

In my anger earlier, I had knocked a sausage and egg sandwich from a plastic plate that Dor had been holding. Now it lay scattered on the gravel beneath my feet. I later heard that Jacinta quite rightly threw a few justified expletives in my direction after I had left.

I deserved a lot worse.

The crew later confessed to being very nervous about my demands in those final few days. Apparently I became very unpredictable in my moods and in my needs. It became a 'what if he wants this,' or 'what if he wants that' guessing game for them. One minute I wanted sausage and egg sandwiches; the next minute an unexpected request for a drink of coke or often a desire not to speak at all.

On the evening run I sought medical attention three times. By now my legs were exceptionally sore, particularly the right shin. That is where the stress fracture was. More KT tape was applied and ice-packs were changed on both legs at regular intervals. That night it really started to get me down. I was in my own words 'getting sad' and reaching my lowest ebb of the entire event. Even the arrival of my Dad and my brother Tom, failed to lift my mood. Having them there meant the world but the pressure, firstly from the injuries and secondly from leading, was enormous.

I would later describe in my diary the ninth marathon experience as 'just horrendous'. That feeling arrived as early as lap two. The night would be nothing if not long, where it would take me 6:52:58 to complete the distance. I think I ran almost all of it although I did have to stop a lot for medical attention.

Of course this must be kept in perspective. I was out there voluntarily. Nothing, apart from my own heart and head, was forcing me to go on. Still, when I am immersed in something, I will give it my all.

The time it took me to run lap two showed how I was feeling. Unlike the first short lap, the second wasn't lengthened by a kit change. On Day Nine the second lap took 11:39, the third 12:52 and the fourth 14:28. Any early optimism for a strong finish to the day drowned quickly. It is hard to explain as I thought I was running well. Although carrying an injury I still felt like I was in fourth gear. In reality I must have looked like I was running in slow motion.

The centre point of the run and bike area was littered with new and arriving competitors, their crews and their supporters. That evening the weather was nice and sunny which certainly helped create a positive atmosphere at this busy location. A 100 mile run (160km) and a 'double iron' event were also now in full swing, making it an exceptionally busy place. Whenever Eddie Ette was on duty, I got raised goosebumps as he roared...

"Ladies and Gentlemen, here comes the leader of the deca, GERRRRRY DUFFFYYYY".

It lives still in my memory.

A stress fracture and an infection that was spreading wildly though was ensuring that this prized medal would be well earned. At times my leg had me close to tears but I tried to block it out and to keep moving forward.

By lap five I was in regular contact with Leigh. On that lap I came in and sat in front of her for 10 minutes where she patiently taped and packed my leg strongly. As I sat there, I watched her for signals of how she felt I was holding up. I wanted to be sure that she was on my side as ultimately she was the boss. Whenever I sat in front of her, I manned up hugely and displayed an air of being in full control. If Leigh had doubts about me, they never showed.

Apart from injury and exhaustion I felt strong in my mind, or at least in most aspects. Even though I had issues in my legs to occupy me, I was still conscious of what was happening all around me. I was hurting physically for sure, but the side of my brain that was in charge of continuing was still unwaveringly headstrong.

Perhaps the shower incident that would shortly arrive (and which I narrated in the opening pages) was because the adrenalin of the day had evaporated. It was also because by then I was unsure how much longer the right leg would hold up. The final 21 laps would heap more pain into it.

Laps six and seven were completed in 13:42 and 15:04. I was slowing at an alarming rate. An eighth circuit in 19:56 was a result of having to apply a fresh ice-pack. I had one strapped on the front of both legs and took on the appearance of a teenage skateboarder wearing knee pads.

One consequence of a bad case of cellulitis is tenderness around the infected area. Even the faintest of contact with my right shin would leave me writhing in pain. I had to ask anyone helping to be exceptionally careful when touching the leg. While Leigh was applying the ice-pack and examining me, I ate.

For the next hour or more, my average lap hovered between 14 and 15 minutes. It was painfully slow but I was making progress nonetheless. As each lap passed, I felt a little more soreness being injected into my right shin. I have been fortunate to have remained pretty much injury free for almost all of my running life.

It was inevitable that in an event of this magnitude and on a course this demanding, something would happen. Coincidentally Mark Padley also picked up a leg infection as well as a stress fracture in his ankle.

The hardest part of the run for me was that 10 metres drop I have mentioned several times. (See run map earlier in the book.) Even in the early days and with two perfect running legs, I had found this seemingly straightforward descent very difficult. On Day Nine I had to stop completely at the top during every lap to plot a routing that offered the least painful navigation. That brief stretch was now taking over 40 seconds. If I was to do it now, I might run it in less than four.

Lap 18 was my slowest of the 226 laps to date, taking almost half an hour. Much of that time was spent seated in front of Leigh.

I crossed the finish line at 11:19pm – a full 37 minutes slower than the day before. This meant the day had taken me 17 hours and 19 minutes. It was a sizeable drop but insignificant in the overall scheme of things.

As Jacinta handed me the recovery drink, I was in a world of pain. For the first time I had no appetite to go back down to the lake to ease my leg muscles and help them recover. All that consumed me was the pain I was feeling in my right leg. It was incredibly sore as I climbed the steps in front of the main house. Every other night I'd taken a different route back to the camper but I figured this route might be 50 metres shorter. Every metre I could save was precious. Climbing, I kept my head faced downwards. To lift it required effort. The crew surrounded me and were very concerned. All I wanted was to wash my body which was filthy and smelly and go to sleep. Conversation held no appeal.

Over the next hour, I really doubted my ability to finish. Perhaps it sounds contradictory but my head was still strong in many aspects. I was just in a lot of pain and I was unsure if my leg would hold up. When I was in the shower I lost myself in thought. The stress of the entire challenge was now bearing itself in full view into my face. A few minutes later as I cried into Jacinta's shoulder, I was at my most fragile ever in a sporting event.

We talked briefly. It was good at that moment to be able to share this with my closest ally. Before I left the block I resolved to just wake up in the morning and to give it my best. What more could I do.

My final words on the audio on the eve of Day Ten?

'So close and yet so far.'

STANDINGS AFTER DAY NINE

Competitor	Cumulative Race Position	Day One	Day Two	Day Three	Day Four	Day Five
Gerry Duffy	1	14:41:07	15:22:12	15:06:49	15:31:04	15:42:57
Mark Padley	2	16:51:49	17:16:45	17:13:52	17:02:06	17:04:42
Tony Raynor	3	16:41:06	18:19:58	19:03:47	19:37:47	18:58:44

Competitor	Day Six	Day Seven	Day Eight	Day Nine	Cumulative Total
Gerry Duffy	15:48:16	15:56:08	16:42:38	17:19:27	142:11:08
Mark Padley	17:12:41	17:18:16	20:23:46	20:19:51	160:43:48
Tony Raynor	19:40:43	19:56:46	19:42:09	20:33:32	172:34:32

WHY?

CHAPTER TWENTY-EIGHT

"Everyone is born with a gift; your journey is to discover it."
Dr Jon Carnegie and Jim Stynes. Finding Heroes

Why?

It is an obvious question. I can understand it. Once upon a time in my life, I might have asked it as well.

Why would someone spend six or eight months chasing such a goal? Why put my ambition on the line by announcing to my family and friends that I was going to do it? Why would anyone want to swim, cycle and run from dawn till dusk and beyond and then have a burning desire to do it all over again day after day?

To focus on what it is I was doing would be to miss the point, I feel. The subject matter is irrelevant to anyone but myself and maybe the other 19 competitors.

This became my goal. I got very excited at the prospect of attempting it the moment I decided to do it. It elevated my heart rate eight months earlier and it never waned. Life is about being happy and happiness amongst others things comes from growth. It certainly challenged me.

I am passionate about endurance sports. The 32 marathons in 32 days consecutive days was a passion from the moment the idea popped into my head in 2008 until we crossed the finish line two years later. During the two-year lead in and for every one of those 32 days I felt so alive.

The truth is the training was never hard, not in the typical sense at least. For every session in my preparation, I was living. It was the same with every hour and every metre of this.

Early in 2012, an Irishman who had lived in Australia for over 27 years sadly passed away at the age of just 45. Such was the legacy he left behind, Australia honoured him with a state funeral. His name was Jim Stynes.

Stynes was a former Irish gaelic footballer who had emigrated to the southern hemisphere back in 1984. He soon made a name for himself when he joined Melbourne football club. Over the following 11 years as a footballer, he became a household name playing 264 game for Melbourne. During his career he also became the first and only overseas player to be awarded the highly prestigious Brownlow Medal in 1991, an award given to the fairest and best player in the Australian football league. For a young Irishman who had grown up playing Gaelic Football, it was an astonishing achievement.

> **Jim Stynes**
> 'I love life. There's always something to overcome, new people to meet. You have just got to find your bliss and go after it. That's where the drive is, that's how you find your special place.'

Apart from his sporting talent, in 1994 Stynes co-founded a youth programme called 'The Reach Foundation'. At its core is the belief that every young person should have the support and self-belief they need to fulfil their potential and to dare to dream. The charity's message has since spread across that entire continent.

Without realising it at the time, that first run that I did back in 1995 was a day that I started to dream. Running gifted me that. John F Kennedy was right.

'Physical fitness is not only one of the most important keys to a healthy body. It is the basis of a creative and dynamic intellectual activity.'

That was the first key to begin unlocking my mind to my own potential. That was also the day I began to dare to make my dreams a reality.

I have learned that the more I am prepared to challenge myself and to exit my own comfort zones, the happier I have become. That is not to say that I feel the need to raise the extreme sports bar ever higher. A similar ambition, from which I may derive equal satisfaction, might be a personal best in a 5k race, a marathon or a business success.

Another non-sporting example of this is in public speaking. Previously it was my biggest fear. The first time I had to do it, it terrified me. Indeed a hypnotist had to offer assistance to give me the courage to stand up and address an audience of four. That's right, four people. Now I do it for a living. What's more, I am passionate about it.

How did I do it doing the first of them? As the author Susan Jeffers wrote in her bestselling book 'Feel The Fear And Do It Anyway', I felt the fear but I still did it. Has the fear completely disappeared? Well yes the fear has. It has been replaced by nervousness but I welcome that. Jack Nicklaus, the most successful golfer of all time said: "The day I'm not nervous on the first tee is the day I will retire." He wanted to be nervous. He played better if he was nervous. He welcomed it and so do I. It keeps me on my toes and I feel I perform better if I am a little nervous starting off. The more I challenge myself now, the more enriching my life becomes.

Just like Stynes, I am addicted to life and to making the most of every day. It is a healthy addiction. Every day I try to challenge myself to get something from that day. It's not to say that some days I don't lounge around the house because I do that too. At least once a year!

I have realised that I have been given a ticket. A golden ticket to live. How I use it is up to me. It's very precious. Only seven billion or so humans have one at any one time. It has a time limit on it though, so I know I must spend that time wisely. I am aware that in the overall scheme of how the universe measures time, it will be gone in a billionth of a blink of an eye. Best to use it well.

It was only at the age of 27 that I slowly started to become aware that it was in my possession. I realised I could stand still and continue living passively or challenge myself to raise my standards and become much happier in the process. Now I try to consciously live every day. I call this active living.

Since I started to ask more of myself, life has given me happiness back in abundance. We have all heard the expression, 'life is for living'. Saying it is easy but if we are unhappy with something but don't subsequently do anything to improve it, then surely nothing will change. Life is just waiting to be asked but the solution is usually found in a place outside the comfort zone.

For all of the duration of training and execution of this event I was in fact relishing every moment. The pleasurable days when everything clicked and the most difficult of days as well. Despite the displeasure my limbs might have been feeling, I knew at all times it was relative and that I was there by ambition.

I feel fortunate to have spent two hours in the company of Jim Stynes back in 2006 and also lucky to have had other inspiring stories touch my life. All of these people have become role models of mine. Their lives are filled with achievements in a sporting context that simply beggared belief.

Running across Canada as 18-year-old Terry Fox attempted to do back in 1980, took incredible self-belief. Competing in an Ironman distance triathlon as Dick Hoyt, a military man from Boston, did in his fifties along with his son Rick, was also highly impressive. All three are on my list of role models' list.

At the starting line in St John's Newfoundland over 30 years ago, Fox was in no doubt of the challenge that confronted him. On top of wanting to run over 3,000 miles, he was also trying to raise Can$1 million for cancer research. He would also attempt it with one prosthetic leg, having lost his right leg to cancer as a result of bone cancer in his right knee. On his crew were his brother and a friend to support him.

Dick Hoyt wasn't alone either as he entered the water to begin his Ironman triathlon attempt. Training alongside him in the months before and being towed behind in a dingy as they began their adventure was his son Rick, a mid-twenties college graduate who had cerebral palsy since birth. In addition to the challenge of completing the distance, Hoyt senior would also carry his wheelchair-bound son for the duration.

Dick, who was in his late fifties, pulled his son in the dingy to complete the swim, and cycled with Rick positioned in a specially designed seat at the front of the bike. For the marathon, Dick would push Rick in a specially adapted wheelchair.

Watching the videos of these three men brought tears to my eyes. It was not just the incredible accomplishments that they set out to achieve. That was astonishing for sure. But there was more to it. Despite the challenges that life had thrown them, they were out there living life to its fullest and refusing to lie down or accept what others saw as limitations. They simply embraced their challenges, identified their ambitions and carried on regardless.

Instantly I realised the first lesson that each story was teaching me was gratitude. The second was ambition and its importance. They were prepared to do whatever it took to achieve their dreams and goals yet they were not blessed with the great health that I possessed. They refused to let it hold them back. They were out there embracing life and everything it had to offer.

It also taught me that conventional wisdom isn't that wise after all. If it was, we would not have sent men to the moon, developed a device that allows us to speak to another human anywhere on the planet, or ever run beyond 26.2 miles.

My inner conventional wisdom once had me thinking that I couldn't be a normal weight, that I couldn't speak in public, that I couldn't complete a full sprint distance triathlon or that I couldn't make a difference.

But I could and thankfully I did.

Their exploits made me realise that I could choose to interpret what I did in sport and in life completely differently. Before these stories, I spoke a language that I no longer use. I used to say I have to cycle tomorrow, or that I have to swim 100 lengths in my local pool, or that I have to run 20 miles on weekends.

Terry Fox and the Hoyts made me realise that I don't have to run, that I don't have to swim and I don't have to cycle. I don't have to take on sporting ambitions such as this book narrates.

I get to.

I am the luckiest man in the world because I woke up to this distinct difference. I am so grateful.

Not only do I get to compete in sports, I get to work, I get to run my business, I get to meet deadlines, I get to give corporate presentations and goal-setting seminars.

I get to write, I get to go to conferences. I get to spend time with family and friends, I get to give back to others who are not as lucky as me. I get to clean my house and I get to keep my garden tidy although it doesn't rock my world. Before this, my mindset told me I had to do most of it. Now I realise that I don't.

I get to.

One word changed in a single sentence, one mindset altered in this man's life.

It is a very simple language, one that I continually have to practise speaking. I am healthy and alive and as long as I am always aware of it, grateful for it and willing to challenge it, then no day can ever be a bad one.

Almost four years ago I was injured. Running was both forbidden and temporarily impossible. A knee operation and a verbal caution from the surgeon a daily reminder not to. Every day I promised myself that when my injury healed, I would be forever grateful. Every day I promised myself that on my return, I would always treasure the gift of simply having the health to run. So many others including some close friends are not as lucky. I have kept this promise. Since I have embraced this philosophy my whole life has become more enriched. I also do it in tribute to these sporting heroes of mine.

Sadly Terry Fox never got to finish one part of his ambition. Half way across Canada the cancer returned and silenced this inspirational teenager forever. His legacy though has since raised in excess of Can$20m through the 'Terry Fox Run,' a series of running events held annually all over the world.

I was inspired by these people but in my mind I knew that if I didn't subsequently do something about this inspiration, then all they were were stories that moved me briefly. That is like agreeing with the expression that life is for living but staying in a comfort zone and never venturing out. Fortunately I was heavily involved in sport before discovering the Hoyts and Terry Fox. These stories though educated me like no academic professor ever could.

They were seizing life and squeezing every last drop out of it. At that time I was active but I was only at the shallow end of my ability, timidly treading the shallow water relative to where I was capable of swimming to. I could see the deeper water. But until then, I never had the ambition or the courage to swim out to it.

After reading these stories I decided to really challenge myself. What was the best of my ability in running, swimming, or in any sport I wished to do. Or in the relationships with my partner, my family and friends, in my career, and in anything that was important to me?

I could only find out if I applied myself more and raised my standards. This wasn't just about running marathons or ultra endurance triathlons. It was about life and everything it had to offer. It was about identifying what was important to me and what I was most passionate about. Then pursuing it to the best of my ability.

My priority list currently has many things on it. Endurance sports is but one. Having the courage to raise my standards, to rewrite my story is what I was encouraged to do by this inspiration. Since then I have grown immeasurably.

Do I always achieve my best in all of these? Certainly not. Do I always give my best? Well, the honest answer is no. Is it my ambition to do so? Yes.

I have also learned not to be too hard on myself. If I don't realise a goal or ambition, I have realised the futility of condemning myself for not achieving it. Nobody apart from Doc Brown in the 1980s 'Back to the Future' movie has ever been able to go back in time.

I just pick myself up and try again.

I'm now experiencing a happiness that I didn't know existed. I realise I will never be 43 again. I need to make the most of 44. How lucky am I. Soon I will hopefully get to be 45. When I do get there, I will consciously make the most of that year.

I have asked myself what are the most important goals in my life and I have committed to striving to do them to the best of my ability. For you, it is whatever rocks your world.

The story in this book was me actively living out one of my passions. The swimming, the cycling, the ultra running, the terrain, the crazy absurd ambition of it all.

Even in those final two days, I was living every minute and enjoying it in a perverse way too. My only real fear in the wash house on that penultimate night was that my right leg might withdraw its co-operation. I was very unsure if it would carry me through one more day. The spirit was still very willing but the leg was very weak.

I decided to sleep on it, to wake up in the morning and to give it my best. What ever happened, happened. I could do no more.

'Control the controllables.'

DAY TEN

CHAPTER TWENTY-NINE

'Nothing worthwhile comes easy'
Hamilton Holt, American Educator and Politician

SUNDAY 12TH JUNE, 2011

When we reflect on our lives we will all have days that will stand out for whatever reason. Our first day at school. There will be the day perhaps when we graduated from college or our first day of employment. No doubt the day we meet the partner that we share life's journey with, will top most people's list.

We will remember days that we pursued and achieved the things that really meant something to us. Goals that are personal to us all. Education, marriage, children, learning the piano, writing a book, giving up smoking, building a house, creating a garden, running a marathon, opening a business, retiring from one, beginning an enduring relationship or friendship.

For me thus far, I have many memories that I will carry to the sky one day. One of these is from June 12, 2011.

My first goal that day was not to be at the lake to hear my name called out as I have narrated. It was to wake up on time. Such was my paranoia about over sleeping, four phone alarms had been set. At 4:55am on that final morning, it was like the stroke of midday outside St Paul's Cathedral. I had managed to close my eyes around 1:30am. One continuous bout of sleep worth a multitude of short siestas.

Extracting myself from the top bunk and manoeuvring down the ladder, I nervously and very tenderly put both feet on the ground. Immediately the pain made itself known but I was still able to apply all 168 pounds of body weight. Small gratitudes.

Dor later told me that Enda had spent most of Saturday night taking the bike apart and then putting it back together again. Let's just say that packing some extra swim hats and that bike service was worth its weight in gold to the cause. Before we left, Enda made me a bowl of porridge. His talents do not extend to the kitchen, but I was hungry so I kept this observation to myself.

Deep down I was concerned and consumed by many things. That breakdown in the shower block five hours before, a physical and visual sign of what was going on in my head. I was very nervous of not being able to finish. I am not saying this just to add drama. It's the absolute truth.

As I walked to the lake I was very pensive. So much was at stake for all of us. Mark, Tony and I were the only three left. All three within sight of joining an incredibly small group of people in the world who had achieved such a feat. On top of all that, this was an official race and I was leading cumulatively by over 18 hours. Half of Ireland knew it. I had to finish.

Earlier in the week, Toby Smithson had confessed how he felt about being in front.

Toby
'Leading brought huge pressure that I hadn't anticipated.'

For the past three days, being in front had weighed heavily on my mind as well. Apart from the magnitude of the event, the prospect of winning and the pressure that it brought was enormous. Victory was now there for the taking. I had the equivalent of a 10 shot lead into the final round of the British Open golf championship. Injury or exhaustion though rarely wiped a professional golfer off the final day's leader board.

The leg that was almost beaten into oblivion just five short hours before now had to be called into action one final time. That's what I was most nervous about in that early hour. I couldn't take anything for granted. Seventeen of the original 20 were gone. There was no sequence or pecking order for their withdrawals. I knew I had to be on my guard and I was determined to do so until the final metre. It goes back to a point I made earlier in the book about having respect for something that is not yet earned. This event was all about the number 10. Day Ten had yet to start.

> **Lao Tzu**
> 'If you wish to be out in front, then act as if you are behind.'

Having respect for what still had to be done was uppermost in my thoughts as I made my way down to the lake for the final time.

Now that I had reached the goal of making it to the lakeshore ready to swim, I identified my next goal. It was to take nothing for granted until I was off the bike and in a reasonable time so as to allow me the necessary time to walk the final marathon if necessary. I prayed the leg would hold and that my bike would as well. I still had not experienced any technical difficulties or even get a puncture.

On my crew for the final day were Jacinta, Dor and Enda. Also there in support was my brother Tom and my Dad. If I needed inspiration then I might draw from my father's commitment to living life to its fullest.

Readers of *Who Dares, Runs* will recall that to celebrate his 70th birthday, he did a bungee jump of over 200 feet in Argentina. Some would say I am the less adventurous of the two. Also there was Andrew Fay, a close friend, who had flown over the day before to lend his support and add humour to the final day.

On that final morning the lakeside was the busiest it had been since the first day. A fog had descended and hid large parts of the lake from view. Jarlath later shared how he viewed it on his first morning.

> **Jarlath**
> 'At an early hour, the lake looked like it belonged in a scene

> from the Harry Potter movie entering Hogwarths at night.
> Dark, covered by trees and no visibility when swimming. A
> perfect place to hide a body.'

You might recall the weather prediction that had been a rumour for several days. We had been warned that a violent storm was due to hit the south of England. At 6:00 am it was dry. Had it missed us? Not a chance. Soon it would pay us an angry visit, but more of that in a few pages.

Returning to see us off were several deca competitors who wanted to wish us well. In addition there were the three remaining 'quin' survivors, as well as 30 competitors who were attempting a single enduroman iron distance event (3.8km swim/186km bike/42.2km run). In all 36 swimmers climbed into the lake on that final morning.

Also there was Brian O'Connell. I recognised his face immediately, but at first I had no idea from where. When he took a large green microphone from beneath his jacket, I realised immediately he was the RTE man I regularly saw on my television screen back home. A short two minute interview followed where he quizzed me on the magnitude of what we had been up to in the preceding nine days. I presumed then that his work was done.

Moments before I entered the water, I hugged my crew. As I did so, I noticed Mark Padley's Dad, John holding a sign which read: 'Good luck Gerry, Mark and Tony.' It meant so much and summed up the camaraderie that existed with those that had soldiered together for so long.

Earlier Enda handed me three swim hats and a vest for wearing beneath the wetsuit. I climbed into the water at 5:59am as I was determined to spend the shortest time possible in there. I knew it would be cold.

Mark Padley
'Day Nine and Ten was all about survival. The water wasn't actually cold. We were exhausted which made it cold.'

It was a special moment to realise that this was our final day. In the lake it was busy, but the extra company was a welcome distraction. As we climbed in, we were greeted by a resounding cheer from all the new competitors.

Twenty seconds later we began to tick off the final swim.

From the very first stroke I felt a chill. I don't wish to be repetitive except to say it was absolutely freezing for almost all of the 77 minutes it took me. It was my second slowest swim time but a completely different experience to Day Two when I had taken one minute longer. Back then I was someone who was cautiously ticking an early box and enjoying a refreshing morning workout.

On that final swim I pushed a little harder, wanting to finish as quickly as possible. The fact that it was the final time gave us all an extra and surprising litre of energy. I knew too I could throw a little caution to the wind.

At all times I felt in control of my faculties but I have never wanted a swim to end as much. It was obvious that Day Ten would be far from a lap of honour. The longer the swim went on, the worse I felt and for the first time my shin ached in the water. I felt it on the first lap. After just five minutes I was stone cold. Every time I came around to shout out my number, I put an extra effort in my verbal communication, for fear of being recognised as someone who was suffering.

Jacinta
'He had a clear strategy for the final few days in the water. That was to purposely avoid direct eye-contact with those in charge for fear they might check up on him. On that final day he mostly breathed to one side and into the middle of the lake so as to hide his face.'

I was very much in control of what I was doing and to a large degree in 'control of the controllables'. An example of this was my awareness to exude positivity as I shouted out my race number at the end of every lap.

I was just so cold.

Finally my last lap arrived and I gave quiet thanks in my head. Mark had climbed out 90 seconds earlier and Tony came in just under the 90 minute mark. Raynor had remained pretty consistent in completing days eight and nine. On those two days he had finished in 19hrs 42mins and 20hrs 33 mins respectively. Indeed almost every day since the opening Sunday, he had finished around 1:00am.

Once Day Eight arrived, Mark's times had begun to fall quite sharply. In the first seven days he had always finished before 11:30pm but on Day Eight he went well beyond midnight. That day demanded three hours longer from him, a clear sign his legs were starting to suffer. Apart from the obvious overuse, I am convinced that this was due to the mechanics of the run course and its continuous right hand turns. Day Nine was slower again for Mark as he finally finished just at 1:41am (19 hrs 41 mins).

Three marshals had to help me out of the water. Once I was out, Dor and Jacinta swooped and wrapped me in a sleeping bag. As we climbed up the field and over the timing mat I was mind-numbingly cold and felt completely helpless. I began to hyperventilate. Once inside the tent the crew tore into action, ripping the wetsuit off me and tried to warm me up at the same time.

Dorothy

'After he emerged from the lake he was shaking and seemed powerless to stop it. I've never seen him in such a state. His whole body seemed to be convulsing. The first thing I thought of was to give him a towel to warm his face. He bit into it so hard, he almost tore it. That's when I got scared.

I knew we had to turn this around for him. Until he warmed up, he was helpless. It was hard to comprehend that his immune system could be so weak. We had a major job to do and we had to do it fast.'

Enda whipped the three silicone hats off my head and replaced them with what can only be described as a hat which was a cross between an Eskimo hat and a real life fur covered mink. Although it looked very unattractive, it was wonderfully warm. After a few minutes he later told me, the veins on my face began to slowly turn from blue to a slightly lighter shade of the same colour.

All the while, I sat there very low and consumed in a lonely place in my head. As I stood bent beneath the canopy of the tent, I thought about what still lay ahead. My motivation remained high but my mood was very low. One part of the brain was reminding me that I had been on the go for nine days and nights and that my body was absolutely exhausted. The same part of my brain was also receiving signals from my legs reminding me of the cellulitis and the stress fracture. My immune system was almost defenceless. I sat there shivering and consumed in a bubble of negativity.

Jacinta
'I was really concerned for him and knew that we had a very important part to play in the next few minutes. We had to get his body temperature back up, we had to lift his mood and get him to eat. He had a nine hour cycle in him. On top of that, just then it started to rain heavily.'

Dale Carnegie (self-help author)
'Feeling sorry for yourself, and your present condition, is not only a waste of energy but the worst habit you could possibly have.'

My negativity was a result of many factors, from near exhaustion to the fact that I still had another 16 hours left to do – and in awful weather at that. Then I recalled something I had learned years before.

Almost all of the time we can choose our mindsets. We can choose to feel low or in a split second we can bounce up and just get on with whatever it is we want to get out of life that day.

I have learned that when this happens, often we can choose where to go in our heads. As I sat there I reminded myself that I had so many things going for me that might help me achieve my goal.

I reminded myself of the 16 years of apprenticeships I had served to get me to arrive at Day Ten with a possibility of finishing. I reminded myself of the eight months of training I had completed including that extra week of 31 hours back in May. I reminded myself that I had ticked nine out of 10 boxes and had only one more left.

I reminded myself that I was one of three who were still going in the event and that for sure, the other 17 who had started would have loved to have been in the discomfort I was in, if it meant they were still in the game.

Then perhaps the most empowering thought of all. I realised that I had *only* 16 hours or so left. Simply a completely different way of looking at the exact same challenge.

By substituting the word *only* for *still* in my brain, I was able to completely reframe the situation I found myself in.

I reminded myself that I was here by ambition and that I had chosen to be here. I reminded myself that my crew had given up their time and made huge sacrifices for me.

I thought of Nick Vujicic, another role model of mine who was born with no arms and no legs. I realised I was the lucky one who had the good fortune to be able to climb up on a bike.

Within those few minutes my focus shifted significantly. The final thing I realised and told myself was that this was Day Ten, the final day. If I completed Day Ten, then I could have a lie in tomorrow.

By now my mood was lifting hugely. Obviously the fact that I was warming up was helping too. The crew had half-stripped me and were warming my limbs by rubbing me profusely with towels. I would have helped but I still couldn't feel my fingers.

In dressing me for the cycle, their difficulty was compounded in two ways. For starters they had to take a tight wetsuit from my body where the final necessity was to pull it down via my legs and off through both feet. It is an understatement to say that both legs and shins were a little put out.

A second issue was having my sister there to witness me undressing. This led to her being sacked from the crew for a brief 90 second period. Believe it or not, that brought a sudden dose of reality and humour to the situation. Even I managed a laugh.

> **Dor**
> 'We hadn't thought of that. While he was freezing he was still conscious enough to tell me to turn around as Enda and Jacinta undressed him.'

The entire changeover took more than 10 minutes. On Day One with Brendan, it was done in three. I was happy to take my time on that final morning as I knew that warming up was vital for the long road ahead. I went into the marquee and sat and ate the entire breakfast. At this stage an extra two minutes in a warm tent was an attractive proposition. I saw it as a reward for my nine days of labour.

As I sat the storm outside began to brew. The forecasters were right. What was about to arrive in the south of England was one of the worst summer storms in over a decade.

> **Jacinta**
> 'As he sat wrapped in a foil blanket, the chatter and banter

from the crowd of 30 competitors, crew, marshalls and supporters was drowned out by the noise of the torrential rain that was now lashing down on the roof.'

After leaving the marquee I noticed in that few minutes, that the wind had picked up and was starting to blow. As we climbed to the tennis court to pick up my bike, there was little chat. There ready to greet me for the final time was Eddie Ette.

"Good luck Gerry," he said. "We will see you when you get back."

By now my mood had lifted considerably but I was cautious out of respect for what still had to be done. I got on the bike shortly before 8am aware I wouldn't dismount until around 4:30pm. Knowing it was the final time helped, but even as I began the rain was already soaking into my clothes.

After the first lap and with a bowl of cereal in my belly, I began to count down the final 104 miles (167km). As I crossed the cattle grid just outside the entrance to the estate, my face contorted with the discomfort that passed through my body.

After more than 180 crossings, now it was like being shaken violently in a tumble dryer. It was only for a brief two-second period though and once I had crossed, I raised my mood by subtracting this from the number remaining. As I settled into mile 13 of the cycle, I calculated that I had only 18 more crossings left out of 200.

On that final day, I began to develop a little paranoia about the fact that the bike had held up so well. Was it really possible to cycle over 1,160 miles (1866 km) and not encounter any problems? Because of this, every minute felt like ten and for much of it, I began to hear imaginary rattlings from the gears and the crankset below.

By mid-morning the storm had turned violent and the strong winds mixed with driving rain, meant we would be asked every question. The elements were now showering quite a lot of debris from the trees onto the course. Any of these leaves or twigs could attach themselves to the tyres. Often I looked down certain that I could feel a flat tyre. But it was never so.

On the bike, I resembled a Patagonian winter hunter with three layers around my upper body, shorts and leggings to cover my legs, two pairs of gloves, two light fleece hats and a helmet. Trouble was, the rain was driving and we were cycling into it.

> **Tony**
> 'Day Ten brought the worst weather I've ever raced in or trained in and I have done a lot over the years. By the second lap I had to put my wife's walking jacket on and she is only five feet tall. I put on a new fleece and gloves but they only lasted a lap.'

Soon after I began to really feel the cold. My fear of a technical issue forcing a stoppage was compounded by the conditions. By 11:30am branches began to fall and at times given the intensity of the rain and wind, I had to squint to protect my eyes. If I had to stop I doubt I'd have survived more than five minutes without going into a state of hypothermia. Even if my cold fingers could dial a number on my mobile, it would take 15 minutes for the crew or marshalls to come to my aid. There was no way my hands would have warmed up sufficiently to allow me to fix anything other than a loosened chain. Like Tony, I had never cycled in such conditions in my life.

> **Mark**
> 'It was an absolute washout with torrential rain from early morning. People competing in the single day event who wore tri-suits were being withdrawn due to hypothermia. In fact their support crews were wearing wetsuits and no, that wasn't me hallucinating. Log cabins were being hijacked for their showers. What a day to realise that we had no choice but to go on.'

Despite the storm, I've nothing but good memories of that final cycle. It was almost as if an invisible force was throwing us one last test. In my head, I laughed at its efforts to derail us and it heightened my resolve to finish.

I was already immersed in the final day. Sometimes the thought of something yet to be done is greater than the physical act itself. I had been so nervous of the final test. Now it was here and already much of it had been ticked off.

From a physical perspective I was on my last embers of energy but mentally somehow I had managed to ignite a new fire. I am certain that this was because it was the final day. My mental state brought fresh energy and as a result extreme determination and a resolve to see this through.

For the duration of the bike I was able to forget about the leg problem. Thankfully I didn't feel it when no weight was applied. Evidence of this is illustrated in my bike lap times. Lap two took just over 48 minutes which was back to the kind of times I was putting in on Day Three. Lap four was two minutes quicker again. Again on lap five I was very consistent completing it in 47:46. It was mental energy that was driving that bicycle chain.

After five laps my crew insisted I come off the bike and change every stitch of clothing. I was completely soaked to the bone. Conveniently there was a portable toilet near the chair. Given that I had to strip to my birthday suit and the fact that it was so cold and wet, the crew felt the shelter might be a good idea to keep me warm.

As I changed with the help mostly of Jacinta and Enda, Dor handled the food while my Dad, my brother Tom and Andrew Fay stood guard over the bike. It was safe. Who on earth would want to steal it and cycle on such a day?

The last thing I wanted to do was to stop. Having to do so meant the next lap took 65 minutes. We never had to stop for a clothes change during the bike up to this, but it was a smart thing to do and a must. It is not that I was being paranoid about wasting time at this stage but I was still concerned about my leg and I was still fearful as to whether or not it would hold up. Part of my reason for such haste on the bike was to leave me enough time for the evening run to allow a walk or a crawl if that is what it would take.

To keep myself from falling asleep on that final day I took to singing on the bike as loudly as I could. One of the songs was the Bill Withers song 'Lovely Day'. The second was an Irish song by an artist called Brendan Shine that most Irish people over 35 years of age would recognise. It has an unusual title, 'Do You Want Your Ould Lobby Washed Down' and was released in the late 1970s. I have no idea why that song came to mind. Funny, I haven't sung it since. I must have sung both of these songs 30 times each as a tactic to keep myself from falling asleep.

When I saw Steve Haywood come out onto the bike course in a car and shadow me from behind with the hazard-lights flashing, I was convinced the organisers had decided to cut the cycle short for safety reasons. After all, cycling an extra four miles each day over and above the deca iron requirement, meant technically we had already cycled far enough. But he was just monitoring us from a safety viewpoint on the debris ridden course.

I recalled the quote from the event website.

'No hiding place.'

Such were the conditions, in the one-day event that was also simultaneously taking place, people were already dropping out. Of the 30 that attempted a single iron distance event on that final day, only 17 of them would make it to the finish.

> **Tony**
> 'By lap six my crew had to scrounge some kit from around the other crews so I ended up in a stranger's waterproof jacket, someone else's gloves, a pair of washing-up gloves over those and plastic bags inside my shoes.

Some 24 miles (39km) after changing all of my clothes, I had to stop and repeat the process. Two full changes of attire in just two laps. I had to do it again after lap nine. To ignore it might have had more serious consequences.

As I stood in the portable toilet on that final occasion, I was helpless. My fingers were partly red and part blue. My teeth chattered but I was distracted as the crew stuffed yet another sausage and egg sandwich into my mouth. I ate seven of them that afternoon.

> **Enda Munnelly**
> 'In the end we had to ask for food. He was eating so many sausages, eggs, bread, pasta, Mars bars and much more. Every morsel of food from the camper was gone so in the end we had to send Tom and Andrew to the shops. By the early stages of the run, the rest of us were shattered and starving as well. As I handed him his sixth sandwich in a five hour window, I prayed he wouldn't eat it all. I was starving too.'

Earlier that morning, Enda had come up with another stroke of genius. I would never have thought of it. After every lap the crew handed me two bottles. One had energy drink and the other had hot water that I would sip for the first 10 minutes of each lap. I had to drink it that quickly as by then it was already getting cold. I am convinced this kept me warm.

On that final lap I became very conscious of the places I would no longer visit. So many geographical relationships about to end but I was very happy to say farewell.

Studying my bike split when compared to the more favourable weather conditions of the day before, offers firm evidence of my theory that I managed to find an extra litre of energy on that final day. Despite having to stop on three occasions for a minimum of 10 minutes each time I was only 10 minutes slower cumulatively than the day before. That final cycle took me nine hours and 19 minutes.

At 4:28pm, I climbed off the bike for the last time.

As I began the run, I could see a television camera pointed in my direction. RTE's Brian O'Connell and his cameraman Paul were here for the long haul. Not content with a brief final morning interview, they were here to see me finish as well.

Even while I was changing into my run gear for the final time, I was calculating times in my head. I had no idea how my leg was going to react once I applied my full bodyweight to it and I was still very conscious of the cut-off. I figured that I had in excess of eleven hours before the cut off, so my mind eased. Barring disaster I would make it. Surprisingly for the first 200 metres I was able to run at a reasonable pace but as I turned the corner to run down towards the rocky track, my leg woke up and immediately shuddered my early enthusiasm to a shuffle. I knew immediately it was going to be a long night.

I didn't care if the run took all of the 11 hours such was my happiness at having no more cycling to contend with. I was also consciously grateful for being able to run – however slowly. My breakdown in the shower was now erased. While continuing to maintain respect and discipline and despite the pain of the stress fracture and infection, I felt that I would make it. So I began to settle in and enjoy the final marathon.

My crew continued to think ahead. Jacinta conceived another strategy to get me home successfully. Once I put on the remaining clothes I had for the run, I had none left. Everything had been used up or borrowed and was soaked through. Saving me from having to run in my birthday suit was a base layer and a jacket borrowed from Enda and a pair of knee length running leggings that belonged to Dor. Interestingly she never asked for them to be returned afterwards.

During the second lap Jacinta handed me of all things a green bin-bag.

"Are you serious"? I asked.

'Yes', she replied and with a smirk on her face.

I knew what she was thinking. Why wouldn't it work ? It was one of those heavy duty ones. If they kept a marathon runner warm on an early morning start line, then why not in a marathon itself?

Jacinta had already cut holes for my arms and one for my head as well. She humourously told me that the hole for my head was much bigger.

I derived great pleasure from wearing that bin liner, and never took it off. Not only would I remain dry for the entire run, it insulated me like a warm blanket.

> **Jacinta**
> 'I thought of it in the afternoon when we were running low on clothes. We needed something quick and simple. I knew he wasn't going to run fast so it wouldn't hinder him. So we put it on the shopping list earlier that afternoon.'

During the second loop, Enda came running by and showed me a picture that he had taken on his phone of the front tyre of the bike. As he was bringing it back to the camper he had noticed a half-inch slit in the tyre with the inner tube protruding out. He was certain that I wouldn't have got another mile without the tyre exploding. Lady Luck owed me nothing in the cycling stakes. He surmised that there was at least a 50 per cent chance the tyre would have exploded as I was descending the fast hill at the beginning of the bike loop.

On the course and under a sky full of anger were quin competitors, triples, doubles, singles and a handful of competitors doing a 100 mile run (161km) event which had started at lunchtime on Saturday. Up to 60 competitors in total. With all the extra traffic on a narrow path and on such wet ground, the course had quickly turned into a quagmire.

On the first run lap we were greeted by a new challenge that we had not experienced to any large degree up to this. The run course had turned into a swamp.

I noticed that some of the particular lines we had taken into various corners for nine days were already impassable and new lines had been devised by those who had already been on the course for hours before Mark, Tony and I.

One route that everyone was intent on avoiding completely was that nasty 10 metre drop I had such trouble with. I was now experiencing pain there unlike anything I had ever felt before. Because of the downward angle of the terrain, it was putting huge pressure on my legs.

As I descended this section the night before, the competitor who would later win the 100 mile race, Glen Hatrick, had accidently bumped into me as he passed at speed. He later told me that such was the roar I let out, he was terrified he had put me out of the event.

On that final night each descent would take me over a minute and a half. For the first hour or more, I didn't realise there was an alternative route. As I went down on the fourth or fifth occasion I saw that a new line to navigate around it had been devised. Given the underfoot conditions the descent was absolutely treacherous. It was like trying to navigate down a children's playground slide covered in oil.

To our left, a wide circle around the descent had been created by those who had been on the course for hours. As I looked over, I saw a competitor meandering in a horse shoe around this line. At the end of that lap I asked Eddie for permission to use the new route. I was paranoid about abiding by the deca rules and exact course that had been set out 10 days before. He assured me that as long as it wasn't any shorter, it was ok to take it.

Earlier the fourth lap had taken me 29 minutes. Over half of that time had been spent with Leigh as she applied more KT tape and two ice-packs at the front of my shins. For the next two laps my right leg was particularly annoyed. After that and for the remainder, it was like having small jagged fragments of glass inserted in my lower leg and base of my foot. However no amount of pain at that stage was going to stop me from finishing.

> **Jacinta**
> 'I never thought for one second he wouldn't get there. There was no way he wouldn't finish but if I had to drag him by the good leg for those last 20 miles I would have done it.'

At 6:15pm Tony Raynor began his final marathon and an hour later all three of us were counting down the final miles as Mark Padley began his final run.

> **Tony**
> 'I finished the bike with six layers on me and I was still freezing. On that final bike lap it was nice knowing it was all coming to an end. Only 26 laps of a course that had turned into waterlogged bog since the night before, was between me and the finish line.'

Given his own state, Mark took two and a half hours longer than I did for that final cycle, finishing just two minutes shy of 12 hours. Like me he was close to a melting point, one lap alone taking him over two and a quarter hours to complete. I am not sure if the cause was technical or if he slept. Right through that final evening, the weather never let up.

> **Mark Padley**
> 'After the cycle, I came into transition. Such were the conditions and my slow pace, I found myself being overtaken by a tent.'

For the first half-marathon Mark was slow but consistent. Each lap took him 15 to 16 minutes. From there to home, it became a major challenge where he feared for a time he might possibly miss the final cut-off.

> **Mark**
> 'Starting the last run I was worried for the first time, knowing that my Day Ten bike split and my Day Nine run split was more than the 22 hours time limit.'

My own last run was horrendously slow but I didn't care. It wasn't important. The first half marathon took me over three and a half hours. Hard to credit but entirely true. Later Dor said that I only appeared capable of taking tiny strides.

> **Dor**
> 'He was on edge, he was exhausted but he was moving forward like a man possessed.'

TICK, TOCK, TEN

CHAPTER THIRTY
The Finishing Line

It was only on my return to Ireland that I realised just how much interest there had been in the event. In those final days and hours, thousands of people from all over Ireland were watching on the official event website for updates. It didn't stop there.

Thanks to the digital age, word had spread to a much wider audience. Ken put up a post on my own Facebook page asking people to comment on where they were following it from. Within 20 minutes the page had been inundated with posts from almost every county in Ireland. Messages were also sent from people watching in the UK, France, Czech Republic, Norway, Sweden, Portugal, Spain, Poland. In America followers posted from New York, Pennsylvania, Oklahoma, and Washington and as far away as Argentina, Brazil, Japan, New Zealand, and Australia.

> **Ken**
> 'The support shown was incredible. By Sunday, each post got hundreds of acknowledgements. It seemed there were people everywhere willing Gerry, Mark and Tony to finish. As the days had passed, the interest grew and grew. We had kept most of it from him, not wanting to distract him. All we told him was that he was getting huge support.'

Doug later told me that he received more Facebook friend requests that last day than he had received in the previous two years. One lady sent him a message saying that she would have made friends with the devil if it meant getting an update.

At around 9:30pm and with about 10 miles (16km) to go, Jacinta applied two fresh ice packs to my shins. The wind continued to blow and the rain poured down but now it didn't play a part. Given my speed it was simply a matter of staying warm and moving forward. Sooner or later I would be told I could stop. Each time I passed the finish line having completed another lap, I could see my Dad and my brother Tom watching eagerly.

The next few hours took an eternity but finally just after 11:15pm, I reached the penultimate lap. As I did, I asked Jacinta to bring my phone out to me. As I ran that second last lap, I called Brendan, Jarlath, Doug and Ken and thanked them for helping me achieve this dream and for being a part of it. I called my Mum as well because I wanted to share this moment with her.

I wasn't aware that my last laps were keeping thousands of people from their beds. Here are a few of the comments that were being posted sometime close to midnight on Sunday 12th June, 2011.

Martin Moore
'Are we there yet, are we there yet, are we there yet?'

Bridget Darcy Scully
'Here we go, here we go, here we go. I'm all alone and singing,'

Tony Salmon
'You're not alone Bridget, All of Ireland is singing. Wahoooo!'

Sean Kelleher
'It's weird watching this live in Facebook,'

Fiona McMenamin Reid
'Absolutely amazing. Sitting in my office in New Zealand, hugely impressed after following you for 10 days.'

Ernest Asensio Blasco
'Congrats Gerry. Wish you the best recovery. Greetings from Barcelona where we have been following you.'

Moss Keane
'I want to go to bed. Hurry up.'

Heather Purcell
'Yeah, I need to sleep too but I can't stop checking for the last few updates.'

Jean Wade
'We are at the finish line waiting to cheer you as you cross the finish line. Well maybe we are not there in body, but we are in spirit.'

Finally at 11:35pm, I had only one lap left. Behind me now was 24 miles of swimming, 1,160 miles of cycling and 261 miles of running. As I completed the penultimate lap, Steve Haywood strode out in front of me and with a smile across his face spoke a few words that were warmly received.

'Turn around, Gerry, and do your final lap in reverse. We will see you when you get back. Good Luck and enjoy it.'

'Is it ok if Jacinta comes with me?' I asked.

"Sure," he replied.

With clearance to proceed from the organiser, Jacinta and I set out on mile number 262 (422 km).

The idea of running the last lap in reverse was to receive words of congratulations from those still out on the course. By now there were still a few dozen competitors trundling towards the finish of their own events. On that last lap I met up briefly with Tony and Mark. Tony seemed exhausted but in control. He would later finish at 2:33am.

Mark really looked to be struggling but would later make the cut off with just 19 minutes to spare. When I met him half way up the rocky stretch he still had 14 or 15 miles to complete. With the exception of the light from our torches, it was pitch dark.

Like me he was moving slowly and awkwardly and he seemed startled and confused by my presence. I'm not even certain if he even recognised me. When my head torch caught him, he was like a startled rabbit caught in the headlights. Maybe he was confused by someone coming in the opposite direction.

I was keen to acknowledge someone with whom I had shared so much terrain for such a long period. He was the competitor I saw the most.

Mark
'I carried into the early hours running as much as I could. It wasn't really until about 2am that I was happy that it was possible to finish within the time limit.'

He later crossed the finish line at 3:41am.

As we left him, I was alone with Jacinta. It was great sharing this with her. She had been on board since I first committed to this ambition many months before. She was soaked to the skin but she didn't care.

With 600 metres to go, I stumbled heavily. Confusion on this reverse lap, complete darkness and exhaustion were the culprits. It didn't matter though as I would have crawled from there. Apart from the fall, I felt like I ran the entire last lap but it still took almost 25 minutes. I thought I was sprinting.

Often I get emotional during training sessions for big events. That is when the magnitude of what I am trying to achieve can sometimes hit me. I rarely get teary-eyed at the finish line itself. I knew I would have the rest of my life to reflect on what I had been lucky enough to achieve. As I crossed the line at 11:59pm, I was entirely calm but eager to savour the joy with all of the crew and my family. Eddie and Steve, the co-organisers were also there.

Moments later Brian O'Connell appeared, microphone in hand just as he had been 18 hours earlier. He was taken by the magnitude of the event and wanted to be there to capture the finish. In fact he and his cameraman had spent much of the day in the shelter and warmth of our campervan. I'm very grateful to them both for it means we have excellent footage of something that will live long in my memory.

In his interview seconds after the finish he asked me why I did it? My answer was instinctive. After all I had no preparation and had no idea what he might ask.

"Because I can, and I just love challenging myself to do things that are maybe a little bit different," I replied.

It was instinctive and from the heart.

STANDINGS AFTER DAY TEN

Competitor	Cumulative Race Position	Day One	Day Two	Day Three	Day Four	Day Five
Gerry Duffy	1	14:41:07	15:22:12	15:06:49	15:31:04	15:42:57
Mark Padley	2	16:51:49	17:16:45	17:13:52	17:02:06	17:04:42
Tony Raynor	3	16:41:06	18:19:58	19:03:47	19:37:47	18:58:44

Competitor	Day Six	Day Seven	Day Eight	Day Nine	Day Ten	Cumulative Total
Gerry Duffy	15:48:16	15:56:08	16:42:38	17:19:27	17:59:29	160:10:07
Mark Padley	17:12:41	17:18:16	20:23:46	20:19:51	21:41:45	182:25:33
Tony Raynor	19:40:43	19:56:46	19:42:09	20:33:32	21:18:18	193:52:51

GERRY'S DECA TIMES AND TOTALS

	Swim	Bike	Run	Total
DAY ONE	01:15:03	08:04:50	05:21:13	14:41:07
DAY TWO	01:18:50	08:44:28	05:18:52	15:22:12
DAY THREE	01:15:21	08:24:43	05:26:43	15:06:49
DAY FOUR	01:16:46	08:40:01	05:34:45	15:31:34
DAY FIVE	01:12:51	08:39:13	05:50:51	15:42:57
DAY SIX	01:12:38	08:57:20	05:38:17	15:48:16
DAY SEVEN	01:12:00	09:00:23	05:43:43	15:56:08
DAY EIGHT	01:14:16	09:16:18	06:12:03	16:42:38
DAY NINE	01:15:53	09:10:34	06:52:58	17:19:27
DAY TEN	01:17:34	09:19:47	07:22:06	17:59:29

TOTAL TIME SPENT...
SWIMMING
12 hours, 31 minutes and 20 seconds

CYCLING
88 hours, 17 minutes and 36 seconds

RUNNING
59 hours, 21 minutes and 31 seconds

COMBINED TOTAL
160 hours, 10 minutes and 7 seconds

CHAPTER THIRTY-ONE

Into The Early Hours And Beyond

I don't recall being in any pain later that night. The distraction of success can be a powerful anaesthetic.

After showering, I returned to the camper around 1:00am. In that confined space were the crew, Andrew, Tom and Dad. Together we celebrated over cups of tea and bowls of cereal. It was the sweetest champagne and tastiest meal of my life. After chatting until about 2:30am we all retired to get some rest. For most of us, it meant only moving about four feet in different directions.

I closed my eyes at 2:40am but they were prised open what seemed like seconds later by an early morning call. From 6:30am until 11am the next morning, I would not leave the sleeping bag nor the phone down for more than five minutes at a time. Every radio station and newspaper in Ireland was eager to learn more about my success and the detail of what we had been through. Pride of place went to The Ray D'Arcy Show and the Morning Ireland radio programme.

I laughed quietly in my head as I talked for about five minutes to close to half a million people live on RTE, while still immersed in the luxury of a sleeping bag on the top bunk.

It was a very important interview though. Shortly after 9am on what was a Monday morning, the charity I was helping to raise awareness and funds for-Irish Autism Action – received an anonymous phone call from someone who later donated €10,000 directly arising from that interview. As a result over €21,000 was raised, exceeding all pre-event targets.

That morning the weather was the opposite to what it had been for most of the previous day; warm and sunny which was pleasant for the official prize-giving ceremony. By midday, a crowd of about 50 had gathered. I took the opportunity to thank the organisers and also the many volunteers including a chap called Dan Watford who had been there every single day. The organisers had a lovely buffet prepared and I ate more than my share of the chef's preparation. As part of the prize giving I was presented with a free entry to the following year's event!

When I volunteered in the afternoon to clean up the mess that was our home, I didn't realise I would have as tough a time as I had on the Sunday. It was pretty horrendous. The 41 bed nights it had provided in the previous 12 days, when combined with the weather of the day before, meant it was a pretty awful sight.

That night we returned to Ireland and were greeted in Dublin Airport and back in my hometown by a huge gathering of family and friends and members of my local triathlon club.

One welcome banner made by Robyn and Meghan Bates, Doug and Sharon Bates's children, read...

"Superman wears Gerry Duffy pyjamas".

I laughed hard when I saw that one.

A few days after, a celebration party was organised and hosted by the Midland Triathlon Club. Special word of thanks to my sister Katherine and also to Noeleen Bourke for organising it and to Ray D'Arcy for coming down from Dublin to emcee it.

On Tuesday, June 14th I went for a full medical with my own doctor. Cellulitis and a stress fracture were confirmed as well as extreme tiredness and a weak immune system. Apart from these, I was in good shape. He recommended an eight week rest period to allow my body to heal.

One statistic worthy of note was when I stepped up on the weighing scales in the surgery. I weighed 170 lbs. I had left Ireland two weeks earlier weighing 168 lbs so this was a sure sign we had got the nutrition spot on. Even after expending 160 hours of energy in such a period, I came back two pounds heavier than I had left a few weeks before.

A few weeks after the deca I got a bout of extreme stomach sickness that knocked me out for three days. The truth is it took a full 12 months to recover completely from what I had put my body through. The cellulitis disappeared but came back again on two occasions which apparently isn't uncommon. My immune system had really taken a hammering. This was demonstrated on a daily basis by having to wear extra layers of clothing right through the summer of 2012.

In the time that has elapsed since the deca, the success of this achievement has followed me and I feel so grateful for it. I tell people that it is a metaphor for what anyone is capable of aspiring to. We are all made of the same ingredients, make no mistake.

Awareness of the challenge spread far and wide. Invites to address the workforces of some fascinating companies, amongst them Google and Facebook, arrived at my door and I was delighted to share my experiences with them of how I approach and take on challenges.

An interview with the sizeable and influential American news website The Huffington Post really brought home the magnitude of the achievement and the awareness it had generated. Almost 20 months on, it still resonates with people and requests to share the story and my experiences continue.

I'm convinced that simple strategies can help us achieve big things. Sometimes we look for huge solutions to big obstacles. It need not be the case.

My tale is a metaphor for your own dream or ambition in life. It is your marathon, your book, your education, your new business, your piano grades, your new career choice, your new language, your charity fundraiser, your new house or whatever your goal may be. Realise that there is almost always a way to achieve it.

At times on that journey you may get hit by obstacles. Those are the times when we find out what we are really made of.

Overcoming these obstacles is what will make achieving so special.

Just remember, you cannot get to 10 without passing through six. All you are doing is passing through.

I wish you every success.

EPILOGUE

One positive about taking over 20 months to put my thoughts and experience into print is that it offers me an opportunity to share a good news update. On June 1st, 2012, Edward Page aka 'Big Ted' had another attempt at completing a deca. Ten days later he successfully crossed the finish line.

Despite not shedding a tear at the finish line in 2011, I must confess that each time I browse through the thousands of messages in support that were sent via whatever means, I have had to bite my lip on a few occasions.

To know that so many were rooting for me as well as every other competitor to succeed is very humbling. I have chosen to finish by reprinting perhaps the most fitting of all which was posted online.

> **Martin Moore**
> 'As we end, let's raise a glass to all of the competitors who were courageous enough to put their foot up to the start line of this amazing challenge. Mark, Toby, Lee, Gerry, Hanno, Russell, Andy, Jean Yves, Roderick, Neil, Andrew, Simon, Keith, Richard, Tony, Michael, Mick, Edward, Keith and Monique. Gladiators all, for without your bravery, we wouldn't have had this mad event.
>
> Take a bow one and all.
> Until the next time.'

Thank you for taking the time to read this story.

GERRY DUFFY'S DECA

January 10th, 2011

	Monday	Tuesday	Wednesday	Thursday	Friday	Saturday	Sunday
Week 1	50 Min Run	1 Hr Bike	90m Bike	1 Hr Bike 30 Min Swim	REST	1 Hr Bike 20 Min Swim	Rest
Week 2	45 Min Run	2 Hr Bike 1 Hr Bike	1:45 Bike 30 Min Swim	1 Hr Bike	1 Hr Run 30 Min Swim	1 Hr Bike	Rest
Week 3	45 Min run	45 Min Swim 1 Hr 55 Min Bike	2 Hr 50 Min Bike	2 Hr 20 Min Bike	50 Min Run	1 Hr Run	35 Min Swim
Week 4	45 Min Run	3 Hr 15 Min Bike 1 Hr Bike	1 Hr Bike 45 Min Swim	2 Hr 10 Min Bike	50 Min Run	Rest	Rest
Week 5	1 Hr Bike	2 Hr 15 Min Bike	1 Hr Bike 80 Min Run 30 Min Swim	65 Min run	75 Min Run	4 Hrs 10 Min Bike	Rest
Week 6	1 Hr Run	90 Min Run	1 Hr Bike 70 Min Run	45 Min Swim	80 Min Run	5 Hr 10 Min Bike	45 Min Run
Week 7	1 Hr Bike	45 Min Run 45 Min Swim	1 Hr 45 Min Bike 45 Min Swim	6 Hr Bike	30 Min Swim	Rest	65 Min run
Week 8	1 Hr Bike 45 Min Run	45 Min Run 45 Min Swim	1 Hr 40 Min Bike 50 Min Swim	6 Hr Bike	45 Min run	70 Min Run	Rest
Week 9	2 Hr Run	1 Hr 45m Bike 1 Hr Swim	55 Min Bike 95 Min Run	2 Hr Bike 30 Min Run	1 Hr Run 1 Hr Swim	3 Hr Bike	10 K Run Race
Week 10	55 Min Run 1 Hr Bike	Rest	2 Hr 15 Min Bike 45 Min Run	6 Hr Bike	1 Hr Run	3 Hr Bike	Rest
Week 11	2 Hr Run	75 Min Bike 1 Hr Swim	1 Hr 45 Min Run 75 Min Bike	7 Hr 30 Min Bike	1 Hr Run	2 Hr 45 Min Bike 15 Min run 1 Hr Swim	Rest

IRON TRAINING DIARY

	Monday	Tuesday	Wednesday	Thursday	Friday	Saturday	Sunday
Week 12	1 Hr Run 2 Hr Bike	90 Min Run 1 Hr Swim	45 Min Run 1 Hr Bike 45 Min Run	4 Hr 15 Min Bike 1 Hr Run	1 hr 45 Min Bike 1 Hr Walk	Rest	Rest
Week 13	1 Hr Run 2 Hr Bike	1 Hr 45 Mins Run 1 Hr 45 Mins Bike	45 Min Run 1 Hr Bike 45 Min Run 1 Hr Swim	8 Hr Bike	90 Min Run	90 Min Run	30 Min Swim
Week 14	75 Min Swim 1 Hr Bike	2 Hr 15 Min Run 2 Hr Bike	2 Hr 10 Min Bike 90 Min Swim	9 hr 15 Min Bike YIKES!!	90 Min Run	1 Hr Bike 1 Hr Run Hr Swim	10Km Run
Week 15	90 Min Run 1 Hr Bike	90 Min Swim x 2	90 Min Swim 1 Hr 45 Min Bike	6 Hr Bike 30 Min Run	2 Hr 30 Min Bike	2 Hr 30 Min Run	75 Min Swim 45 Min Walk
Week 16	Rest	Rest	1 Hr Run	2 Hrs 25 Min Run 1 Hr 5 Min Run	80 Min Run	2 Hr 30 Min Bike	Rest
Week 17	4 Hr Bike 90 Min run 38 Min Swim	4 Hrs Bike 90 Min Run 38 Min Swim	4 Hrs Bike 90 Min Run 38 Min Swim	4 Hrs Bike 90 Min Run 38 Min Swim	2 Hr Bike	45 Min run 1 Hr Run 1 Hr Swim	1 Hr 45 Min Run
Week 18	2 Hr Run 38 Min Swim	6 Hr Bike	1 Hr Run	90 Min Bike	1 Hr Bike	29 Min Swim 3 Hr 10 Min Bike 1 Hr 28 Min Run 5:11 Half IM Distance	Rest
Week 19	90 Min Run Hr Swim	2 Hr Bike 1 Hr Run	2 Hr Bike	Rest	Rest	2 Hr Bike	30 Min Run
Week 20	75 Min Run 1 Hr Run	2 Hr Bike	90 Min Bike 45 Min Run	75 Min Swim	1 Hr Bike	30 Min Run	25 Min Bike
Week 21	1 Hr Bike				DECA Begins		

HOW THE 20 DECA STARTERS FINISHED

Name	Day One	Day Two	Day Three	Day Four	Day Five	Day Six	Day Seven	Day Eight	Day Nine	Day Ten	Total	Days completed
Gerry Duffy	14:41:07	15:22:12	15:06:49	15:31:04	15:42:57	15:48:16	15:56:08	16:42:38	17:19:27	17:59:29	160:10:07	10
Mark Padley	16:51:49	17:16:45	17:13:52	17:02:06	17:04:42	17:12:41	17:18:16	20:23:46	20:19:51	21:41:45	182:25:33	10
Tony Raynor	16:41:06	18:19:58	19:03:47	19:37:47	18:58:44	19:40:43	19:56:46	19:42:09	20:33:32	21:18:19	193:52:51	10
Monique Hollinshead	19:28:49	19:23:00	20:29:56	19:51:12	20:28:52	21:26:13	21:15:51	21:38:45	DNF	DNS	164:02:38	8
Roderick Elder	16:25:49	17:11:33	17:32:33	18:10:07	17:59:33	18:54:39	DNF	DNS	DNS	DNS	106:14:14	6
Michael Trew	16:57:45	17:15:34	18:00:58	18:12:28	18:08:08	18:59:56	DNF	DNS	DNS	DNS	107:34:49	6
Hanno Nickau	14:16:25	16:33:11	17:13:00	18:41:22	21:51:24	DNF	DNS	20:19:48	DNS	DNS	108:55:10	6
Mick Barnes	17:46:47	19:27:11	18:05:38	17:50:25	18:04:36	18:07:59	DNF	DNS	DNS	DNS	109:22:36	6
Richard Ginn	16:38:51	17:45:44	18:36:07	20:23:23	21:27:43	DNF	DNS	DNS	DNS	17:44:15	112:36:03	6
Edward Page	18:11:34	21:19:14	21:39:45	20:43:18	21:27:44	21:49:14	DNS	DNS	DNS	DNS	125:10:49	6
Toby Smithson	12:53:33	15:12:30	14:29:19	19:22:54	20:55:07	DNS	DNS	DNS	DNS	DNS	82:53:23	5
Tony Fisher	16:34:58	17:38:23	17:33:54	18:27:21	20:26:30	DNF	DNS	DNS	DNS	DNS	90:41:06	5
Neil Kapoor	16:26:21	DNS	DNS	DNS	14:37:32	16:24:23	DNS	DNS	DNS	DNS	47:28:16	3
Russell Clarke	15:17:11	20:28:48	DNS	DNS	DNS	DNS	DNS	DNS	13:27:03	DNS	49:13:02	3
Andy Kemp	15:39:39	17:14:05	20:52:19	DNF	DNS	DNS	DNS	DNS	DNS	DNS	53:46:03	3
Andrew Moore	18:17:38	20:16:14	DNS	DNS	DNS	DNS	DNS	DNS	DNS	18:18:53	56:52:45	3
Simon Pearson	DNF	DNS	DNS	DNS	DNS	18:17:02	20:24:11	21:14:26	DNS	DNS	59:55:39	3
Keith Laing	19:37:26	21:19:13	21:30:15	DNF	DNS	DNS	DNS	DNS	DNS	DNS	62:26:54	3
Jean Yves Even	16:14:53	DNS	17:03:08	DNS	DNS	DNS	DNS	DNS	DNS	DNF	33:18:01	2
Lee Wigzell	13:48:14	DNS	DNS	DNS	DNS	DNS	DNS	DNS	DNS	DNS	13:48:14	1

NB: Some competitors came back after some rest days to do another day or two

Fancy Running A
Half Or Full Marathon?
Welcome To The
'Training Zone'

Firstly please read through some important tips/advice and considerations. After you have read them, simply log on to www.gerryduffyonline.com and download your free specially-prepared training programme. Don't worry. There are a multitude of programmes to suit many abilities.

MEDICAL ADVICE
Firstly consult with your Doctor in advance of beginning any training programme.

SOME OTHER ADVICE BEFORE YOU START...
Training for your marathon or half marathon will be challenging, but should also be fun and enjoyable. Finishing a marathon is an accomplishment that less than 1% of people in the world can say they have achieved. You are about to be one of them.

Are you a beginning runner? Already a runner? Haven't run in a long time? Regardless, you can finish a marathon. Reading through some of the pointers below will help you along the way.

MOTIVATION
Whether you are training for a marathon or half marathon, it takes a lot more than good old determination and willpower to get you through training and the big day. Let your mind lead the way, not your body. Try to determine the big picture of why you want to do this. By the way, why do you want to do this? Don't let yourself off by stopping at your first answer. Dig deep.

Why do you want to run a marathon or half marathon? When you go beyond that first answer, you will begin to realize what is really driving you. When you learn what is really driving you, then you can use that to push yourself through willpower and determination. You will build the foundation that will get your subconscious mind working for you, not against you. In short, you are in for an incredible experience.

WEAR THE RIGHT GEAR

Treat your feet to a good pair of running shoes as these will be your most important piece of gear. Shoes are designed to fit feet with different arches, pronation, width etc. Visit a local specialty running store to find the best shoes for your feet. A comfortable, well-fitted pair of runners will add to your enjoyment and may also prevent painful and costly injuries.

PRE-TRAINING

Before you begin your training, you should be able to run for at least 30 minutes without stopping. Distance is not important, you just need to get your body used to running. Combinations of run/walks are great to use during pre-training because they ease your body into the exercise and minimises the chance of experiencing a running injury.

AVOIDING INJURY

Use your non-running days to rest and recover. If you feel a niggle, back off the training for a day of two. Better to miss two days than two weeks. Ice down any soreness a few times per day for 15-20 minutes.

TRAINING

Your mileage should gradually increase each week before tapering off in the final weeks leading up to the marathon / half marathon to allow your body to recover from training and so you will be strong on the big day. Having the long runs under your belt will give you a major psychological advantage on the day.

STRETCHING

Stretching regularly should be part of your running routine. Stretching offers many benefits including helping to prevent muscular aches, pains, cramping and injury. It will also reduce the possibility of muscular fatigue and increasing the muscles efficiency/effectiveness of movement. Although it is generally considered more important to stretch after a run than before, if you feel that you need to stretch before your run you should ideally jog or walk for 5 or 10 minutes before stretching to warm the muscles up and to get blood flowing.

SOME STRETCH BASICS

• Stretch the muscle to the point of its greatest range of motion, but do not overextend. You should feel very minimal tightness/discomfort (but not pain).
• Hold and control the stretch for at least 30 seconds (and maximum 60 seconds).
• Stretch all the major leg muscle groups (e.g. calves, hamstrings, quadriceps, groin, hip flexors).
• Stretch uniformly (after stretching one leg, stretch the other).
• Don't overstretch an injured area as this may cause additional damage

LONG RUNS

The key to these programmes is the long run on weekends. Consistency is most important. You can skip an occasional workout, or juggle the schedule depending on other commitments, but try not to cheat on the long runs. Notice that although the weekly long runs get progressively longer, every few weeks there is a "recovery" week, where mileage is reduced to allow you to gather strength for the next phase.

RUN SLOW

Do your long runs at a comfortable pace, one that allows you to converse with your training partners, at least during the beginning of the run. Toward the end, you may need to abandon conversation and concentrate on the act of putting one foot in front of the other to finish.

However, if you find yourself finishing at a pace significantly slower than your pace in the first few miles, you probably need to start much slower, or include regular walking breaks. It's better to run too slow during these long runs, than too fast. The important point is that you cover the prescribed distance; how fast you cover it doesn't matter.

WALKING BREAKS

Walking is a perfectly acceptable strategy in trying to finish a marathon or half marathon. It works during training runs too. You could walk one minute out of every 10, or one minute every mile. Walking gives your body a chance to rest, and you'll be able to continue running more comfortably.

CROSS-TRAINING

Cross-training is any other form of aerobic exercise that allows you to use slightly different muscles while resting (usually) after your long run. The best cross-training exercises are swimming, cycling or even walking. Cross-training for an hour the day after your long runs will help you recover.

REST

Rest is an important component of any training programme as it is during the rest period (the 24 to 72 hours between hard bouts of exercise) that the muscles actually regenerate and get stronger. Hard running (such as the long runs) allows you to improve, however, you'll find that you can't run hard unless you are well rested. If you're constantly fatigued you will fail to reach your potential.

This is why rest days are vital. If you need to take more rest days – because of a cold or a late night at the office or a sick child – do so. The secret to success in any training programme is consistency, so as long as you are consistent with your training during the full programme, you can afford, and may benefit from, extra rest.

KEEP TRACK

It is advisable that you keep track of your training efforts and results during race preparation. This will allow you to analyse your improvement. Looking at your "diary" can also help with motivation.

TAPER

This is a golden rule of marathon or half marathon training, which forms one of the main cornerstones of all the schedules. If you don't taper (ease off) sufficiently for the race, you may find that you've wasted all those hard sessions. You will find that these schedules reduce your weekly and long run mileage during the final weeks to ensure that you will be fully recovered from previous workouts while at the same time be completely rested for the big event.

HITTING THE WALL

You've heard the phrase, you may have even experienced those energy-sapping effects 18 miles or so in, affectionately known as "hitting the wall". The weak legs, light-headedness and strong urge to stop are caused by a depletion of glycogen (carbohydrate stores) and an almost complete reliance on fat for fuel.

While fat can power a runner for days in theory, it can't maintain the same speed and intensity as carbohydrate. Couple that with dehydration and it can bring you to a sudden and grinding halt. Fortunately, there is an effective weapon against the wall.

NUTRITION

Understanding how nutritional status affects the body during exercise is very important. And it's not just about race day. Eating the right foods at the right time, before during and after long training sessions will compound to make your overall training programme that much more effective.

Be sure to get the nutrition you need (carbs, proteins, unsaturated fats) to keep you strong and allow for adequate recovery. Cut down on junk food such as biscuits, sweets, soft drinks and the like. You're going to be asking a lot of your body over the coming weeks and months so you want to make sure to fuel it properly.

HYDRATION

On runs of an hour or more, carry fluids with you and consume 6-8 oz. every 20 minutes. During training it can be advisable to weigh yourself before and after each run and get your body weight back to the weight it was before the run by drinking water or sports drink within the first hours after the run. Always hydrate well – you will lose a lot of water through sweating (even if it's cold outside).

So What Level Are You At?

Are you a completer beginner? If so please log on to www.gerryduffyonline.com and download the 'Get Me Started' programme. This will help to give you a base level of fitness and get you up to 30 minutes of exercise over eight weeks.

If you're already there or have now completed this base fitness, then simply log on and choose whatever marathon or half marathon training programme you feel best suits your goals.

HALF-MARATHON OPTIONS

LEVEL 1 TRAINING SCHEDULE

Not worried about how long it'll take, just want to finish? This plan is for you...

LEVEL 2 TRAINING SCHEDULE

Already running three–four times per week? Think you can finish in c. 1:50? Check this plan out.

LEVEL 3 TRAINING SCHEDULE

Suitable for the experienced runner targeting a sub 1:30. Already running three–five times per week with a c. six mile long run.

FULL MARATHON OPTIONS

LEVEL 1 TRAINING SCHEDULE

The 'Get Me Around' plan. Time is not important here.

LEVEL 2 TRAINING SCHEDULE

Best suited to runners looking to break the four-hour mark and who have been running a few times per week for the last few weeks.

LEVEL 3 TRAINING SCHEDULE

Can you run 8 miles in one go? Think you can finish around the 3:30 mark? Running c. 20 miles per week already? If so, this is the plan for you.

LEVEL 4 TRAINING SCHEDULE

Are you looking to dip beneath the 3:00 mark? Already running four-five times per week and would find two eight-mile runs a week no problem.

Now log on to
www.gerryduffyonline.com
and download your free training programme

Good luck and enjoy...

Iron Distance Triathlon Training

Most people have the ability to complete an Iron distance triathlon. But be under no illusions, it is not just about the race day. All of the hard work is done in the weeks and months prior. Your first challenge when training is to ensure you know what is required, and then that you still have the desire to do it.

SOME QUESTIONS TO ASK

• Are you ready and able to commit 10–18 hours a week for training?

• Are you prepared to get up early, do a session before and after work?

If you are up for the challenge of training then keep reading. If the thought of this commitment puts you off, you may need to reconsider. Taking on a 3.8km swim, 180km cycle and 42km run in one day is going to be tough not matter how well prepared you are. That said, the better prepared you are, the more you will enjoy the day. With that in mind I have illustrated on the website an example of a training plan that should get an athlete who follows it, to arrive at race day in peak condition.

Before you study the plan, I need to share some important points. Firstly it is impossible to design a training plan that will suit all levels. We have all different levels of base fitness, respond differently to exercise, push ourselves to different limits. We are motivated by different things (e.g. simply to finish before the cut off or finish in under 10 hours). Some of us need more time to recover than others and of course regular commitments can have a big influence on our time, energy and ability to train.

With this in mind, outlined on the website is a 20-week training plan that should suit most. I have assumed a high level of fitness and experience starting the programme. When I did my first Iron distance I had spent the previous year competing in many triathlons from sprint distance up to half iron distance. I highly recommend this. I also highly recommend a consultation with your doctor to get expert advice on your ability to undertake such an ambition.

Week one starts off with a 2km swim and includes a 70km cycle towards the end of the week. If you feel that the distances shown are ambitious, then either start your build phase four/six weeks earlier so that you can follow this plan from week one, or scale back the distance of the sessions shown.

You will see that most weeks have nine sessions made up of three swims / bikes and runs. This is not set in stone. If you have the time, energy or motivation to complete all of them, great. If not, feel free to tweak the plan to suit your current level of fitness, time availability, finishing time goal etc. It might suit you better to only do two sessions of each discipline each week.

I recommend that you print the plan out and tweak it to suit you. Then stick it on the fridge.

SOME FINAL POINTERS

• If you miss a session or two each week, don't stress about it. It is important that you listen to your body. If you are tired, then rest.

• If you are hungry, eat. You are going to burn through a huge amount of fuel during training. To have enough energy for the next session and to give your body the sustenance it needs to repair damaged muscles, you will need to continuously fuel your body with the right foods. Also practice your nutrition strategy during training.

• Mondays are rest days – enjoy them. As the distances build up you will really look forward to these days.

• Getting enough sleep is essential.

The training period not only trains the body, it also trains the mind. Use the long sessions to prepare mentally for race day. Envision yourself in the race, how you're going to feel at various points during it and picture the transitions etc.

SWIM

- Don't just jump in the pool and swim length after length thinking that you are going to improve your swim technique. Swimming well takes a lot of work and practise. That is why I have included a variety of swim sessions and drills in this plan.
- The time trial ("TT") swims are useful for gauging your progress throughout the 20 weeks. They also help to set your target 100m and 200m times for the later sessions.
- When doing the longer warm ups ("w/u") and cool downs ("c/d"), continue to focus on technique drills, e.g. kicking drills, arms etc.
- Introduce open water swims from at least week 15 to help you get used to sighting, wetsuit etc.

BIKE

- If the weather is unkind, revert to an indoor 'turbo' for bike sessions. Choose a good film!!
- "Tempo" Pace = Race Pace
- If you are going to use a TT (time trial) bike in the race, introduce the TT bike from week 10 of the plan to help your body get used to the more extreme position.
- Don't neglect bike maintenance.
- Practise eating on the bike.

RUN

- Practise eating during the run. Find out what nutrition/fluids will be available on race day and then practise running with the different options. For some runners Coke works, for others it's gels.

Whatever the case, it is essential that you practise – you don't want stomach cramps to ruin those lovely last few miles.

For your comprehensive Iron Distance
Triathlon Training Plan, log on to
www.gerryduffyonline.com
and download your free programme

Good luck and enjoy...